D1716730

Doing Research that Matters

Shaping the Future of Management

DOING RESEARCH THAT MATTERS
Shaping the Future of Management

BY

MARCO BUSI
Carisma RCT Ltd, Aberdeen, United Kingdom

Emerald

United Kingdom – North America – Japan
India – Malaysia – China

Emerald Group Publishing Limited
Howard House, Wagon Lane, Bingley BD16 1WA, UK

First edition 2013

Copyright © 2013 Emerald Group Publishing Limited

British Library Cataloguing in Publication Data
A catalogue record for this book is available from the British Library

ISBN: 978-0-85724-707-0

ISOQAR certified
Management System,
awarded to Emerald
for adherence to
Environmental
standard
ISO 14001:2004.

Certificate Number 1985
ISO 14001

INVESTOR IN PEOPLE

And it ought to be remembered that there is nothing more difficult to take in hand, more perilous to conduct, or more uncertain in its success, than to take the lead in the introduction of a new order of things.

Because the innovator has for enemies all those who have done well under the old conditions, and lukewarm defenders in those who may do well under the new.

This coolness arises partly from fear of the opponents, who have the laws on their side, and partly from the incredulity of men, who do not readily believe in new things until they have had a long experience of them.

— Niccolò Macchiavelli, The Prince, Chapter 6, 1537

Contents

FOREWORD

As the head of the Drucker Institute, I've had the chance to ponder the subject of Marco Busi's book on more than a few occasions. After all, the man whose vast body of work forms the intellectual foundation of my organization — affecting everything from our overall worldview to individual activities — had a decidedly trenchant take on the topic.

"I have a deep horror of obscurity and arrogance," Peter Drucker once said of his writing, "so I presented it in a form that people could apply." This was, of course, Drucker's way of declaring that he did *research that matters.*

It was also his way of asserting that all too many of his university colleagues, bent on piling up articles in peer-reviewed publications with no regard for whether their contributions made a bit of difference beyond the ivory tower, did not. (It is a view shared by many of those Busi interviewed; see, especially, Chapter 7 on the huge disconnect between the way the academy measures achievement and any real-world relevance that a scholar's work may have.)

"Sure, we want and need research," remarked Drucker, who passed away in 2005, barely a week short of his 96th birthday, with 39 books to his name and countless consulting clients who felt they owed him a great debt. "But consider the modern medical school, which began in the late 18th century. The emphasis in medical school is not on ... publication but on the ability to treat patients and make a difference in their lives." In a similar manner, he added, "business educators should be out as practitioners where the problems and results are."

It's not that Drucker, who over a span of more than six decades taught at four major institutions of higher learning (Sarah Lawrence College, Bennington College, New York University, and Claremont Graduate University), failed to appreciate the research going on around campus. Yet he perceived its value differently than many others did.

"Intellectuals and scholars tend to believe that ideas come first, which then lead to new political, social, economic, psychological realities," Drucker wrote. "This does happen, but it is the exception. As a rule, theory does not precede practice. Its role is to structure and codify already proven practice. Its role is to convert the isolated and 'atypical' from exception to 'rule' and 'system,' and therefore into something that can be learned and taught and, above all, into something that can be generally applied."

Drucker also worried about the drift toward hyper-specialization, maintaining that many of the most significant advances were to be attained by forging links among different areas of knowledge. (Busi makes the same point in a section of Chapter 4, aptly titled "Search at the Intersections.") "'Only connect' was the constant admonition of a great English novelist, E. M. Forster," Drucker wrote in his 1993 book *Post-Capitalist Society*. "It has always been the hallmark of the artist, but equally of the great scientist — of a Darwin, a Bohr, an Einstein. At their level, the capacity to connect may be inborn and part of that mystery we call 'genius.'

"But to a large extent," Drucker continued, "the ability to connect and thus to raise the yield of existing knowledge ... is learnable. Eventually, it should become teachable. It requires a methodology for *problem definition* — even more urgently perhaps than it requires the currently fashionable methodology for 'problem solving.' It requires systematic analysis of the kind of knowledge and information a given problem requires, and a methodology for organizing the stages in which a given problem can be tackled — the methodology which underlies what we now call 'systems research.' It requires what might be called Organizing Ignorance — and there is always so much more ignorance around than there is knowledge."

Drucker wasn't always so sour on the state of scholarly research. Relatively early in his career, he was confident that management theory and practice were on their way to becoming mutually reinforcing. "The manager wants to know what kind of structure he needs," Drucker observed in *The Practice of Management*, his 1954 landmark. "The organization theorist, however, talks about how the structure should be built. The manager, so to speak, wants to find out whether he should build a highway and from where to where. The organization theorist discusses the relative advantages and limitations of cantilever and suspension bridges." The good news, according to Drucker, was that these two distinct perspectives — both of which had much to offer — were beginning to converge. "Indeed," he wrote, "we are speedily closing the gap by creating a unified discipline of organization that is both practical and theoretically sound."

By the mid-1980s, though, things had changed for the worse. "Being incomprehensible has become a virtue in academia," complained Drucker, who famously forswore writing for scholarly journals, preferring instead to see his byline grace the pages of *The Atlantic*, *Harper's*, and *The Wall Street Journal*.

To be sure, there were exceptions, and Drucker pointed to them admiringly. For instance, he said that he found Michael Porter's theories on strategy particularly useful. He called Phil Kotler's work on marketing, especially among nonprofits, "pioneering." And he lauded C.K. Prahalad and Gary Hamel's insights on core competencies as "pathbreaking."

Tellingly, all of these Drucker favorites are academic outliers, alchemical blends of thinker and doer — just like Drucker himself. Busi (who, not coincidentally, interviewed Kotler, holds up Hamel and refers to Porter and Prahalad) has discovered a similar magic in that mix. "In fact," he writes, "I have learnt that people who have the potential to do research that matters, especially in the management field, are those who sit in the space between the two ends of this continuum.

"They are neither the 'pure' Academic nor the 'pure' Practitioner," Busi explains. "They are *just* the typical engineers of the future." They are, in other words, innovators — and, as such, Drucker's advice for this group seems perfect: "Because innovation is both conceptual and perceptual, would-be innovators must also go out and look, ask, and listen. Successful innovators use both the right and left sides of their brains. They work out analytically what the innovation has to be to satisfy an opportunity. Then they go out and look at potential users to study their expectations, their values, their needs."

In the end, this surely would have been Drucker's test: Has someone actually been able to put your findings to good use? Do they satisfy a genuine need? If the answer is yes, that's worth more than a thousand journal citations. If the answer is no, then it's just research, not *research that matters.*

Rick Wartzman
Executive Director, The Drucker Institute

ACKNOWLEDGMENTS

When I set out to do the research for this book, I never expected that my request for an interview with Nobel Laureates and Management Gurus would have been met with so much politeness, friendliness, and just a true desire to help *me* and more generally to help make this a better world. I am not sure what I was expecting but I know I could have not wished for more.

The interviews have been extremely insightful and the people I interviewed made a patient effort to go into as much depth as possible to help me understand where they were coming from, where they are going, and why they do what they do. They provided me with information, articles, and support prior to the interview and after it as well, without which this book would have never been possible. I truly feel privileged to have been given the chance to pick their brains, learn from their experiences and be inspired by their motives.

For that reason, I am and forever will be indebted to the exemplary people who have so kindly agreed to be interviewed and, in doing so, allowed me to have the most amazing learning experience of my life.

Collaboration, as I have learnt, is often a key element of meaningful endeavors. If it weren't for my collaboration with Nancy K. Napier, my original idea would have never blossomed in this book. Nancy is Professor of International Business, Executive Director of the Centre for Creativity and Innovation at Boise State University, and the author of *Insight: Encouraging Aha! Moments for Organizational Success* (2010) and *The Creative Discipline: Mastering the Art and Science of Innovation* (2008). She contributed significantly to shaping my ideas and also to writing some of the sections in the book, in particular based on research of literature and the Nobel Laureates' biographies (thanks also to her research assistant Bianca Jochimsen for helping with the desk research). She also was extremely patient throughout the project, when my day job delayed the research process and stretched our collaboration to breaking point. When she finally had to leave the project, she did so gracefully and, in perfect mentoring style, she pushed me to finish what she has always defined as "my own important project." Any young scholar who may have the possibility to work under Nancy's mentorship, I warn you: treasure the experience!

I would also like to express my most sincere gratitude to my commissioning editor, Kim Eggleton, for the continuous support, feedback, and encouragement throughout the process. Kim also kept feeding me with extremely useful references and information, some of which have eventually made it into this book. I don't know how many other editors would have endured the same challenging process and I can only say that you have acted truly as the ideal *Insight Distributor* I discuss later in this book. For that, I am deeply grateful and I hope that the final product justifies your patience and efforts. Thanks to Juliet Harrison, Katie Spike, and the rest of the team at Emerald Group Publishing as well for making this project a reality.

Several academic colleagues have contributed at the very beginning of this research journey, when we were still testing our original ideas and designing the study. In particular Mary Lacity, Bjørn Andersen, Roger D. H. Warburton, Rudy Hirschheim, Shikhar Sarin, Scott Lowe, Sian Mooney, Gundy Kaupins, Christopher Lonsdale, Anthony Boardman, Mark Cowan, Erran Carmel, Gerald Ferris, Marijn Janssen, Janet Murray, Jan de Vries, Tom Gattiker, Michael Harvey, and Anne-Wil Harzing offered insightful views that informed the research that followed. Thanks also to Bernard Marr, who found the time to take a break during his holidays to answer some of my very last minute questions (and who also tried and succeeded to making me rather envious by telling me he had just watched the sun set over the Indian Ocean while I was making the final adjustments sitting at my office in cold and gray Aberdeen, UK!). And, of course, I am grateful to all the other people — too many to mention — who contributed with insightful discussions and brainstorming sessions throughout the project. You know who you are.

Practitioners who strive for innovation and continuously attempt to translate cutting-edge ideas into practice, helping refine those ideas in the process, are among the heroes often mentioned in this book. Steve Chisholm and Peter Swanson certainly deserve a special mention here. My original business partners with whom I have laid the foundations of Carisma RCT, they have been extremely important in my transition from academia to industry, both personally and professionally. I would like to thank Steve for helping me learn the ways of industry and the importance of practical application while pushing me never to lose sight of the value of research-driven big ideas; a true mentor and a friend, he has always been there to challenge me and, at the same time, to support me. And thanks to Peter, for being an important advocate of my grand vision since the very beginning, for inspiring me to make a commercial venture out of my passion for research and for helping me understand how to communicate research ideas and findings to a practitioners' audience. His help has certainly increased the chances that my research insight may be adopted and, eventually, have impact.

My thanks also to John Wheatcroft for reading and commenting on the early drafts of this work and to Dave Mackay and Veronica Martinez for helping me find relevant literature on the topic of research design and methodology.

I would also like to thank the people I love. My family, who have always believed in me and supported me, no matter how crazy my ideas. They taught me to always be the best I can be, and led by examples rather than empty words. They also worked hard to ensure I had it easy in life, and that is a better head start than anybody can ask for. I can only hope not to have let them down too often.

And to Maria Chiara, my partner in life, for always believing in me, for pushing me to live the life I want to live and for being there to support me at every step of the way. She also contributed to this book in many ways. She endured numerous — probably boring at times — conversations about the many ideas and doubts I have had throughout the process. She never complained for the very little time I dedicated to our private life as a result of having to write this book at nights and weekends while also having to do my day job during the day. But she also contributed directly, giving me ideas and suggestions for how to make this book better.

Last, but not least, I would like to express my most sincere gratitude to all the people I have met along my way who have all helped shaping me, my personality, and my thoughts. Those who did the 'right thing,' because they inspired me; and those who did the 'wrong thing,' because they gave me the opportunity to realize I had to search for a better way to do it.

To the braves, who try to shape the future

To my family, who inspires and empowers me to give it always my best shot

To Maria Chiara, who makes my journey worth travelling

Prologue — My Declaration of Intent

I don't feel like working on any issue that isn't going to be important and meaningful to the world. I only have ... so much time on this planet and the question is: do you want to do useful stuff or not? My answer is, for sure, the useful stuff!
— Roger Martin, Dean, Rotman School of Management

Desire is the key to motivation, but it's the determination and commitment to an unrelenting pursuit of your goal — a commitment to excellence — that will enable you to attain the success you seek.
— Mario Andretti, Italian born American race driver

This book is for all those who, like me, are a bit revolutionary, who want to create a box just so that we can think out of it; who do not accept the status quo just because it is, ehm, the status quo; who are willing to fail over and over in the attempt to succeed at least once; and who constantly question the underlying assumptions of the environment around us searching for something worth finding.

In other words, this book is for those who believe that what we do as individuals must count for the world as a whole and who desperately want to leave something behind through our actions.

This is most definitely not a book for those who rather walk the beaten path than defining one worth walking on; who waste brainpower to gaming a poor system to their advantage rather than to changing it for the better; who believe that 'everything is just fine the way it is'; and who don't need inspiration from others.

If you are a practicing manager who thinks that innovation happens only in the field and that academics live in Cloud Cuckoo Land, you probably picked this book up by mistake. Likewise, if you are an academic who thinks to know it all, throw the book in the bin, now!

Having said that, it is difficult to find a clear-cut classification for this book. Yes, it certainly is a book aimed at academics. At the same time, it is also a book for management practitioners and others who have an interest in management innovation. Although, it might also entertain others who are not interested in management innovation at all but who want to understand what makes successful people, successful. And yes, it is definitely a book on how to do good quality research, regardless of the field of application. It does not, however, provide any suggestion whatsoever on how to select the right population, how to conduct a longitudinal case study, or how to complete a linear regression analysis, to mention but a few of today's apparently 'most wanted' research methods.

In fact, it is important you understand that this is not at all a 'how to' book. I don't aim to be prescriptive and tell you how you should conduct your research studies, or how you should foster innovation in your business. Neither do I claim to have found the answer to one of the biggest and most important questions of our time — at least in my opinion — that is, how can we shape the future by doing more *research that matters*?

On the contrary, this book is a type of memoir, a recount of my very personal quest to date, carefully planned and excitingly lived, searching for inspiration and guidance on how I could do *what I want to do*, better.

What *I do* is management research, consulting, and training.

What *I want to do* is create new and valuable knowledge that through its very existence contributes to creating a better future for those who might be touched or influenced by it. It's a grand aim, but one that I feel immensely passionate about.

Throughout this book, I refer to this ultimate objective as *doing research that matters* and I use "meaningful insight" and "*research that matters*" interchangeably to refer to the final outcome of *doing research that matters*. "Matters" to whom? Well, since the focus of my own research is management, I expect it to matter primarily to organizational leaders, management researchers, publishers, educators, and practicing managers with responsibilities spanning research and/or innovation. At the same time, the principles that I am going to explore for *doing research that matters* are also relevant to disciplines other than management.

Also, throughout the book, I often discuss and refer to academic or scholarly research. I do not intend though to imply that research can only be carried out within the academy. As a matter of fact, I am strongly convinced — rightly or not — that, especially in the field of management, most valuable research and innovation these days are done by practitioners, consultants, and independent scholars from outside the realm of academia.

It follows that, should I be successful in influencing how people *do research that matters*, regardless of their affiliation, the impact should extend far beyond the boundaries of a handful of companies or universities and into society, government, schools, and, eventually, the life of every one of us.

Don't get me wrong. I am not so big-headed to think one single book (my first book, that is) is going to change the world. One single action or project in isolation would never suffice to achieve such an extraordinary goal. Rather, I want to make sure that *my* contribution, small or — hopefully — big, helps shape the future of the world *I* live in.

My intent, therefore, is not to tell you *what* you should do or *how* you should do it to make your work, your research, matter. It is simply to push you to critically review and question what you do, to give you some food for your thoughts by sharing the experiences of incredibly smart and passionate people that have devoted their life to the very same objective and that I was lucky enough to talk to, exchange ideas with, and research in depth.

These people and their stories have inspired me *to be* better and *to do* better. I invite you to join me as I attempt to structure what I have learnt from the journey upon which I embarked over three years ago and which has been, without the shadow of a doubt, the most wonderful and insightful (and challenging) learning experience of my life.

This Book's Tower of Babel

During my interview with Constantinos (Costas) Markides, Robert P. Bauman Chair in Strategic Leadership at the London Business School, he told me that we need to be precise with the terms we use when speaking about management research. He explains why: "Depending on the disease, the doctor has to prescribe a different medicine. It's the same with innovation. We have different types of innovation. We have product innovation, process innovation, management innovation, technological innovation, business model innovation, strategic innovation … You name it. And also there are different degrees of innovation. You can have incremental or radical product innovation. You can have incremental or radical business model innovation. My argument would be that depending on what type of innovation you want to achieve, we'll have a different medicine … We cannot prescribe a medicine until we get very specific [about] what exactly we want to achieve."

Throughout this book, I often refer to "management research," "management researchers," "management innovation," and I ask the question of how we can become better at doing management research to shape the future of management.

Following Costas Markides' advice, I therefore thought it important to offer my own definitions for these key terms to enhance clarity and understanding.

I define "management" as the act or process of coordinating and using tangible and intangible resources to transform an input into an output toward a predetermined set of goals. Depending on the goal, the time horizon of the decisions being made, the information available to the decision makers, and the area of influence of the resulting actions, management can 'be done' at a strategic, tactical, or operational level.

This is a rather wide area and it includes many different scientific disciplines. Naturally, each of us will tend to define some boundaries around such area based on our own experience and knowledge. That would be a mistake though. Henry Mintzberg, John Cleghorn Professor of Management Studies at the Desautels Faculty of Management, McGill University, believes that, strictly speaking, "management ... is about what managers do, how they do it, how they should do it, how they can't do it and the nature of management. When you extend that to organisational issues, they may not be managerial issues per se, like control systems in organisations ..." Costas Markides offers a different slant and specifies: "Management is not business. Definitely not ... Management ... is the art of ... galvanising a group of people towards a common goal. It is an art, not a science ... A group of people ... can be small or big, domestic or international ... And the goal can be a private goal or it can be a public goal or it can be a social goal. That is what management is. We need to expand it beyond business." In line with Markides, Peter Drucker also underlines how: "Management is not 'Business Management'; it is the ruling organ and decisive function of EVERY modern social institution."[1]

Consequently, to me, "management research" is research, scholarly and not, into any aspect relating to management. This includes anything from leadership to operations management, human resource management to production management, etc. I agree with David Ulrich, Professor at the Stephen M. Ross School of Business, at the University of Michigan, that "Management research is so broad to include almost anything from business context to strategy to financial systems to technology to organization, etc. Good management research starts with a phenomenon ... that being a real issue or concern rather than theory. The purpose of research is to offer theory to explain why something happens so that it can be replicated and/or to empirically study and explain why something works." Similarly, Philip Kotler, S. C. Johnson & Son Distinguished Professor of International Marketing at Chicago's Northwestern University Kellogg School of Management, defines, "Management research [is] research into all aspects of managing an enterprise, including how strategies and plans are formed; how organizations recruit, train, motivate, and compensate; how organizations relate to their stakeholders and to their competitors; and so on." Whereas for Costas Markides, "Everything that has to do with [galvanizing people toward a common goal], to me, is management research."

Management research, therefore, can be as wide an area as management itself. Not just that but, ideally, research in management should evolve as rapidly and adaptably as the practice of management itself. So much so that Henry Mintzberg actually suggests avoiding any pre-determined definition: "You show me some research and I will tell you whether I think it's management or not. I just had a doctoral student fit in some research on … the relationships between culture and globalisation. Is that management research or actual policy research or international business research?"

In this context, I use "management innovation" in relation to any type of innovation that basically transform, incrementally or radically, how we manage and what we know about management.

Last, when I ask how we can become better management researchers, I am aiming to find out how we can foster more management innovation doing management *research that matters*.

These definitions serve the purpose of establishing a common vocabulary and an understanding between author and readers. At the same time, I do ask that you do not use these to constrain the dominion of applicability of the lessons and ideas I am going to discuss in this book. As Mintzberg says: "Who cares [about these definitions]? If it's insightful and interesting and important, it's all that matters. I don't want to draw phoney lines around these things." Neither do I! Neither should you.

The Beginning of a Journey

I began this journey following my own critical self-assessment and resulting dissatisfaction with the impact (or lack thereof) of my own research and my personal discontent with the organizational cultures of some universities I had worked for.

Frustrated by the lack of impact of my own work and the explicit encouragement by my employer to do research that mattered (only) to meaningless research assessment exercises (RAEs), rather than to the real world, I left academia and set out to create an organization where *doing research that matters* would be the underlying and guiding ethos.

I was encouraged when I discovered from the interviews and research I did for this book that my frustration with the academic system was common across many others, as was the solution I had opted for. Gary Hamel, for example, founded the strategy consulting firm *Strategos* and "worked with companies like Microsoft, Whirlpool, and Campbell to help them not only fix problems but also learn fresh approaches and new ways of thinking."[2] And Konosuke Matsushita

Professor of Leadership, Emeritus at the Harvard Business School, John Paul Kotter, together with an ex-Microsoft executive, founded *Kotter International* whose vision is *"millions leading, billions benefitting"* and whose team is trying to understand what type of unusual advisory and educational services will work in the future.

Most share Gary Hamel's realization that "the future is coming faster than you think" and that one may "cling to traditional assumptions about business at [her] own peril."[3] That is why the motivation behind these initiatives seems to be always the same, as so very nicely and powerfully summarized in Roger Martin's quote at the start of this chapter: the desire to work only on issues that are "important and meaningful to the world."

Driven by the same desire and having made the jump to a life as a practitioner and an "independent scholar" — to use Ronald Gross' terminology indicating any person pursuing scholarly research without salaried academic positions or academic endorsement[4] — I decided I needed to learn more about what underlying conditions I should put in place in my organization to increase our chances to do important and meaningful work.

Using the only approach I knew, which I had learnt from my days as a Ph.D. student at the Norwegian University of Science and Technology in Trondheim, Norway, I started defining my research questions. I wanted to understand one simple — and at the same time extremely complex — thing: *How can I do research that matters? Research that has the potential to change people's lives and how organizations function?*

There exist plenty of research methodology books: were they not good enough? Maybe so, but asking the question and trying to find alternative instructions on how to do good research could not really do any harm, as the many articles being published on the topic of 'research impact' (or lack thereof) prove. If anything, trying to understand how to generate more impact would only contribute to improve what is widely referred to as the current dramatic situation.

It was then time to design my research methodology. This was trickier. The beauty of working for oneself is being able to choose what to do and how to do it, without having to worry about fitting in within organizational cultures and objectives that do not fit with one's own. Or, as Ronald Gross puts it: "you have freedom to follow your own bliss without regard to fashions and trends."[5]

Totally unconstrained, I could therefore attempt to think laterally. The cunning plan that emerged was worrying in its simplicity: *To find out how to do research that matters, ask those who have done it before. They'll have the answer.*

My research was always going to be based on two pillars. First, I wanted to look 'inside the box,' the management box to be more precise. To do that, I would have to ask management researchers who are well known for having created a lasting impact through their work.

Second, I wanted to look 'outside the box,' that is, beyond the management field. If you ask a production manager how to improve the production output, she might tell you to optimize the material flow or change the plant layout. If you ask the same question to a human resource manager, she might tell you to create an environment where people are happy and motivated. Both answers are true and important. And if it were you in charge of improving production in your factory, you would want to be aware of both points of view and follow both sets of recommendations. Similarly, looking at the concept of *research that matters* and how to do it from more than one viewpoint, I thought, could prove insightful.

My plan was therefore to ask management experts, of course, but also Nobel Laureates from fields outside of the management box, aiming to identify common (or uncommon) patterns.

The embryo of this project was born. From that embryo to this book, the journey has taken a rather tortuous path of collaboration.

Enters Nancy Napier, Professor of International Business and Executive Director of the Centre for Creativity and Innovation at Boise State University.

As so many unexpected collaborations do, my collaboration with Nancy began over dinner at a conference in Aalborg, Denmark: an 'Italo-Scott' budding entrepreneur with a near past as an academic and a passion for research and an American academic with a past in industry and a passion for starting new academic ventures.

I had never written a book before. Nancy had written many. I wanted to learn from Nobel Laureates how I could do better research. Nancy was inspired by Gary Hamel's challenge to academics to find big "romantic problems" to work on. I had the energy and mad ideas typical of a less experienced player. Nancy had the measured consideration typical of a more experienced one.

For as odd a duo as this was there were enough striking common interests and different traits to make the two complementary and, consequently, to make us think that the collaboration would work to the benefit of the final product.

What begun as an individual journey of self-analysis later became a dinner conversation, then a series of brainstorming sessions, email exchanges, Skype sessions, and face-to-face conversations in some very interesting places around the world, including a hotel lobby near the beautiful Hoan Kiem Lake in the Old Quarter of Hanoi, Vietnam; at a wonderful cottage near McCall, a resort town on the western edge of Valley County, Idaho, United States; and at a bar near the suggestive Edinburgh Castle in Scotland. All of this helped planting the seeds that eventually blossomed in this book.

Getting to this book did not happen without its difficulties and unexpected turns though. In all honesty, I never thought writing a book would take this much energy and dedication. First, as often is the case for independent scholars, having to earn my living through a day job soon made it impossible for me to dedicate nearly as much structured time to this project as I wanted or as it deserved. This meant continuously slipping deadlines and, eventually, made it impossible for Nancy to continue the journey with me (there was a lesson about collaboration here for me to learn, to which I will return later in the book). It also made it very difficult for me to see the light at the end of the tunnel. I later learnt though, from the stories of some of the exemplary researchers I have studied, that they have gone through much thicker and taller walls than I have encountered, some through war even, yet they all managed to generate the meaningful insight they had committed their life to. So, really, I could not use my being busy as an excuse!

Enters Kim Eggleton, my Senior Commissioning Editor at Emerald Group Publishing.

Thankfully, I was lucky to receive continuous and unconditional support by Kim, who thought it important this book would see the light of day. If it hadn't been for Kim, I am not sure this book would have ever been completed. Kim gave me a structure for the writing process and the always healthy pressure of having to meet deadlines.

Collaboration is a theme that I am going to discuss later in the book. My very own experience collaborating with Nancy and Kim has allowed me to look at the journeys of some of the interviewees from a different perspective. As they say, experience is the hardest kind of teacher but also the one that gives birth to the more valuable lessons. It also provided me a first validation of the idea that I am going to put forward in a later chapter that *research that matters* can only truly happen as a result of having a certain set of personal characteristics, working with a certain type of people and within a certain type of environment and choosing to disseminate ideas through specific types of distribution channels.

If it hadn't been for my collaboration with Nancy, I would have never had the chance to discuss our different point of views in so much depth, to compare personal experiences, and to come up with new ideas on how to go about doing this project. If it hadn't been for my collaboration with Emerald and Kim, I would have never been able to complete this project.

Collaboration is what made this journey possible. Collaboration, under the right circumstances, with the right person, on the right topic, at the right time, is also indispensable to make good research *better*.

Where I Looked for Answers

In my journey to understand how to do *research that matters* and to have lasting impact, I decided that studying in-depth a small set of the 'best specimen' would be more effective than surveying a large sample. Finding the right people to interview was always going to be a challenge. First, because I still had to understand what elements define the concept of *research that matters*. Without knowing what makes up the concept, it was going to be difficult to identify those whose work would represent it. Second, because it was quite clear that these were going to be people either extremely busy, or in the spotlight or, more likely, both.

Various sources publish rankings of the world's best management researchers, best business leaders, and best thinkers. One such source which is often cited both in academic and industry circles is the website Thinkers50, whose editors compile a biannual ranking of 'management gurus.' "The ranking is based on voting at the Thinkers50 website and input from a team of advisers led by Stuart Crainer and Des Dearlove. The Thinkers50 has ten established criteria by which thinkers are evaluated — originality of ideas; practicality of ideas; presentation style; written communication; loyalty of followers; business sense; international outlook; rigor of research; impact of ideas and the elusive guru factor."[6]

I used the Thinkers50's lists up to 2011 to identify potential targets for the interviews. I complemented that with the Sveriges Riksbank Prize in *Economic Sciences* in Memory of Alfred Nobel — popularly but imprecisely referred to as the Nobel in Economics — that since 1968 "is awarded by the Royal Swedish Academy of Sciences, Stockholm, Sweden, according to the same principles as for the Nobel Prizes that have been awarded since 1901."[7]

At the same time, as mentioned earlier, I wanted to look outside the management box. The idea of interviewing Nobel Laureates came about because of the common association of the Nobel Prize with the concept of 'life changing research,' which is in line with the meaning I give in this book to *doing research that matters*.

At this point, you might be thinking: "What the heck do Nobel Laureates have in common with management researchers?" You wouldn't be the only one asking that question. As a matter of fact, Professor Barbara Kellerman, James MacGregor Burns Lecturer in Public Leadership at Harvard University's John F. Kennedy School of Government, thinks the idea "sounds almost loopy." And Gerhard Ertl, who in 2007 received the Nobel Prize in Chemistry, pointed out, quite rightly, that "management research seems to be of quite different character than research in the natural sciences."

Granted, Nobel Laureates normally come from the hard sciences, but their work has nevertheless been acknowledged by their peers and beyond as having made a lasting difference.

Besides, Gary Hamel recognizes how "any field — whether it is medicine, engineering, or business — can become stuck in a paradigm trap over time. Everybody's been trained the same way. They think the same way, and they take the same things for granted ... business faculty need to be very conscious of the inherited dogmas that may underlie their views."[8]

The idea of looking for underlying patterns in these management-outsiders' approach to research seemed to have merit then, as it would allow me to see 'my' world (i.e., that of management and management research) through a different set of lenses not biased by the self-reinforcing culture which inevitably affects the views and opinions of people working in the management field alone.

Thus, this research set me on a journey that would see me spending several hours immerged in the most interesting conversations, picking the brains of the smartest and best thinkers from the management field and from a unique group of world-renowned scientists from medicine, biology, astronomy, and other disciplines.

I have spent much time thinking of a way to refer to these exemplary scientists and management thinkers throughout the book. In the end, I decided to use the term "*Futureers*," from 'future' and 'engineers,' following a realization that these are the people who commit their lifetime to engineering the future we will all live in, be that through advancing science, technology, management, or whatever other field they work in. I am going to use this term interchangeably with "exemplary researchers" or "exemplary scientists."

The gracious willingness of well-known, surely very busy people to give their time and insight astounded me. In a world where the time to stop and think about fundamental questions way too often seems a resource scarcer than diamonds on earth, the fact these people were able (and keen) to spend their precious time helping me with my quest, without expecting nothing in return, made me wonder: what is it that pushes them to act this way? Why are they helping me?

When I asked them the same question, their answers in a way encapsulate the very reason why these people do what they do and are who they are, their winning characteristics. They have passion for *doing research that matters*: "this is a topic that I feel great passion about," said David Ulrich. They are inherently curious, like 2009's Physiology or Medicine Nobel Laureate Professor Jack Szostak: "I've never been quite sure what factors led to my own success in research and I have always been curious as to whether there are general principles that could guide one to success." They never stop questioning what they do: "[your research] forces me to think a little bit about the way I do research and whether I have an impact or not. It is a self-reflecting exercise," told me Costas Markides. They want to help shape the future: "If I would see that it is in some way helpful for the scientific community ... I would certainly agree to giving this interview," said the 2008 Physiology or Medicine

Nobel Laureate Professor Harald zur Hausen. Although they are never arrogant about what they think it is they do: "it is an interesting project, could be important so it is a pleasure to try in a *very, very, very* small way to be of assistance," told me with admirable modesty John Kotter.

In the end, I was fortunate to personally interview and learn from 5 Nobel Laureates, 10 of the world's top 50 management thinkers and 1 internationally renowned astrophysicist. To complement the interviews, I used information available from other sources, such as the Nobel Foundation, universities' websites, scholarly and managerial literature, and studying numerous biographical notes, interviews, newspaper, and magazine articles. In addition, I talked with two-dozen of our academic colleagues, perhaps somewhat less well known but equally thoughtful about seeking to do research that is meaningful. Finally, I spent countless hours discussing the content of these interviews and brainstorming on the ideas that I present in this book with several "idea practitioners" close to me. I am borrowing the phrase "idea practitioners" from Tom Davenport, Laurence Prusak, and James Wilson to "describe industry practitioners who are intrinsically motivated to assess and translate existing ideas and develop new ones to bring into their organisations, and then fight for them with those who resist the change that these ideas inevitably bring about."[9]

In the end, I was able to collect around 100 hours of interviews, 150 hours of videos, hundreds of pages of personal notes from several meetings and conversations with the various people from all over the world who contributed in one way or another to my research, and thousands of pages of relevant scientific articles, biographies, etc.

The book, then, offers insights from these *Futureers* who have done and do *research that matters*, who produce meaningful insight and who continuously impact their field of research and, ultimately, the way we manage organizations, the way we live and prosper. I have chosen to include many original citations from the interviews with these remarkable people to help illustrate some of the themes that run through their own experiences in *doing research that matters*. Some are rather lengthy, as I wanted to transfer as much as I could of the more or less positive and negative emotions that some of my questions elicited in them.

I intentionally left out two sets of people from my research. First, I excluded those exemplary academic researchers and "independent scholars" who have contributed greatly to their fields of research or practice but who rather stay 'in the shadow.' These people never make it in any list of top thinkers or top influencers not because they do not deserve it but rather because they do not want to. For that reason though, there was simply no way for me to find them. Second, I excluded management and strategy consultants. As I said earlier, I have an assumption — a very strong one — that management consultants are as important (and probably more productive) in the generation of research ideas and insight as academic researchers (as Kiechel III's

Lords of Strategy[10] so elegantly shows us). However, I wanted to test this assumption first with some of my interviewees before extending my research to this group as well. I should clarify though that many management thinkers and academic researchers I interviewed for this book also practice as consultants.

If there were ever a follow-up to this book, this would be my starting point.

The good news is that there are many similarities in the way the *Futureers* do what they do, whether they are physicists, chemists, or management experts. At the same time, there are also enough differing perspectives on some of the issues that have emerged to leave space for your own self-reflection so that you can make your own decision as to which line of thought you see yourself better fitting in with.

I have spent much time looking for such similarities and differences and I have structured them in such a way that you may find it easy to compare your own thinking and doing against indisputable benchmarks of excellence.

That's One Giant Step for Man (Me); One Small Step for Mankind?

My underlying frustration, therefore, stems from the realization that *I* am not doing enough; *we* are not doing enough.

With increasingly complex problems that need smart brains' attention and the presumably growing supply of intellectual power worldwide, isn't it time that researchers in and out of academia start *leading* the race to innovation, rather than *following* it? Shouldn't we, as researchers, push the boundaries of the *known* to open a window on the *unknown,* rather than driving forward by looking in the rear view mirror?

To me, these are all rhetorical questions.

As a practitioner by profession and an inspired researcher by nature, I think it is essential to do (more) *research that matters* and helps change people's lives. I also think that searching for, investigating, and creating new knowledge should be more than a job: it should be our mission, as researchers and management innovators.

I found this same credo in the world's top management thinkers and Nobel Laureates whom I interviewed: even though they have already achieved status and recognition in and beyond their fields, they remain insatiable for new, insightful, and impactful knowledge.

So, rather than asking ourselves "Shouldn't we do it?", mine and this book's romantic problem is "How can we do it?"

I do not claim to be a pianist who puts individual notes together to create everlasting musical memories, nor a chef who transforms raw ingredients into a unique palate delight. No, I claim only to have modestly tried to do to the concept of *doing research that matters* what a glass prism does to a beam of white light, attempting to decompose meaningful insight and the process of generating it into its constituent spectrum of essential elements.

In doing so, I had (and have) three distinct objectives.

First, I wanted to satisfy a personal desire to learn how to do better what I love doing. This, I can confidently say to have met.

Second, I wish to inspire researchers and educators (and, why not, practicing managers) to take more responsibility and self-accountability for their role in investigating important problems and creating valuable insight.

Third, I wish to offer some ideas for how to translate that inspiration into actions. About this last point, let me repeat that this is not a 'how to' book: as it emerged clearly in the interviews I conducted, no one single 'best' approach exists for *doing research that matters*. It would be meaningless, therefore, to try and distil a number of 'do's and don'ts' hoping these would suffice to help the keen researcher do her job better. The ideas herein aim only to make you think harder about what and how you can change and do better what you are already doing.

To know if I have met these last two objectives, I have to be patient. One of the theses I will defend in Chapter 1 is that management innovation and, in particular, management research are in dire straits. To come out of such dark period we need a tsunami of the minds as well as of the system.

This book, then, will only be as valuable as the ripple effect it will manage to initiate. For now, I can only say that this has been one giant step for me.

Sharks and Life-Vests

This is a book written by a practitioner that is probably going to be read mostly by an audience of academics. I feel like a wounded man stranded at sea, bleeding out and waiting for the sharks to arrive and take a bite.

Some of the more methodologically focused and traditional researchers among the readers will no doubt note methodological limitations or flaws in my approach. Some will even find gaps in my knowledge of the state of the art. And some will probably feel impelled to let the world know of the many shortcomings they find.

If you are one of them, I want to help you.

Is this research based on a statistically valid sample? Probably not. Are the answers I suggest here based on a quantitative data analysis of variance? Nope. Would the design of this research pass the scrutiny of the typical double-blind review process of an A-Level journal? Certainly not. Is citing this book going to help you increase your citation index? Not by the slightest margin. In fact, I am sure you could write an entire paper about all these limitations. If that is what you feel impelled to do, you should follow your heart but don't feel obliged to let me know about it.

For the rest of my readers though, academics or not, I am the one asking you to throw me a life-vest. The 1921 Nobel Prize in Literature awardee Anatole France once said that "to accomplish great things, we must dream as well as act." Dreaming is not difficult. Acting, much more so. I initially dreamt of talking with tens or hundreds even but when I started, I realized how challenging it was to even find the time, resources, and energy to talk with just a few. In the end, I decided to write this book as I firmly believe that the experiences of even just a few people whose work has shaped the world as we know it today can teach us important lessons. Sharing these, I thought, is far too important to let myself get delayed in pursue of methodological excellence.

Mind you, I have tried to be as rigorous as I possibly could be in my research. But in the end, I followed the advice of Dr. Milton Chen, Executive Director of the George Lucas Educational Foundation, Edutopia, to "do your best even though it may not be perfect or good enough today. Making a real effort is what makes it a valuable learning experience, not just the outcome."[11]

But, of course, as is always the case, there is much room for improvement.

And here is where you come in: there is no doubt in the validity of the dream but your help can improve the action. I want to kindly ask that you contact me with as many suggestions and contributions as possible for improving this work's methodology, knowledge base, data set, interpretations, and whatever else you might think might matter.

Together, we can change the world.

Marco Busi
Aberdeen, United Kingdom
mygoalis@doingresearchthatmatters.com

Personal Introduction To The *Futureers*

Try not to become a man of success but rather try to become a man of value.

— Albert Einstein, Nobel Prize in Physics in 1921

The interviews with the *Futureers* are what made this project possible. They are the stars. Details about their life, scientific discoveries, and research insight will emerge here and there throughout the book. Therefore, although none of them needs an introduction, it makes sense that you meet them here. I am going to refer to the *Futureers* by their name, sometimes mentioning their main affiliation or award just to make it easier to remember who has done what and when, and rarely by their full affiliation or professional titles as that would mean killing many more trees than I want to.

So, please meet the *Futureers* (ranked in alphabetical order by their family name):

Gerhard Ertl[1] is a German scientist who won the 2007 Nobel Prize in Chemistry for his studies of chemical processes on solid surfaces. He was one of the first scientists to concentrate on the new field of semiconductors, and developed the methodology for modern surface chemistry, which uses high-vacuum experiments to observe the behavior of atoms and molecules on the uncontaminated surface of a metal. Among others, Ertl determined that chemical reactions on the surfaces of tiny ice crystals in the stratosphere cause damage to the Earth's protective ozone layer, and his work has advanced scientific understanding of why iron rusts, how fuel cells function, and how to clean auto emissions. Ertl has received so many honors this book would probably not be enough to contain them all. He is ranked number 6 among the Superstars of Science, a website celebrating "the scientific heroes of our age — those people that through their research, discoveries and theories have helped tackle some of the world's greatest problems, cure and prevent illness, heighten our understanding of nature and the universe, and inspired others to pursue scientific excellence."[2] Ertl studied physics at the Technical University of Stuttgart and completed his Diploma in Physics in 1961. He received his Ph.D. from the Technical University of Munich, Germany, in 1965. In 1986, he became director at the Fritz Haber Institute of the Max Planck Society, Berlin, Germany, where he remained until his retirement in 2004.

Rob Goffee[3] is one of Europe's leading experts on organizational culture, leadership, and change. He was named by Thinkers50 among the world's top 50 business thinkers (2009). He is Professor of organizational behavior at London Business School, where he has led several of the School's major executive programs, acted as Chair for the Organizational Behaviour Group, served as Deputy Dean and Governor, Director of the Innovation Exchange and Faculty Director of Executive Education. His work has covered a range of industries with a focus on leadership, change, corporate performance, entrepreneurship, business formation and growth, and managerial careers. An internationally respected teacher and facilitator, Rob has taught executives from some of the world's leading companies, including Unilever, Nestlé, and Sonae. He also consults to the boards of a number of FTSE 100 companies. Goffee has published over 70 articles and 10 books, including *Entrepreneurship in Europe*; *Women in Charge*; *Reluctant Managers*; *Corporate Realities* and *The Character of a Corporation* (1998) written with Gareth Jones. His articles feature in *Harvard Business Review*, *Leader to Leader*, *European Business Forum*, *Business Strategy Review*, *Management Today*, *People Management* and the *Financial Times*. Goffee is past winner, together with his long-time research partner Gareth Jones (a Fellow of the Centre for Management Development at London Business School and a Visiting Professor at INSEAD, Fontainebleau and IE Business School in Madrid), of the prestigious McKinsey Award for the best article in the *Harvard Business Review*, entitled, "Why Should Anyone Be Led by You?" The massive interest the article generated led to a five-year journey exploring authentic leadership. His book by the same title is a culmination of that research.

Margherita Hack[4] is a world-renowned Italian astrophysicist and popular science writer whose work has contributed significantly to what the world knows today about the stars and theirs spectra. So much so that her scientific contribution earned her a place among the stars, literally (!), with the asteroid 8558 Hack, discovered in 1995, being named in her honor. In 2012, on her 90th birthday, the President of Italy Giorgio Napolitano invested her of the honorific title of Knight Grand Cross of the "Ordine al Merito della Repubblica Italiana", the highest ranking honor and most senior order of the Italian Republic, for merit acquired by the nation. Born in 1922 in Florence, she received her Laurea in Physics from the Arcetri Observatory, in 1945, with a thesis in astrophysics on Cepheid variables. She was Professor ordinarius of Astronomy from 1964 to 1997 at the University of Trieste and Director of the Department of Astronomy there; she retired in 1998. She administered the Trieste Astronomical Observatory from 1964 to 1987, making it become internationally well known. Hack has worked for numerous observatories in the United States and Europe and she has also been a member of several working groups, most notably at ESA (the European Space Agency) and NASA (The National Aeronautics and Space

Administration). A member of several Physics and Astronomy associations, Margherita Hack is a national member of the "Accademia Nazionale dei Lincei," the oldest academy in the world (founded in 1603) and the highest Italian cultural institution, which in its ranks has featured members as prestigious as Galileo Galilei.

Robert S. Kaplan[5] is the Marvin Bower Professor of Leadership Development, Emeritus at the Harvard Business School and founder and Director of The Palladium Group, a strategy consultancy. In 2011, he was named in the top 15 among the Thinkers50 list of today's most influential business thinkers. He joined the HBS faculty in 1984 after spending 16 years on the faculty of the business school at Carnegie-Mellon University, where he served as Dean from 1977 to 1983. Robert Kaplan is known worldwide as the co-originator of ground-breaking management concepts like activity-based costing and the Balanced Scorecard, both among the most successful and widely used management tools in the world. Kaplan's current research focuses on two topics: measuring and managing organizational risk and, in a joint project with his Harvard colleague Michael Porter, measuring the cost of delivering health care and linking patient costs to outcomes. Later in the book, you will have a chance to read about this collaboration as he recounts it. Kaplan received a B.S. and M.S. in Electrical Engineering from MIT, and a Ph.D. in Operations Research from Cornell University. He has received honorary doctorates from the Universities of Stuttgart (1994), Lodz (2006), and Waterloo (2008). He has published 14 books and over 150 papers including 23 in *Harvard Business Review*. Recent books include *The Execution Premium: Linking Strategy to Operations for Competitive Advantage*, the fifth *Balanced Scorecard* book co-authored with David Norton, and *Time-Driven Activity-Based Costing* with Steve Anderson. The list of Kaplan's awards and honors is endless. Most recently, he was elected to the Accounting Hall of Fame in 2006, and was given the Lifetime Contribution Award for Distinguished Contributions to Advancing the Management Accounting Profession from the Institute of Management Accountants in 2008, and the Lifetime Contribution Award from the Management Accounting Section of the American Accounting Association (AAA) in 2006.

Barbara Kellerman[6] is the James MacGregor Burns Lecturer in Public Leadership at Harvard University's John F. Kennedy School of Government. She was the Founding Executive Director of the Kennedy School's Center for Public Leadership, from 2000 to 2003; and from 2003 to 2006 she served as the Center's Research Director. Kellerman was ranked by Forbes.com as among "Top 50 Business Thinkers" (2009); by Leadership Excellence in top 15 of 100 "best minds on leadership" (2008–2009) and in the top 50 world's management thinker by Thinkers50 (2009). She is on the Advisory Board of the Leadership Research Network, on the Advisory Panel of the White House Leadership Project Report, on the Advisory Board of the Brookings Institution Leadership Initiative, and on the Publications Committee of the International Leadership Association. In 2010 she was given the Wilbur M. McFeeley award by the National Management Association for her pioneering work on leadership and followership. She received her B.A. from Sarah

Lawrence College, and her M.A., M.Phil., and Ph.D. (1975, in Political Science) degrees from Yale University. Kellerman was cofounder of the International Leadership Association (ILA), and is the author and editor of many books including *Bad Leadership*, *Followership*, *Leadership: Essential Selections on Power, Authority, and Influence*, and *The End of Leadership*. She has appeared often on media outlets such as CBS, NBC, PBS, CNN, NPR, Reuters, and BBC, and has contributed articles and reviews to *The New York Times*, *The Washington Post*, *The Boston Globe*, the *Los Angeles Times*, and the *Harvard Business Review*.

Philip Kotler[7] is the S.C. Johnson & Son Distinguished Professor of International Marketing at the Northwestern University Kellogg School of Management in Chicago. He is hailed by Management Centre Europe as "the world's foremost expert on the strategic practice of marketing." In 2009, he was ranked 9th in the Thinkers50 list of the world's top 50 business thinkers. He was a Member of the Board of Governors of the School of the Art Institute of Chicago and a Member of the Advisory Board of the Drucker Foundation. Kotler has consulted for some of the largest companies in the world, such as IBM, General Electric, AT&T, Honeywell, Bank of America, Merck, and others in the areas of marketing strategy and planning, marketing organization, and international marketing. He received his Master's degree at the University of Chicago and his Ph.D. degree at MIT, both in economics. He did post-doctoral work in mathematics at Harvard University and in behavioral science at the University of Chicago. He has also received honorary doctoral degrees from 14 universities worldwide. Kotler has published over 150 articles in leading journals, several of which have received best-article awards. He is also the author of many books: *Marketing Management: Analysis, Planning, Implementation and Control*; *Principles of Marketing*; *Marketing Models*; *Strategic Marketing for Nonprofit Organizations*; *The New Competition*; *High Visibility*; *Social Marketing*; *Marketing Places*; *Marketing for Congregations*; *Strategic Marketing for Hospitality and Tourism*; *The Marketing of Nations*; *Kotler on Marketing*; *Building Global Biobrands*; *Attracting Investors*; *Ten Deadly Marketing Sins*; *Marketing Moves*; *Marketing Insights from A to Z*; *Chaotics*; and *Market Your Way to Growth*.

John Kotter[8] is a world-recognized expert on change management and leadership. He is the Konosuke Matsushita Professor of Leadership, Emeritus at the Harvard Business School, a graduate of MIT and Harvard, and co-founder of consultancy Kotter International. He joined the Harvard Business School faculty in 1972. In 1980, at the age of 33, he was voted tenure and a full professorship, making him one of the youngest people in the history of the university to be so honored. In 2011, he has been ranked among the Thinkers50's list of the world's top 50 most influential business thinkers. Kotter has been the premier voice on how the best organizations actually *do* change. His international bestseller *Leading Change*, in which he outlines an actionable, eight-step process for implementing successful transformations, has become the change bible for managers around the world and was listed by *Time* magazine as one of the 25 most influential books ever written on business management. In 1996, *Leading Change* was named the number one management book of the year. He is the author of 18 books, 12 of which have been business best sellers and two *The New York Times* best sellers. His works have been printed in over 150 foreign language editions and total sales exceed three million copies. His books are in the top 1% of sales on Amazon.com. His articles in *The Harvard Business Review* over the past 20 years have sold more reprints than any of the hundreds of distinguished authors who have written for that publication during the same time period.

Howard Gardner[9] is the John H. and Elisabeth A. Hobbs Professor of Cognition and Education at the Harvard Graduate School of Education and Senior Director of Harvard Project Zero. His theory of multiple intelligences, outlined in his book *Frames of Mind* (1983), granted him worldwide recognition. Gardner's research revealed the existence of other forms of intelligence, such as kinesthetic intelligence possessed by athletes, and higher musical intelligence among musicians. The author of 28 books translated into 32 languages, and several hundred articles, Gardner is best known in educational circles for his theory of multiple intelligences, a critique of the notion that there exists but a single human intelligence that can be adequately assessed by standard psychometric instruments. In the business world he is widely known for his book *Five Minds for the Future* (2007) where he identifies the five minds as disciplined, synthesizing, creative, respectful, and ethical. In 2011, Gardner received the 2011 Prince of Asturias Award for Social Sciences; the same year, he was ranked number 37 on the Thinkers50's list of the world's most influential business thinkers. In 2005 and again in 2008, he was selected by Foreign Policy and Prospect magazines as one of the 100 most influential public intellectuals in the world. Among the many honors, he received a MacArthur Prize Fellowship in 1981 and was awarded honorary degrees from 29 colleges and universities from around the world. During the past two decades, Gardner and colleagues at Project Zero have been involved in the design of performance-based assessments; education for under-standing; the use of multiple intelligences to achieve more personalized curriculum, instruction, and pedagogy; and the quality of interdisciplinary efforts in education. Since the mid-1990s, in collaboration with Psychologists Mihaly Csikszentmihalyi and William Damon, Gardner has directed the GoodWork Project — a study of work that is excellent, engaging, and ethical. Gardner's current research focuses on effective collaboration among non-profit institutions in education and a study of conceptions of quality, nationally and internationally, in the contemporary era. Professor Gardner asked me to emphasize that his discussion of funding and carrying out research — which has emerged from his interview and which I present in this book — is done from the perspective of the United States.

Constantinos (Costas) Markides[10] is Professor of Strategic and International Management and holds the Robert P. Bauman Chair of Strategic Leadership at the London Business School, whose MBA program was ranked number one by the *Financial Times* in 2009, 2010, and 2011. In 2011 he was listed among the top 50 world's business thinkers by Thinkers50. His research interests include the management of diversified businesses and the use of innovation and creativity to achieve strategic breakthroughs. He advocates continual corporate innovation —

even when a company is doing very well. His books include *All the Right Moves: A Guide to Crafting Breakthrough Strategy* (2000); and *Fast Second: How Smart Companies Bypass Radical Innovation to Enter and Dominate New Markets* (2005) with Paul Geroski. *Fast Second* used the metaphor of a landscape to describe the business world, dividing organizations into "colonists" and "consolidators." The former are good at exploring new business opportunities, but the latter are better adapted to commercializing them. He has published extensively in *Harvard Business Review*, *Sloan Management Review*, and many other scholarly and managerially relevant journals. In recent years, increasingly Markides has turned his attention to how management ideas can be used to address social issues such as reducing drug-related crime and improving education. A native of Cyprus, Markides received his B.A. (Distinction) and M.A. in Economics from Boston University, and his MBA and DBA from the Harvard Business School.

Roger Martin[11] has served as Dean of the Rotman School of Management at the University of Toronto, Canada, since September 1, 1998. He is best known for his work on integrative thinking as a means of solving complex problems. In 2011, he was named by Thinkers50 as the sixth top management thinker in the world; one of the 27 most influential designers in the world by *BusinessWeek* in 2010; and "B-School All-Star" by *BusinessWeek* in 2007 for being one of the 10 most influential business professors in the world. He regularly contributes to *Washington Post's On Leadership* blog and to *Financial Times' Judgment Call* column. He has published 15 *Harvard Business Review* articles and numerous books, of which *The Opposable Mind: How Successful Leaders Win Through Integrative Thinking* (2007) is the best known. His other most recent books include *Playing to Win: How Strategy Really Works* (2013), co-authored with former P&G CEO AG Lafley; *Fixing the Game, Bubbles, Crashes, and What Capitalism Can Learn from the NFL* (2011), *The Design of Business: Why Design Thinking Is the Next Competitive Advantage* (2009), and *The Future of the MBA: Designing the Thinker of the Future* (with Mihnea Moldoveanu, 2008). He received his A.B. from Harvard College, with a concentration in Economics, in 1979 and his MBA from the Harvard Business School in 1981. In his most recent research and book, Martin focuses on the state of American capitalism and the effects of coupling the "real" market — designing, making and selling products and services — with the "expectations" market-trading stocks, options, and complex derivatives. The economic train crash of 2008, he says, was a direct result.

Henry Mintzberg[12] is currently John Cleghorn Professor of Management Studies at the Desautels Faculty of Management, McGill University in Montreal. In 2011 he was ranked number 30 in the Thinkers50 list of the world's top business thinkers. He is best known for his work on management and, in particular, on the work of managers, how they are trained and developed. He is also one of the leading figures publicly criticizing modern management education and in particular traditional MBAs for not giving managers the knowledge and skills they need to manage effectively. Mintzberg's claims to fame are too many to include here. Among others, in his first book, *The Nature of Managerial Work* (1973), he challenged the established thinking about the role of the manager, examining what managers do, rather than what they should do. His work on organizational forms identified five types of organization: simple structure; machine bureaucracy; professional bureaucracy; the divisionalized form; and the adhocracy. Furthermore, he is also credited with advancing the idea of emergent strategy — whereby effective strategy emerges from conversations within an organization rather than being imposed from on high. Mintzberg is the author to over 150 articles and 15 books. Some of his best known books include *Managing* (2009), *Tracking Strategies* (2007), *Managers not MBAs* (2004), *The Nature of Managerial Work* (1973), *The Structuring of Organizations* (1979), *Mintzberg on Management: Inside Our Strange World of Organizations* (1989). He is a former President of the Strategic Management Society, Distinguished Scholar Academy of Management and an Officer of the Order of Canada and of l'Ordre national du Quebec. In addition to teaching at McGill, he has been a Visiting Professor at the Université d'Aix Marseille (France), Carnegie-Mellon University, École des Hautes Études Commerciales (Montreal), the London Business School (England), and INSEAD (France).

Douglas Dean Osheroff[13] was the recipient jointly with David M. Lee and Robert C. Richardson of the 1996 Nobel Prize in Physics for their discovery of superfluidity in helium-3. This discovery was made in 1971, when Osheroff was a 26-year-old graduate student at Cornell. He earned his Bachelor's degree in 1967 from Caltech. There his freshman and sophomore classes learned Physics from the famous three-volume set by Feynman, Leighton, and Sands that was produced in response to Feynman's lectures to the freshman and sophomore classes at Caltech. He received a Ph.D. from Cornell University in 1973. In 1972, Osheroff accepted a position at Bell Labs in New Jersey at Murray Hill. He joined the Department of Solid State and Low Temperature Research under the direction of C. C. Grimes. In 1987, after 15 years, Osheroff left Bell Laboratories to accept a position at Stanford University. In 1991, Stanford honored Osheroff with the Gores Award for excellence in teaching. From 1993 to 1996, he served as Physics Department Chair, and stepped down in September 1996. He is now J. G. Jackson and C. J. Wood Professor Emeritus of Physics and (by courtesy) Applied Physics at Stanford University, Department of Physics.

Elinor Ostrom[14] was awarded the Sveriges Riksbank Prize in Economic Sciences in memory of Alfred Nobel in 2009 jointly with Oliver E. Williamson, for her analysis of economic governance, especially the commons. She challenged the conventional wisdom by demonstrating how local property can be successfully managed by local commons without any regulation by central authorities or privatization. She was the first woman and remains the only woman to be awarded the prize. Professor Ostrom sadly died on June12, 2012, age 78 leaving a wonderful legacy for scholars and humankind. She was Indiana University Distinguished Professor, Senior Research Director of the Vincent and Elinor Ostrom Workshop in Political Theory and Policy Analysis, Distinguished Professor and Arthur F. Bentley Professor of Political Science in the College of Arts and Sciences, and Professor in the School of Public and

Environmental Affairs. In April 2012, she was named to the *Time 100*, *Time* magazine's annual list of the 100 most influential people in the world. Together with her husband, Vincent Ostrom, in February 2010 she was awarded the University Medal, the highest award bestowed by Indiana University. An Indiana University faculty member since 1965, Ostrom has conducted research on topics ranging from the effectiveness of urban police departments to the management of groundwater basins, irrigation systems, pasture lands, forests, and fisheries. In addition to her positions at IU, Ostrom was the Founding Director of the Center for the Study of Institutional Diversity at Arizona State University.

Jack William Szostak[15] was awarded the Nobel Prize in Physiology or Medicine in 2009 "for the discovery of how chromosomes are protected by telomeres and the enzyme telomerase" jointly with Elizabeth H. Blackburn and Carol W. Greider. He is a U.S. citizen although he was born in London, the United Kingdom, and grew up in Canada. He studied at McGill University in Montreal and at Cornell University in Ithaca, New York, where he received his Ph.D. in 1977. He has been at Harvard Medical School since 1979 and is currently a Howard Hughes Medical Institute Investigator, the Alexander Rich Distinguished Investigator at Massachusetts General Hospital, and Professor of Genetics at Harvard Medical School. He is also affiliated with the Howard Hughes Medical Institute. He is a member of the Biological Sciences Class of the American Philosophical Society, which is considered the oldest learned society in the United States. Past members have included Benjamin Franklin, Charles Darwin, Louis Pasteur, and Linus Pauling. In addition to the Nobel Prize, Jack Szostak is the awardee of the 2008 Dr. H.P. Heineken Prize for Biochemistry and Biophysics and the 2006 Albert Lasker Basic Medical Research Award for his work on telomerase. His current research is on the origin of life.

David (Dave) Ulrich[16] is as a Professor of Business at the University of Michigan and a principal partner at the RBL Group, a consulting firm focused on helping organizations and leaders deliver value. His research and professional interests relate to how organizations build capabilities of speed, learning, collaboration, accountability, talent, and leadership through leveraging human resources. He has consulted and done research with over half of the Fortune 200 helping leaders build their personal and organization leadership brand, HR departments and professionals deliver value, and organizations align their culture with customer expectations (e.g., he and a team of colleagues helped GE and the then CEO Jack Welch to design the bureaucracy cutting Workout program). Ulrich is the co-author of over 100 articles and book chapters and 23 books. These include HR books (*Human Resource Champions*; *HR Value Proposition*; *HR Transformation*; *HR Competencies*); leadership books (*Why the Bottom Line ISN'T!*; *Leadership Code*, *Leadership Brand*) and organization books (*Boundaryless Organization*; *Learning Organization*; *GE Workout*). In his latest book *The Why of Work: How Great Leaders Build Abundant Organizations That Win* (2011), Ulrich, with his psychologist wife Wendy, examines people's motivation for working and what they get out of work. He was the Editor of *Human Resource Management Journal* (1990–1999), served on the editorial board of four other journals, is on the Board of Directors for Herman Miller, is a Fellow in the National Academy of Human Resources, and co-founder of the Michigan Human Resource Partnership.

Harald zur Hausen[17] was awarded the Nobel Prize in Physiology or Medicine in 2008. The Nobel Prize was divided, one-half awarded to Harald zur Hausen "for his discovery of human papilloma viruses causing cervical cancer," the other half jointly to Françoise Barré-Sinoussi and Luc Montagnier "for their discovery of human immunodeficiency virus." Zur Hausen studied Medicine at the Universities of Bonn, Hamburg, and Düsseldorf and received his M.D. in 1960. After his internship he worked as post-doc at the Institute of Microbiology in Düsseldorf, subsequently in the Virus Laboratories of the Children's Hospital in Philadelphia where he was later appointed as Assistant Professor. After a period of 3 years as a Senior Scientist at the Institute of Virology of the University of Würzburg, he was appointed in 1972 as Chairman and Professor of Virology at the University of Erlangen-Nürnberg. In 1977 he moved to a similar position to the University of Freiburg. From 1983 until 2003 he was appointed as Scientific Director of the Deutsches Krebsforschungszentrum (German Cancer Research Center) in Heidelberg. He retired from this position in 2003. He received numerous national and international awards and he received 23 honorary M.D. and Ph.D. degrees from various universities in the world. He is an elected member of various academies and research organizations, and became an Honorary Member of a number of biomedical scientific societies. From January 2000 to December 2009, zur Hausen was Editor-in-Chief of the *International Journal of Cancer*, and from 2006 until 2010 he was member of the Board of Directors of the International Union against Cancer (UICC). From 2003 until 2010 he was Vice-President of the German National Academy for Natural Sciences and Medicine LEOPOLDINA in Halle. Since 2006 he is member of the Scientific Council of the National Science Transfer and Development Agency in Bangkok, Thailand.

CHAPTER 1

SHAPING THE FUTURE OF MANAGEMENT BY REINVENTING MANAGEMENT RESEARCH

For business faculty to move from being merely scribes and conceptualisers to being inventors, we need the courage to commit ourselves to really romantic goals, to problems for which there are no obvious and immediate solutions.[1]

— Gary Hamel
Ranked world's #1 most influential business
thinker by the Wall Street Journal

Does the Management Field Really Need More Insight?

Gary Hamel thinks that "Most of modern management as we know it today ... was invented in a very brief period of time, from about 1890 to 1920. Ironically, we expect great leaps in other kinds of technologies but we assume that management has to stay the same. If we think of management as a social technology, there is no reason to believe that it couldn't be reinvented ... As researchers, we need to become more experimental. As human beings, we are always interested in what the next great breakthrough in medicine or technology will be. I don't know how many people are asking, 'What's the next great breakthrough in management? ...' And I ask, 'Where are the management and business school faculty in all of this? How are we making a real difference in the way businesses are run, rather than being interested only in incrementally improving their effectiveness?' "[2]

The notion of questioning the impact of current research and fostering more impact for future research has been around for years, although the heat and attention on it seems to be ratcheting nowadays. The current widespread discontent with the quality and relevance of academic research in management is undisputed.

Much of the discontent comes from outside the academy's walls, spurred by business, professional organizations, and the press. Ben Schiller's *Financial Times* article by the title "Academia strives for relevance"[3] is just one of the more recent diatribes urging professors to focus research on topics that appeal to and can help managers. Indeed, the *Financial Times, Wall Street Journal* and other institutions regularly question the current state of business education and often cite the disconnect between research and its link to the organizational world. Even the Association to Advance Collegiate Schools of Business (AACSB), in their "Final Report of the AACSB International: Impact of Research,"[4] noted how "business schools have recently been criticized for placing too much emphasis on research relative to teaching, and for producing research that is too narrow, irrelevant, and impractical"[5] and called for "impactful research" to become a guiding principle for business schools.

But the discontent comes from within the academy as well. For nearly four decades, some of the most deliberate and urgent calls for research relevance and usefulness to practice came from those producing research.[6] Over 35 years ago, in the article "Towards more meaningful research" published on *The Personnel Guidance Journal* by Leo Goldman,[7] the then City University of New York's professor made some observations that are still as valid today. Among others, he noted that: "research rarely tells us anything about the cutting edges of our field, or about the current major needs and wants of our customers — the individuals, institutions, and communities that we serve." He lamented the lack of "meaningful research" and then posed a question: "what is responsible for this state of affairs?" The answer stemmed in part from the diverse worlds of researchers and practitioners, which in his time rarely intersected (still true today). That diversion caused Goldman to see the inevitable outcome, that is: "we don't study important topics" —

> "... [researchers] go on and on asking the same tired old questions or asking questions about smaller and smaller matters ... why is this? Partly because so often the research is done by people who indeed do live in a different world from that where counsellors [or "managers"] are struggling."[8]

Like Goldman, many others have since lamented such apparent problems. Remarkably, no matter how many academics or practitioners have noted such a terrible state of affair and no matter how many outstanding authors have proposed solutions that could help eager academics do *research that matters*,[9] even after 30 years, the situation remains largely unchanged. If anything, it is getting worst.

Why is that? This is one of the questions I ask in this book.

In a moving personal discussion of his "intellectual journey," the ITT Professor of Creative Management at the Stern School of Business (New York University), William H. Starbuck[10] recounts how he came to a surprising and disconcerting realization: in trying to create a 'real' science in the management field, using computer simulation, mathematical and experimental research approaches, he missed his goal of having impact. Instead, he decided to conduct research that *changes* rather than simply *describes* what he sees. To do that, he suggested more recently that perhaps researchers should seek out opportunities to cooperate with managers as a way to ask better questions, obtain better data, and more meaningfully interpret their findings.[11]

Starbuck's suggestion is not to be interpreted necessarily as research needing to be applicable to matter. Some actually challenge the idea that practical applicability is an inherent dimension of good research. Most notably, Henry Mintzberg is convinced that "meaningful doesn't mean applicable by practitioners" and that research should not "help practitioners ... make more money ..., [but] simply ... enable them to see more deeply into the problems they face."

Although, there exists a stream of thought — in which I personally recognize myself — that gives particular importance to generating knowledge that can be used in practice. Rob Goffee, Professor of Organisational Behaviour at London Business School, recognizes the need to "connect big ideas formed up in the stratosphere with actions down in the trenches."

As part of this book, I thought it worthwhile to ponder on this *apparent* contrast in views.

Last, there is the important matter of time. The editor of the *Journal of Managerial Psychology*[12] recently called for "creating knowledge that makes important contributions to society" that will enhance well-being of individuals, organizations, and society. In his Academy of Management Presidential Address, Professor Tom Lee argued that the "value of scholarly contributions should be evaluated by the subsequent knowledge they inspire,"[13] which can take decades of programmatic focus in a topic area.

This brings up another important issue I look at in the book about the apparent contrast between a game that requires its players to quickly and continuously publish to stay and prosper in the academe and a widespread agreement among management gurus (be they from the academy or from industry) and Nobel Laureates from fields other than management that to do *research that matters* and to generate meaningful insight require years of hard work and dedication.

What Do You Want to Be: A Storyteller or a True Innovator?

Not much has changed since Goldman's remark 35 years ago and today still, rarely do we encounter management articles that astound us, theories that explain what is happening or could happen, new approaches and ways of thinking, or ideas that will help change lives. Too many articles focus on the past — reporting or re-telling or re-testing knowledge that already exists, rather than building theories or ideas for the future.

In 2008, in my role as editor of *Strategic Outsourcing, an International Journal*, I conducted an assessment of articles submissions to the title together with colleague and editorial advisory board member Ronan McIvor, Professor of Operations Management at the University of Ulster, Northern Ireland. As we looked in particular at the theories most often cited and used in those articles, we concluded somewhat disconcertingly that: "The worrying observation is that, even though the amount of information available and the amount of published papers have increased, we must admit that the end of last century and the beginning of the 21st century have seen a marked decline in the amount and significance of theory formulation." We then posed a challenging question: "Is this a warning signal that researchers are taking more of a reporter or a story teller role, describing what happens in the real world, rather than providing innovative thinking and thought leadership to shape the future not only of the ... discipline but of practice as well?"[14]

And even when articles report on seemingly 'new' insight, the argued novel knowledge represents only a minimal incremental addition to the body of knowledge or practice. And yet, Gary Hamel warned us that "to fulfil our potential as innovators and inventors, we have to be willing to look beyond today's best practices and commit ourselves to making a difference in organisations."[15]

Are we simply at another cycle of hand wringing about research and its value to the broader world? And why are we still facing the same challenges and limitations as four decades ago? What if this is too big a problem to solve? Gary Hamel again thinks that "We need to solve problems that today seem almost insurmountable. It's hard work, but courage comes from the willingness to tackle a problem that may not be easy but that's inherently worthwhile."[16]

Remembering that what led many of us to work in research in the first place was a thirst for discovery, I decided to try and understand how we could reverse this depressing trend. That is why I look at the concept of *big questions* versus *small questions* and the role of research in generating *incremental* versus *radical innovation* later in the book.

Dissemination and knowledge transfer is also facing some serious challenges. There are strong pressures from within the scientific community to "publish or perish," the idea being that career advancement and prosperity in academia is strongly linked to, and solely dependent by, one's ability to publish. At the same time and consequently, publishing in scholarly outlets is getting increasingly difficult — rejection rate is absurdly a measure of quality for certain scholarly outlets — and lengthy. Even assuming we could produce a masterpiece, it could take years before we can see it in print.

Today's research quality measures and scientific publishing trends are also enforcing an idea of research rigor and quality that is narrowing more and more the type of problems we investigate and the approaches we use to solve them. As a matter of fact, academic publishing in particular, for no good reason, is turning into too fine a filter that while it allows thousands of valueless sand particles to go through, it often stops gold nuggets from ever reaching the light of day.

Not least, whilst scientific writing style might be conducive to communicate with other academics, it is less conducive to creating excitement and interest in practitioners and the wider audience. Interestingly, I found during my research that the current communication style does not even generate interest and excitement in other academics. Plus, many academics confirm that the sheer amount of new journals and articles being published every month is making it impossible for them to read much anymore these days.

All this begs the question as to how we can hope to influence anybody's behavior if nobody — not even other academics — reads what we write. It also begs another question as to why, if nobody reads what academics write, are they being pushed to write and publish more and more?

This has led me to investigate dissemination in the context of enabling *research that matters* and what other ways exist to spread ideas and innovation.

The System of Management Research: A Hard to Change Equilibrium

In preparation for my interview with him, Harvard University Professor Robert Kaplan kindly sent me a few of his articles that he thought I should read.

First, I read the one he published in 1998 in the *Journal of Management Accounting Research*, entitled "Innovation action research: Creating New Management Theory and Practice."[17] Recounting retrospectively the work he had done years before and that had led him to develop ground breaking concepts like the balanced scorecard, in that article he proposed a "theory of a [specific] mode of knowledge creation" based on using what he referred to as "innovation action research." He explained that what pushed him to propose innovation action research was the realization that, where problems encountered in practice could not be solved with available ideas and theories, "extensive studies of existing practice would merely document obsolete and ineffective practice, not the innovative practice [that are in these cases] needed.

"In innovation action research, scholars work with client organisations to enhance and test an emerging theory that has been proposed to improve organisational performance. Innovation action research is very much experimental, especially in the early stages of developing a new theory, since both the scholar and the client organisation want to learn more about the emerging theory and how it can be successfully implemented ... The scholars become active change agents, helping to create phenomena that did not exist before ..."

Kaplan's observed that "for research intended to improve management of organizations, scholars should find it natural to contemplate changing the underlying phenomena, not just study existing practices."

I couldn't but feel slightly dismayed then when I read the other article he had sent me, which he published in 2011 by the title "Accounting Scholarship that Advances Professional Knowledge and Practice."[18] In there, he noted how scholarship in his field seems to have failed to address "important issues that have risen in the past 40 years of practice."

I would have hoped that those working in a field, the very though leader of which proposes a mode of research that evidently works, would follow the lead. But almost 15 years later, the theory Kaplan had proposed, failed to be adopted successfully.

Not that this situation is limited to accounting research alone. Just two years before, in 2009, one entire issue of the *Journal of Management Inquiry* was dedicated to discussing the irrelevance of organization theory and research studies.[19] Wondering what had happened to organization theory, some noted how scholars in this field as well had failed to develop insight that can inform practice and argued that "this is a very serious problem that was avoided by the founders of our disciplines."[20] Whereas others suggested that "a growing preoccupation with theoretical and methodological rigor [may] underpin the increasing generation of theory and research that is irrelevant to managers."[21]

When I asked Professor Kaplan why he thought this was the case, he put forward an interesting thought:

Kaplan's view is that academic scholarship is a complex system comprising many parts that have nowadays converged to equilibrium. In his words, "it is a very stable equilibrium, even if it is an unfortunate equilibrium guided towards a very narrow view of research ... All journals converge to a narrow set of research methods. Promotions can then depend upon whether you get articles published in that set of journals. And so the people who are promoted have bought into that theory of research. Then they train doctoral students ... and the negative cycle continues.

"It's very hard to break out of that system. It's very stable, it's reinforcing and it is able to withstand a lot of criticism from outside because it is internally consistent and sustainable.

"And so that's our whole system of academic scholarship now, and it converges to things that people can do easily. ... We can buy databases and sit in our offices and write statistical analyses, we can do mathematics on yellow pages on our desks or run experiments with our students in laboratories and write them up and publish them. It's scholarship without tears."

I am, quite clearly, not the first person to suggest that management research needs to change. For years, scholars and business people have debated *how to* make research more relevant. The classic 1971 article "That's Interesting!" by Murray S. Davis[22] was an early call for examining "interesting results," those that deny assumptions or challenge theories. Since then, many eminent researchers, including several of our interviewees, have called for creating new theories, for doing research that can be applied[23] or implemented[24] and can be assessed beyond "journal rankings"[25,26] or the "rigor-relevance" argument.[27]

Many question whether business schools and professors have "lost their way" in the focus on theoretical rather than more relevant research[28] and suggest that collaboration across disciplines[29] or between academia and business would help "cross the chasm" to enhance relevance.[30,31]

And so it can too often be seen that, although it is good practice to include a discussion on implications for practice at the end of scientific publications, this is often little more than a check mark, since the implementation in practice rarely happens or if it does, it receives little attention.[32]

What is concerning though is that it is not just the contribution of research to practice that is hard to find. Besides the many existing reference to this issue that can be found in literature, I actually witnessed it first hand as editor of a scholarly journal myself.

In an effort to draw out the relevancy of published research, Emerald Group Publishing started a number of years ago to demand that all articles published in their journals be introduced by a structured abstract. This includes, among others, three sections: "Research limitations/implications"; "Practical implications"; and "Social Implications." You would be surprised to know — or maybe not — that the number of authors leaving blank these three sections far surpasses those who actually know how to defend their contribution to knowledge, practice, and society.

This is, therefore, an old problem that I try in this book to look at from a different perspective. Validating Kaplan's 15-year-old view, my interviewees pointed out that one key characteristics of *research that matters* is its ability to change the underlying paradigm of the system under study. Using Markides' words: "… the first step … to generate more innovation in academic research is to change our purpose or paradigm, which says that our goal is to publish or perish. It is not! Our goal is to generate ideas that help change the world, that create value. And if you don't develop a new paradigm or use new mindsets you are never going to have progress in academia."

I would therefore like to throw a challenge at those brave enough to face it, which is to think about what you can do to change the system of management research in its current unfortunate equilibrium so accurately described by Kaplan. In other words, how can you do *more* research that matters *more*?

Focus on Building a Meaningful Journey and You Will Inevitably End Up at a Meaningful Destination

One clear theme that has emerged during the interviews is that the remarkable people who unquestionably succeed in *doing research that matters* always know what they are aiming for: some call it doing insightful research, some call it generating usable knowledge. Although they might end up with what most in the end hope is something that will transform the future (and it often does), when I spoke to them I understood that these people are passionate about what they do (i.e., the journey) more than for what they aim to achieve (i.e., the explicit destination). Especially if and when the actual destination is unclear, the passion for the research journey is paramount.

I heard somewhere that we may as well dream to achieve great things in life as we don't consume less calories by dreaming small. The people I talked to certainly have shown the ability to think big and to try to solve "romantic problems," that is problems that matters. However, looking across the *Futureers*' experiences, the one thing they all have in common is that they find — or, better, they look for — satisfaction and self-reward from the journey they go through to solve such life-changing problems, not from finding the solution to those problems.

They don't look for fame or status, although certainly these are enjoyable aspects of their careers. They don't even look for the freedom to work where/when they want, although these as well certainly contribute to making the journey pleasurable. And they don't desperately seek financial gains, although some of them are enjoying great riches from the commercialization of their research work.

Robert Kaplan exemplified what I heard from many. The driving question for all of his research work is: "Does this research help me think differently and better about a problem that I care about? And so wow, ... based on this research I really understand the problem much better, I can understand the solution better." Joy and satisfaction, therefore, come from doing something well, generating new insight, and pursuing truly new discoveries.

I am going to share many ideas I gained from these interviews but, if I had to choose just one suggestion I would like you take away from this book, this would be it. Don't spend too much energy on the end-result and rather focus on enjoying the journey.

London Business School's Markides puts it well: "If you start by saying: I want to do this research because I want to publish in the top journals, I guarantee you that you have a very low probability of success that you are going to come up with interesting questions or interesting answers."

Even if you have the grander aim in mind of *doing research that matters*, keep your eyes firmly on the road and don't you worry about your final destination. Henry Mintzberg seems to take exactly the same approach: "I don't ever remember asking myself [whether my research was going to change people's life]. On the other hand if I am doing research that's insightful of course it's going to change people's behaviours."

Because of these observations, I have structured the book using a loose metaphor to a journey. I start looking at how the *Futureers* prepare for their journey, in terms of: how they know what to aim for, i.e., the concept of *research that matters*, and what drives them to choose the road of research. I then look at how they approach and design their journey. I try to understand how they find those romantic problems that are worth investigating; how they go about solving them; and how important is collaboration in what they do. Then, I try to understand how they share their experience, focusing on issues like getting the word out and publishing (or perishing?). Finally I attempt to reach the end of my personal journey pondering on what *I*, first and foremost, and more generally individuals, institutions and publishing organizations could do to encourage and do more *research that matters*.

CHAPTER 2

DESTINATION PARADISE: UNDERSTANDING WHAT TO AIM FOR

Tell me what you yearn for and I shall tell you who you are. We are what we reach for, the idealized image that drives our wandering.

— James Hillman

Great research, over short or long periods of time, demonstrates some knowledge of how the world works and proves itself out by people taking action ... So it's not just ... laborious work that gets you to $E = MC^2$, it's the fact that people have been able to use that insight to create nuclear power which works. It's not just a theory. It actually works.

— John Kotter, Harvard Business School

"*Research that matters*" is the central topic of this book. But what does it mean? As you might imagine, it means different things to different people. What might be obvious to one might be completely alien to another. Equally esteemed colleagues have equally valid but slightly different views on the characterizing features of an excellent piece of research. Rob Goffee told me: "you can define [research] excellence in many ways. You have decided to drive your definition with this notion of life changing. I kind of like that idea and I do think that's the kind of ambitious vision that ought to be shaping at least some of our research if not all of it."

Although it might seem contradictory to start from the very point that I earlier suggested not to spend too much energy thinking about, that is the destination, I need to do this to clarify what I aim for and what the subsequent chapters will try to lead to.

Hence, in this chapter I present my understanding of the concept of *research that matters* and I put forward a model based on the research behind this book.

Exploring What Makes Us Proud

The first step toward understanding *how to* do *research that matters* is to understand what this concept means. Specifically, what are the characteristics of an excellent piece of research?

I begun my investigation by asking some of my colleagues from various universities around the world to answer one single question:

What is the piece of research (published or unpublished) that you have completed in your career which you are most proud of and why are you so proud of it?

I asked one single question by email using words like *proud* to instigate a quick emotional response, rather than a well thought through scientific dissertation. It worked, generating results that were enlightening on several levels.

First, my colleagues' initial comments were on the question itself. Most found it *difficult, interesting, important, exciting, stimulating, fundamental and thought provoking,* validating the idea that I was onto something meaningful. Even more compelling was the realization that (at least these) academic colleagues want to contribute to shaping the future of management.

I analyzed all answers searching for keywords patterns. This analysis allowed me to start mapping the concept of *research that matters* and its key dimensions and characteristics, which fell into several categories.

A first interesting observation, in line with the depressing state of academic research that I discussed earlier, was that many respondents associated the concept of *research* with that of *publication* and the concept of *research that matters* with that of *research published/cited in high-ranking journals.* As a matter of fact, all who responded cited one or more of their published articles as examples of research they were most proud of. Many cited (1) publications that appeared in top-rated journals or (2) citations of their work by others as two important measures they used to rate how much their research mattered.

Next, others too cited the type and amount of publications and citations as inherent characteristics of insightful research but gave us a different perspective on the reasons why these are so: in their views, when a piece of *research that matters* attracts interest of other academics, they in turn *initiate further research* activities that might end up in multiple publications and start a cyclical development that eventually lead to uncovering more insight on the topic. This increases the potential for impact because of greater attention on the topic, increased number of observations, more testing and more publications. All of these steps help create and spread theories/concepts/tools and, potentially, support their wider adoption in the world of practice. In essence, they suggested that *the amount and scope of influence* was of importance and a number of *publications* and *citations* were valid measures of performance in the academic world.

For others yet the attention should be put more on the ability of a piece of research to generate further research. What I call the *viral* dimension also emerged in some of the answers, implying that good research should change the way other researchers think of a particular topic or field as a result of its findings. Comments included, for example, "the paper was the first to argue against the general perception in the field," "the research stands in direct opposition to an earlier publication."

In addition to scope of influence, the *methodological aspect* of research was referred to as an important dimension of excellence. In particular, *research that matters* must be methodologically rigorous and well executed.

Following from this, many agreed that good quality and impactful research has better chances to be carried out in *collaboration* between colleagues, as co-authors and co-investigators. According to some, not only impactful research often emerges from a collaborative effort but, it should also instigate more collaboration and networking by other academics and practitioners.

Another characteristic of excellent research was its ability *to be pioneering*. Clearly, the more pioneering the research, the higher the chances that — once it is accepted — its impact could be widespread. "Pioneering," in this context, referred to several aspects. First, the research could be on a question no one had asked before. Second, the research could examine an old question in a new way, with a new method. Or finally, the research results could be different from what others have found. Regardless of the interpretation, for research to matter, it needs to break new grounds, lead to surprising results and/or open up a whole new range of approaches.

Surprisingly, a more controversial dimension was *applicability* and *practical usability* of theory or research. On this issue, some agreed that good management research should make society and industry better by addressing an important managerial and practical problem, the solution to which can be used by people in the field. For this reason, industry support of and participation in the research effort as well as feedback from industry practitioners and/or users seem to be intrinsically related to the concept of *research that matters*.

For others, though, a good piece of research could simply generate both *opportunities for learning* and *lessons to be learnt* without necessarily being linked to a practical problem. According to this view, research could be evaluated by simply answering two questions: "Did the world learn something new from it?" and "Did I learn something new from it?"

Some also mentioned that being *first* in the competition of ideas was important: "the driving force for me — it is the only one in the world like the one that I have — doing so earns one a measure of *respect in the discipline*." Reading this answer, one might think that some interpreted the concept of *research that matters* from a highly materialistic and self-centered perspective.

As I reviewed other responses tough, I realized there was often more than mere personal gratification in gaining peer recognition. In fact, some respondents felt that when research garnered awards or kudos, it had the potential to become more impactful. When people talk about a piece of research, the ideas spread and, consequently, the probability increases for it to generate impact through more research, funding, publications, etc.

Indeed though, an important dimension of valuable research is its ability to *generate a return* for the researcher. Some indicated that *research that matters* should be *challenging* but *rewarding* (e.g., "I was just thrilled to discover I was actually able to write something that was worthy of publication"), provide a *sense of achievement* and personal growth (e.g., "it was entirely self-started, self-written, self-handled") and be *fun* and make the researcher *proud* (e.g., "It all comes together and when you read the proofs you are glad/proud that you wrote that").

The reverse side of self-growth was helping others to grow as well, professionally and intellectually. A clear pattern emerged from the answers that *research that matters* should also create opportunities for more senior scholars to *mentor* and *teach* the 'next generation'.

Another interesting dimension concerns *time* and *timing*. For a piece of research to be impactful, it takes time to be done properly (e.g., "it took me more than 15 years to accomplish"), the world must be ready to welcome it ("it was just at the right time") and it takes time for others to use it and appreciate it ("it is too soon to tell whether the world feels it has learned something of value as well").

When looking at the importance of time and timing factors, many respondents warned us to keep in mind that what might be important to researchers to advance their careers might take their focus away from what really matters to those who read or use their research (e.g., "what 'matters' to your career vs. what 'matters' to others that may read your research can be two very different things"). Especially for younger researcher, the ability to do research that can generate a true positive impact in this world is limited by their need to progress in their career. What you do in the earlier phases of your career might be — and indeed often is — driven by factors other than meaning and impact, such as departmental politics, culture, traditional expectations, etc. This, I think, is itself a seriously worrying signal of the state of academia.

Mind mapping the concept of "Research That Matters."

The figure above shows a mind-map diagram of the keywords that my academic colleagues used to describe *research that matters*. Line thickness loosely reflects the number or quantity of comments linking dimensions: thicker lines mean more people commented on the relationship of two or more elements.

To validate and enrich the preliminary findings and to understand better the concept of *research that matters* I developed an interview protocol to guide the conversations with the *Futureers*.

Keeping in mind the journey metaphor I decided to use, I grouped the answers from the preliminary investigation in three key sections: (1) before the research journey starts (even before life as a researcher starts), (2) during the research journey, and (3) at the end of the journey. This structure enabled me to look for similarities and differences among the various interviewees' experience. The table on next page shows the structure and questions I used for the interviews.

The interviews' blueprint.

Interview Questions

General about research and about research questions/problems

1. *(if relevant)* How do you define the concept of "management research"? And what do you think are THE problems that have the potential of greatest impact and that should be investigated today in this field?

2. Why do you do the research you do? What triggered you to start and what keeps you going?

3. How did you find or chose (and how do you keep finding/choosing) those research problems to investigate which were/are not just interesting to you but also useful and important for people and/or organizations? Problems which, so to say, are worth researching?

4. Do you ever ask yourself or do you think it is important to know whether your research has transformed organizations or the way people work and live?

About the research process

5. How do you do your own research? In what way do you approach the research process? Do you think research approaches differ from field to field or do you think there exists a set of factors or characteristics typical of excellent research independent of the field of interest? Last, can you explain why certain approaches/methodologies yield to better results than others, if they do?

6. What sorts of things "go wrong" during research projects? What happens when they do and how do you "fix" the situation?

7. Do you work mostly independently or with others? What lessons on collaboration in research have you found most useful? Why?

About dissemination of results

8. What drives you to disseminate your research outcomes? And how do you disseminate your research outcomes?

9. How do you see the current "publish or perish" trend and what do you think are the long-term effects this focus will have on academic/theoretical production, practical innovation and our day-to-day life?

10. We're also talking to and studying Nobel Laureates for lessons on these questions — do you think there's anything to be learned from them, their approaches or processes? What would a "Nobel Prize" for management research look like?

Finally: How do you define the concept of "excellent research"? What would you say are the characteristics of a piece of excellent research?

Is There Light at the End of the Tunnel?

The short answer is: yes.

Although there is no doubt that scholarship across the management-related disciplines are currently going through a rather dark tunnel, this research has given me hope that we can see the light at the end of it.

We might have trouble *doing* research that matters to shape the future of management but I believe we can *understand* the underpinnings of it. And if we can understand what it is, there is no reason why we should not be able, eventually, to do it.

As the remainder of this book will hopefully illustrate in detail, my interpretation of the *Futureers'* experiences validates for the most the observations raised by my academic colleagues summarized briefly above.

Futureers define *research that matters* in several different ways. Some, like Costas Markides, focus on the original seed of the research to explain what makes for excellent research: "an important and relevant question for which I don't know the answer already." For Harald zur Hausen, it is "an original idea [intrinsic] into a long-waiting research problem." And to Jack Szostak, "the best research opens new doors to discovery."

Others, like Gerhard Ertl, consider excellent research something that generates knowledge we do not already have on both new questions and old questions, in this case answered by using new techniques. Philip Kotler, on the other hand, focuses on how rigorously the research is carried out: "Excellent research applies the scientific method of gathering and analysing data capable of establishing evidence for or against a hypothesis or theory."

And many others, like John Kotter, Robert Kaplan, and Roger Martin, argue that *research that matters* should prove to work, be useful and be used. On the other hand, some, like Henry Mintzberg, do not share the same view on the importance of methodological rigor (as the world of academia has come to understand it these days) and of applicability of results. Instead he associates the concept of *research that matters* simply with research that is insightful. Although Dave Ulrich admits that "more often [he] thinks the goal of good research is impact more than just insight."

When moving from *what* research that matters is to *how* to do it, complexity soon arises. Kaplan suggests looking at the current problem of stagnating innovation in business and management research as a whole, with "a lot of parts that have to change to come up with a solution."

In my research, I have attempted to identify these "parts" that Kaplan talks about. I have come to see it as a three-pronged issue with responsibility — and opportunity — coming from the following areas: (1) the person, e.g. the researcher or the practitioner, (2) the system, e.g. the university, company, research lab, etc. where the person works, and (3) the distribution channels, e.g. the outlets available for disseminating research results.

To put it differently, when it comes to understanding how to do *research that matters* and who has the responsibility for its generating a meaningful outcome, it can help to distinguish between the respective responsibilities of the individual researcher or practitioner (responsible for *creating*), the system (responsible for *enabling*), and the distributor (responsible for *spreading*).

I argue that *research that matters* can only be truly achieved (i.e., it will eventually change people's lives) if the three elements co-exist and if their values are aligned.

A keen researcher truly committed to *doing research that matters* may be challenged in her objective to changing people's lives if the university (or company) employing her adopts a value system promoting *incrementalism* and a "publish or perish" culture. Similarly, whilst the right personal attitude and the right environment might lead to interesting and valuable results, the value of these results would get lost if the researcher chooses a distribution channel valuing, for example, methodological rigor over balance of rigor and impact.

Of course, these examples should be interpreted the same way if the roles were inversed: a university trying to shape the future of management would find it difficult to do so if the researchers working for it favored personal status among peers rather than research impact; and a scientific journal aiming to publish more insightful research would be challenged if no researchers (or universities) would support its aim because, for example, the journal had a low impact factor.

"I call these three elements of the system: the *Insight Generator* element, referring to the researcher doing the research; the *Insight Incubator* element, referring to the environment where the researcher does her research (that could be a company or a university); and the *Insight Distributor* element, referring to the entity responsible for disseminating the research (that could be a publisher, an editor, a scientific journal, a practitioners' magazine, etc.)

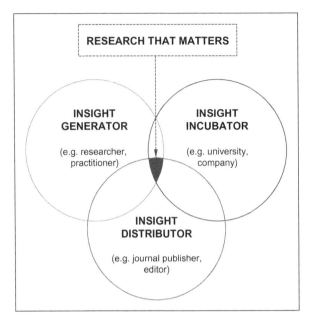

The "Research That Matters" model.

Unless the vision and values of the three elements align, any effort to do research that will shape the future of management will encounter many hurdles.

Realistically, this also means that the chances are slim that we will ever be able to produce research that truly matters. Is this a good enough excuse to stop trying? Not at all, it isn't! As a matter of fact, perseverance is one of the most important personal characteristics that I observed in those who managed to have a lasting impact, as Harald zur Hausen clearly shows when he says: "I think one of the important aspects is really to think a little bit anti-dogmatic and to be remarkably persistent in following your aim because every researcher will experience some frustration [at times], and will have some periods when things do not work out too well, but you need to be able to tolerate these periods as well and to continue nevertheless to work on your answers."

It does not matter which of the three roles we identify ourselves with, e.g. if we are researchers, university leaders or journal editors/publishers. If we are honest in our attempt to shape the future of management we must recognize that we have the ethical responsibility and moral duty to work both *introspectively* to learn how we can do better and *extrospectively* to do what we can to positively influence the cultures of the other two elements.

In the remaining chapters, I am going to discuss and compile a collection of key features that I have learnt are typical marks of excellence with regards to *Insight Generators, Incubators*, and *Distributors*. In the final chapter then, I am going to return to this model and bring all the lessons together into an easy to understand and actionable "Research That Matters" framework. Whilst not wanting to be prescriptive in any way, this model will hopefully help you to analyze and understand the role you play within a larger context.

This is how I see it working:

The *Insight Generator* element of the model looks at our personal characteristics, our choices as individuals and our commitment to changing the world through what we do. As such, working on this element of the model to change our behavior will have the highest impact on the way we decide to look for our research questions and the approach we choose to doing and disseminating our research. That is, measuring ourselves against this element means asking ourselves the question: "*Do I have what it takes to do research that matters?*"

The *Insight Incubator* element of the model, on the other hand, refers to the characteristics and culture of the system within which we operate. For management researchers and scholars, this would be their university; for management consultants, their advisory firm; for practitioners, their company. Learning from this element of the model helps us understand whether our system is dominated by a culture of excellence and meaning or if it values other objectives (e.g., number of publications). For those of us privileged enough to be in positions giving us power to influence our organizational culture (which, in truth, I believe means all of us), this element of the model will hopefully guide us toward changing the underlying values of our own system. By doing so, we are building an environment where researchers working with us or for us can apply their personality and creativity to producing meaningful results. Measuring our system against this element of the model therefore means asking ourselves the question: "*Does my system value research that matters?*"

Finally, the *Insight Distributor* element of the model focuses on spreading *research that matters*. Understanding this element's characteristics therefore should help us understand how we can better spread our own research (if we are the researchers) or research done by others (if we are journal editors, for example) in a way that increases its chances of having an impact. Measuring our values against this element of the model therefore means asking ourselves the question: "*Am I choosing or creating the best conditions for research that matters to spread?*"

Ignoring any one of these elements will equally affect our chances to do (or to contribute to) *research that matters*; our chances to play a role in shaping the future of management.

I must make a point of clarification about the role of practitioners in *doing research that matters*. Gary Hamel observed that "advances in management practice often come through a partnership between two groups. In one group are the theory-oriented practitioners ... who are in the world of practice but have a passion for new ideas and willingness to experiment. In the other are the practice-oriented theoreticians ... who have a real desire to change the world of practice."[1] In the book *What's the Big Idea*,[2] Tom Davenport and co-authors support a similar view. As a matter of fact, it would be appropriate to look at Davenport and co-authors as Hamel's "practice-oriented theoreticians" and to their book protagonists (whom they call "idea practitioners") as Hamel's "theory-oriented practitioners".

In this book, I look at Hamel's "practice-oriented theoreticians" in the *Insight Generator* element of the model and at Davenport's "idea practitioners" in the *Insight Incubator* element. My focus in terms of understanding the personal characteristics that might be more conducive to *doing research that matters* lies more on the former. For what concerns the latter, my focus is more on understanding the characteristics of the system, rather than the individuals, for which I think Davenport and co-authors have made an excellent job already.

The *Insight Generator* Element

On a continuum of people who do research in management or practice management, we can place the 'pure' academic-type at one end and the 'pure' practitioner-type at the other. There are inherent strong cultural differences between the two types, and generalizations are always dangerous but, I will make them in a stark way, for the sake of showing what I understand are the characteristics of the researcher who has the potential to do meaningful research.

In a way, the 'pure' academic-type is so far apart from the 'pure' practitioner-type as Apple is from Microsoft, although the work of neither one of these two types bears any resemblance with the lasting impact these two excellent companies were able to generate. Apple and Microsoft's cultural differences were made famous by Apple's hilarious "Get a Mac" advertising campaign. This series of adverts showed a rather laid-back and cool looking bloke introducing himself as a Mac ("Hello, I'm a Mac."), and a more formal, all suited-and-booted, almost stiff man introducing himself as a Windows personal computer ("And I'm a PC").[3]

(I do hope that you will excuse me for the gross generalization and pessimistic exaggeration I am about to do.)

The "I'm an Academic" type is purely driven by analyzing data and thinking up new theories from within the walls of his own office and pays little or no attention to their relevance to the real world on the outside. I am not arguing for a minute here or in the remainder of the book that we do not need more fundamental type research. However, for what concerns management, if we leave aside the very few Einstein's among us, most of the traditional pure academics are likely to (or indeed aim to) generate incremental advances, rather than coming up with radical innovation. The "I'm an Academic" type is usually driven by number of publications, journal ranking, and peer consideration.

The "I'm a Practitioner" type, on the other hand, has no interest whatsoever in theories and is driven more by 'doing'. Their world is generally limited to the four walls of their factory or office. They are not aware (nor are they interested to find out) of best practices from elsewhere in their own industry or transferable from others. Let alone spend time investigating how they could revolutionize their industry. The problem at hand, on that day, at that very moment is all that matters and the number of scars from the field is the only meter of choice to decide whether anybody can be part of their club or not.

The one type generally looks at the other as a complete waste of time and space and an inferior human being.

In this case however, neither one of the two wears the cool blue T-shirt!

In fact, I have learnt that people who have the potential to do *research that matters*, especially in the management field, are those who sit in the space between the two ends of this continuum. They are neither the 'pure' Academic nor the 'pure' Practitioner.

They are *just* the typical engineers of the future.

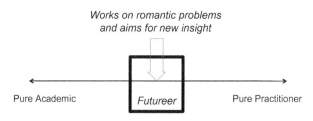

Where *Futureers* Sit.

These are the people who see value in generating insight that relates in one way or another to real world issues — although applicability might not be what immediately drives them — and who work hard to change the way others look at those issues. In the words of Henry Mintzberg: "I totally reject the idea that research has to be applicable ... but I also totally reject the idea that any kind of theoretical research is acceptable, because a lot of theoretical research is monumentally uninteresting and will never help anybody."

Costas Markides takes a slightly different slant on the issue suggesting that, to have impact: "you have to ask managerially relevant questions, but you need to explore them in an academically rigours way."

These are the people who are unsatisfied with generating incremental knowledge and who aim instead for radical innovation. They aim to generate *or* apply learning that can benefit a wider audience beyond just the realms of the academic world or of a specific organization. They aim for more than just solving the problem at hand, on one hand, or presenting a paper at a conference in Kuala Lumpur, on the other.

John Kotter has a refreshing take on where he positions himself on this spectrum: "I don't want to do research for research's sake. I don't want to do studies that will be interesting to a few thousands academics. No, I want to do something that is useful for the world. There is no question about that. That is on my mind all the time."

These are the people who are patient enough to invest the time it requires to truly create something worthwhile.

These are the people, in other words, who are defining the future.

The *Insight Incubator* Element

The culture, requirements and general ethos of the system where we operate influence our own culture and how we work. I am not going to enter into the old "nature versus nurture" debate. There is little doubt though that the more a system recruits and develops excellent people; the more it fosters meaningful research or innovation; and the more it rewards efforts based on values of excellence and impact; the greater the chances that those working in it will enjoy their work and achieve meaningful results.

Philip Kotler talks of the challenge of building a successful innovation culture that keeps an organization ahead of its competition. So too in institutions where research and innovation occur. In his own university, Robert Kaplan sees the type of system that encourages excellent research: "Fortunately, [Harvard Business School] does reward scholarship that advances the knowledge of practice and can be applied. But that's a particular nature of Harvard Business School. Most other business schools don't have that same value system." How so very true!

Certainly, the dominant publish or perish mentality has been pinpointed as a key shortcoming of the current academic system. According to London Business school Professor Costas Markides: "Unfortunately we have become so dominated by this publish or perish attitude that makes us very short-term oriented and willing to ask stupid questions."

Such mentality typically affects younger researchers more than tenured professors, making it harder for untenured scholars to do *research that matters*.

Absurdly, the fact younger scholars have less chances to do *research that matters* is not due to their alleged lack of experience or training but rather to system politics and promotion mechanisms.

The wrong reward system drives the wrong behaviours, and ultimately the wrong outcomes. According to Barbara Kellerman, "Most young scholars do find that they have to satisfy ... senior professors, many of whom tend to be very traditional in what they consider good enough work to get tenure and that, obviously depends a lot on publishing."

Robert Kaplan explains how it works: "What happens, and this is very unfortunate, is that almost all other academic institutions have basically outsourced their most important academic process which is the promotion of faculty. Rather than do the job themselves about who is doing the best work, and use people who are most creative, they have outsourced it to journal referees and editors. They'll say: 'well, if we could find those eight or ten papers that have made it through the [review] process — that is completely outside the control or influence of the university — we'll promote you and give you tenure!.'"

However, if my "Research That Matters" model holds, the responsibility for doing meaningful research is not only the system's, but also the person's. Jack Szostak seems to agree on such dual responsibility: "Very few research Institutions will support someone for 5–10 years on a long range project, with little or no publishable intermediate results. There are also not that many people who would be willing to tackle such difficult problems. It is perhaps more of a problem that some people feel they have to flood the literature with minor reports. The diversion of effort from substantive projects to trivial polishing work is clearly bad."

Those of us who are in the position to do so: what can we do to change the system? This is not a simple question to answer, but Harald zur Hansen has an idea: "If we do not provide an initial period of freedom to young gifted researchers ... and provide them with sufficient support for a period of ... at least 3 to 5 years [and give them] the necessary freedom to select their field, and to ... experience their own ideas which they develop during this period of time, ... I don't think the situation is going to change. And this I find is a bit deplorable."

The *Insight Distributor* Element

Costas Markides is convinced that "we all assume that a good idea will always catch on [but] this is not always the case. [Many] die before they have an impact.

Some ideas obviously spread and they influence and have impact." What can we do then to ensure our research and meaningful ideas find their way to influence others?

Chris Argyris is one of the most influential scholars in the field of organizational development whose ideas and research "have had a tremendous impact upon the field."[4] Roger Martin said that one of the most important notions he received from Argyris, whom he refers to as one of his academic mentors together with Michael Porter, Michael Jensen, and Jim March, is that of "knowledge for action, [that is:] knowledge that doesn't produce action is barely worth having."

Regardless of whether one might interpret "action" as Kotter's application in practice or as Mintzberg's input into further thinking, the point is that for a piece of research to have impact, its outcomes must spread: even the most ground-breaking discovery would be useless unless its insight were made known and accessible to others.

It is within this context that I see the distribution of insight as an inherent element of the concept of *research that matters*. As researchers and/or idea-practitioners, we should choose the best possible distribution channels for our ideas, i.e., that which will give us the widest reach. At the same time, as editors, publishers, and reviewers we should do whatever we can to help develop distribution channels that best serve the purpose of spreading *research that matters*.

Although this might seem simple enough, we know that in reality there are many factors that influence, or limit, our choices and actions, regardless of whether we sit on one side or the other of the fence.

I discussed earlier the "publish or perish" mentality from the point of view of the system. Here, I look at it from the point of view of the distribution of research and ideas.

Professor Howard Gardner, quite uncompromisingly, says: "If you do scientific research, you are expected to publish in peer reviewed journals or to write articles or chapters that satisfy the rigors of scholarly research. If you don't publish, you are not part of the scientific community."

Most universities have created this predominant idea that one has to publish in scholarly so-called A-journals to advance their career (more on this in Chapter 7). Roger Martin describes this process as a hazing ritual similar to those used by the legendary Crips and Bloods criminal mobs: "you get methodologically hazed for five years, and unless you put up with the hazing ritual you don't get into the club. … The Crips send you out and tell you that you have got to kill somebody. If you are not willing to do that you don't get to be a Crips … So [in Academia] there is a hazing ritual. I don't know how to describe it better than that. You have to either accept the hazing ritual or die."

And yet, as Kotter says: "Einstein didn't write his original papers to get him promoted from associate to full professor! People do good work and when they write it down ... it's because they want to, not because they're in the system where they're forced to ..."

Furthermore, publishers, editors, and so-called expert reviewers have all got used to judging the quality of a piece of research not much by the insight it generates or indeed the impact it might have but rather by other menial indicators such as whether it cited the 'right' articles, whether it utilized certain methodologies, etc.

Not to mention the very strong 'halo effect' that dominates the review process in place at most of these A-listed journals. Like with supermarket loyalty points, the more articles you have published already the higher the chances that you are going to get one more published, regardless of its insight. And, of course, the opposite is also true.

Such approach or mentality to using the author's name as a criterion for quality and editorial decisions has recently gained popularity and a name in its own right: "The Oppenheim Effect."[5] Such name follows a disgraceful incident that involved information science's guru Charles Oppenheim, professor at Loughborough University, when he decided to submit an article to a well-reputed journal. In a 2005 article published on *The Times Higher* by the rather telling title: "Early careers spent grinding teeth, not cutting them," Chris Bunting recounts how Oppheneim described the incident himself:

> "Some time later a very good friend of mine got in touch with me. This friend had been sent my article to referee. He thought that, in all honesty, he could not referee it because we were so close and he telephoned the editor to say that he would have to find someone else. The editor responded: 'Don't be silly, this is Charles Oppenheim. We both know we are going to publish it anyway. This is really just a formal exercise, so could you just go through the motions?' Oppenheim chuckles: 'The editor had kind of given the game away. Now I know I can send him any old rubbish and get it in.'"[6]

Not only that. Roger Martin's view, shared by many others, is that "journals are completely methodology obsessed, and if you don't use acceptable methodologies then you just can't get published ... We are teaching researchers to be slaves to the methodology. Rather than the methodologies helping them figure stuff out, the methodologies encourage them not to figure out stuff for which their methodologies can't be rigorously applied. ... Methodologies ... *restrict* our ability to understand the world rather than *enhance* our ability to understand the world."

At the same time, most *Futureers* warn us that, by enforcing this narrow view of research we may be dangerously leading and being led to miss out on more elegant research and more meaningful research outcomes. As Kaplan points out: "... academic journals get locked in to a style of research and [they are not] open to other forms of research. Elegant forms of research. ... Elegant research is mathematics and statistics and strong, powerful impressive hypotheses and we value those like the highest level of scientific knowledge. It can start to feel that that is the only kind of research that they should be publishing and that's when they miss out on more exploratory research, rich descriptions, taxonomies ... I think what made my career over the last 30 years possible was that being a full professor at Harvard Business School I basically could bypass the academic journals."

The highest-ranking journals are also known to be exclusive clubs priding themselves to have the strictest membership selection process: the higher the ranking, the tougher is the review process and the lower is the rate of submissions' acceptance.

I do not want to start a debate on journal ranking here, I simply want to raise a question as to whether this approach of exclusivity is conducive to spreading *research that matters* or if, on the contrary, it serves as too thin a filter.

Perhaps though, the most worrying outcome of this predominant mentality is that we are pushing and being pushed to generate small incremental innovation rather than inviting people to address more fundamental questions that could lead to radical innovation.

As John Kotter observes, "The problem ... is that you start to think about the system and how you gain the system and how you play, how you win by the rules of this system as opposed to the research itself."

In their study of heads of Management Studies departments in UK universities, Professors Stuart MacDonald (University of Sheffield) and Jacqueline Kam (University of Bristol) suggest that such gamesmanship is common. In their well-worth reading *Journal of Management Studies*' article by the title: "Ring a Ring o' Roses: Quality Journals and Gamesmanship in Management Studies"[7] they illustrate some entertaining, although depressing, examples.

Personally I have seen that playing the system to advance in academia can happen in many ways, of which I mention here only four (ranked according to increasing innovation-damaging potential, unethical behavior, and depression levels).

Firstly, writing general material like a literature review on a specific topic so that it might attract more citations just because it is so general (sounds silly? It is).

Secondly, addressing small, menial questions that can be answered and written up quickly. Academics manufacturing scientific papers like journalists produce daily news items. Costas Markides' point of view on this point is that "the difference between [academics] and journalists is that we [academics] have years and years to do our research whereas they have 24 hours. So, we might as well utilise the fact that we have all this time in a constructive way."

Thirdly, choosing a safe methodology, a safe set of references and a non-too-controversial outcome.

Fourthly, exchanging favors with other academic colleagues, like mutual citations and what I refer to as tagging along (i.e., "you put my name on your paper and I'll put yours on mine").

The result? To quote Mintzberg: "Journals are full of a lot of marginally interesting stuff."

I have also learnt that meaningful research is the result of many rounds of tweaks, feedback and revisions, all of which take time. This is one of the key reasons why practically all of the *Futureers* favor writing books rather than scientific articles, as John Kotter explains: "When I write up my work I write it up almost entirely in books because it seems to be the best way to try to communicate … I usually publish my 30th draft. The number of people who will see my work and comment on it before anything goes to publishing can be 50 to 500 people."

The revenue model of publishing companies also poses a challenge as they must continuously increase the number of titles and the number of articles being published per year in order to increase revenue. And yet, Costas Markides puts into words a feeling well known to most of us: "The problem is that nobody reads anymore! We have so many … academic journals. I get 50 journals every month here. With 50 articles each. Do I read them all? Of course not! So, the question is: if nobody reads what you publish, how are you going to spread the word about your idea?"

There is also the issue of cost as a limiting factor to spreading of insight. Scientific journals' collections are expensive and only the most civilized and wealthier nations can afford including them in their academic libraries. With today's global connectivity and cheap access to the Internet, wouldn't good ideas spread much further afield if only they weren't constrained by costly mediums available to only the wealthiest among us? Shouldn't we all — universities, publishers, authors, etc. — do whatever it is in our power to make sure everybody can access research that, potentially, matters? Philip Kotler, e.g., is making more use of "Twitter, LinkedIn, Facebook and other Internet sources to inform more persons about [his research]."

In conclusion, this widespread strategy of pushing people to publish frequently and on so-called A-journals drives incrementalism and minimal impact. This seems to me as being in clear contrast with the notion that, in order to have impact, we must address big romantic questions and spread our research outcomes as widely as possible.

It seems like most agree this is the wrong way to go about promoting *research that matters* and yet, those who could do something to change this damaging behavior are not actually doing anything about it. All the *Futureers* I interviewed agree that the implications are serious, wide-reaching and threatening.

But this book is not as much about pointing out what does not work as it is about finding ideas to do it right:

Kaplan, for example, thinks one way to improve the current approach is for schools to facilitate younger researchers by creating "some publication where we can allow even junior scholars to do ground, descriptive research, work at the problem level, give us some insights based on small samples and write it out in ways that are rigorous, that people will accept and hope that over time that type of publication will give value."

To conclude, I would like to share Costas Markides' advice:

"Get away from this publish or perish mentality and get in the business of generating ideas that will help us make this a better world. That is the goal."

CHAPTER 3

THE THRILL OF DISCOVERY

The important thing is not to stop questioning. Curiosity has its own
reason for existing. One cannot help but be in awe when he contemplates
the mysteries of eternity, of life, of the marvellous structure of reality.
It is enough if one tries merely to comprehend a little of this mystery
every day. Never lose a holy curiosity.

— Albert Einstein, Nobel Prize in Physics 1921

My research has always been driven by curiosity.

— Gherard Ertl, 2007 Nobel Prize in Chemistry

"What do you want to do when you grow up?" Many of us have been asked
that question. I bet few guessed it right the first time we answered it though. I wanted
to be a truck driver when I was a kid — what drove me was the curiosity to see the
world and to me, as a kid, driving a truck was the easiest way to do it.

Reassuringly, *Futureers* as well rarely begin their careers knowing they will be
studying the questions that eventually led them to the top of their field. Certainly
almost none began their careers thinking they would be awarded management gurus'
status or the Nobel Prize. Some, of course, like Albert Einstein, eventually come to
believe that they are destined to be among the few. Einstein was so confident of
eventually winning the award that, during his divorce, he promised the $32,000 in
prize money to his future ex-wife.[1] But most start in their professions with other
thoughts in mind.

When Margherita Hack started her studies at the University of Physics, she
did not think too hard about it: "In those days — I graduated in 1945 —
[schools] were not used to organise seminars to explain what was going to be
taught in the various faculties, what possible future [jobs] one would be most

likely to get. My parents had not been to university and I knew almost nothing about universities. I signed up for physics just because that was the subject I was enjoying the most. ... Maybe, if I had chosen a different topic, I could have liked it even better. I don't know. Let's just say that mine wasn't a thoughtful decision."

For Barbara Kellerman, on the other hand, it was "an autobiographical impulse": "I grew up in a political household where some leading figures of the day were often discussed and I also remember as a child oddly being interested in the dynamics of how kids behave, you know which little girl or boy was the more powerful, why were other ones weaker, so forth and so on."

Regardless of what pushed them to start researching their topic at the very beginning, once the *Futureers* get going, there is a sense they can hardly stop. Gerhard Ertl's opinion is widely shared among the people I interviewed: "a scientist is never, never at the end, and when we solve a problem, five other problems develop anew. So that's why a scientist will always think about his work and what he can do next. ... You never should give up, you should always try to solve the problem as far as it is possible. And you must be patient. You *must* be patient. That's very important."[2]

Among these exemplary researchers, some seem to have had a passion for their research topics from early on in their childhoods or high school days, others seem almost to have stumbled across their topics, and still others came to their subjects as a result of personal and/or professional experiences.

It is in fact not *how* they chose their topics but rather what pushed them to become *Insight Generators* in the first place and, even more, what keeps them pushing to continue being *Insight Generators* and to build a legacy that reveals remarkable similarities.

This is what this chapter is all about: recognizing the non-uniqueness of their (or our) backgrounds and being inspired by what continuously drives these excellent researchers from fields ranging from management to hard sciences to generate meaningful insight. Three questions are at the core of the chapter: (1) how did they get started? (2) what drives them to choose their research journey? and (3) what keeps them going over the years?

Writing this chapter gave me the opportunity to ask myself: what pushed *me* to do research? What's pushing me now? And most importantly, do I have what it takes to enjoy the journey?

I found it valuable to spend time pondering on these issues and I would suggest you to do the same.

Once Upon a Time: How Does It All Begin?

Raise your hand those of us who think that members of those exclusive clubs like the Nobel Laureates, Ernst & Young's Entrepreneurs of the Year, the Thinkers50 — just to make a few examples — had it all figured out early in their lives? How many of us picture these exceptional people as super-humans with a life-plan clearly defined at age 10? And finally, how many of us may use those assumptions as our excuse to not try our hardest? I certainly admit to having been guilty of this at least once or twice in my life!

Doubtless, many of us feel tempted to slack off or give up when we hit snags or compare ourselves to those who seem to have stepped into outstanding careers. The truth is, though: that's not a good excuse! In fact, those at the top also started at the bottom, many with little sense of where their work would take them.

Studying the Nobel Laureates' and management gurus' interviews, speeches, and life stories reveal that, remarkably, the reasons they offer for doing what they do, seem nonlinear and like Margherita Hack's comment earlier, not always "well thought through." So how do they find their way?

My research indicates several similar pathways, most notably: *curiosity, serendipity, ability to see opportunities where others may only see problems* and, finally, *inspiration from others.*

Curiosity

Many of the *Futureers* I talked to started doing what they do simply because they wanted to work on a topic they found interesting. Roger Martin "just thought strategy consulting would be an interesting thing to do." Jack Szostak declares never to have asked himself "whether the problems were important to anyone else or to any organisation." He simply chose questions that he "found interesting, important, tractable, and not too competitive."

Following one's interest, however, often leads *Futureers* to change their minds or us to changing ours, sometime often. Some of the people I studied started with a direction in mind and ended up going a totally different way. This was the case for John Kotter, for example, whose experience is proof that our choices are seldom irreversible: "I started off in physics because the Russians put up Sputnik, the United States Congress voted a good deal of money for science training. In my high school, the only interesting courses, therefore, were in the sciences. That led me to physics and the sciences. I discovered when I arrived at MIT that I was never going to be a brilliant physicist so I started looking for where I could make a contribution. Electrical engineering school at MIT was without question back then, probably still today, the best in the world ... I used that as a staging area for looking [around] and [eventually] I found a course and a teacher that really intrigued me. That was Labour

Economics and that led me into the study of organisations, which led me eventually to questions that have to do with leadership and questions that have to do with why organisations perform well. [This] led me to the whole question of change and the changing world. Once I settled in to that arena, I just found it very fascinating for whatever physiological reasons."

Robert Kaplan also followed an unplanned series of events. He started in operations research before moving to management accounting and eventually generating insight that go well beyond accounting into business and management. As he says, "My Ph.D. was in a field called Operations Research ... but when I went to Carnegie Mellon for my first appointment, they asked me if I would teach accounting to MBAs ... and I'd only had one course in this ... I said 'yeah that would be fine' and ... I just read the book and kept ahead of the students. ... I shifted fairly quickly from my operations research field to accounting because ... if I were able to generate insights, ... there would be opportunities for people to put those ideas into practice. So if I think about 40 plus years ago ... when I [made] the transition what was motivating me was to do my research, come up with ideas and concepts and insights that would be applicable to manage organisations better."

Serendipity

Serendipity is an unsought discovery or experience that has value if leveraged. Whether one takes advantage of the event depends largely upon the openness and past experience of the person who becomes aware of it. Interestingly, the hard sciences talk openly about the value of the unexpected discovery while the management literature seems more reticent to acknowledge it. While some entrepreneurship literature discusses it, and most business people say they have encountered serendipitous events, only a few management researchers have tackled it (much) as a valid topic for study.[3] Entrepreneurs, for instance, may see opportunities coming from events that to others may be interesting but lack meaning. *Futureers*, however, sometimes come at serendipity from a side angle, referring to luck or small choices that made a big difference to them in their research direction and choices.

Lee Hartwell, 2001 Nobel Prize in Physiology or Medicine, describes one such "fortunate event" that changed his life direction (italics added)[4]: "From age 13 to 17 I was preoccupied with sports, girls and cars. But midway through high school *a fortunate event happened*. I became unhappy with the football coach and bored of carousing with my car club friends. A close friend of mine suggested we transfer to the cross town high school and my accommodating mother moved apartments so I could do so. At the new school I was fortunate to find some teachers that challenged me, particularly a physics teacher and my grades improved dramatically. Since no one in my family had ever been to college, I had little in the way of career guidance. However, I was good at math and physics and I liked mechanical drawing, so I thought I might become an engineer. I went for one year to a two-year junior college,

Glendale Junior College, in preparation, taking math, chemistry and physics. I did well, and my counselor encouraged me to meet with a recruiter from the California Institute of Technology. This was *my next major break*. I took the entrance exams and was admitted into the sophomore class."

Hartwell's boredom with cars and football (if not girls!), his friend's suggestion that they move to another school, and his mother's willingness to change living quarters to allow that laid the ground work for him to experience the serendipity of meeting teachers who challenged him. In addition, the encounter with a counselor who saw his potential and encouraged his application to Cal Tech were "fortunate events" that Hartwell was smart enough to see could make a difference in his future.

For Jack Szostak, on the other hand, it was a fortunate encounter of a different sort: "My Nobel Prize winning work began as a collaboration with another investigator whom I met by chance at a scientific meeting."

For others yet, the serendipitous moment was stumbling across unexpected results and being willing to welcome and pursue the unexpected discovery. Harald zur Hausen, for example, was studying human cancers in relation to infections when he tried to apply the same methodology to other systems. He soon got disappointed that he found no evidence in support of his hypotheses. Keeping an open mind, however, zur Hausen found something unexpected that led him in a different direction: he "noted some genetic warts that contained a totally different virus, namely particles of the human papilloma virus group and that occasionally such warts may convert into ... tumours and this triggered the idea that the same agent may cause human cervical cancer". So he changed the course of his research to follow that lead. Alas, he was disappointed yet again: "When we finally had it, it was 1979/1980 ..., we were very disappointed not to find it in cervical cancer. On the other hand, with a related probe ... we demonstrated that there are some loosely related sequences in cervical cancer cells as well ..." And that was it: "Basically from that point on, it was then easy ... to study the mechanism by which these viruses transform cells." That work was the foundation for the research that led to his Nobel Prize some 30 years later.

An Unfair Disadvantage, or Seeing Opportunities Where Others See Problems?

Many of the *Futureers* I researched did not have an unfair advantage when they started, as some might think (and as some might ultimately wish for). At least not in the way 'advantage' is usually intended. As a matter of fact, some might say they had an unfair *dis*advantage.

Mario Capecchi (Nobel Prize in Physiology or Medicine, 2007), did not go to school and did not learn to read and write until he was nine years old since he grew up in war-time Italy. Yet, when asked about this unfair start and how it affected his life, he answered[5]: "I think what it provided was resourcefulness, and I think just the drive to keep yourself, maintain yourself, and survive. I think it led me to be able to use my own resources, to be able to get through life. And I think now I'm also very grateful, in a sense it's fantastic. I mean most children didn't make it, I think I was extremely lucky."

Similarly, Toshihide Maskawa of Japan (Nobel Prize in Physics, 2008) has said that post World War II, when he was raised as a researcher, it was "after a brutal and reckless war and before the calmer period of the 1960s."[6] He heard from teachers and parents that because "there are no natural resources in Japan, [the Japanese people] must survive on the strength of science and technology. It was within [that] atmosphere that ... I gained a yearning and an affinity for science."[7]

A little less dramatic example, perhaps, is the story of Donnall Thomas (Nobel Prize in Physiology or Medicine, 1990) who lived in a small town in New York State. He remembers[8]: "... the long cold winters, absence of commuting problems and opportunity for long discussions [as being] conducive to our work." We could blame in part Mother Nature's forcing Thomas and his colleagues to remain indoors, the smallness of their town (and relatively easy commute) for them being able to get to work in bad weather, and their camaraderie for the ideas and discoveries that emerged.

Or, we could simply acknowledge that a distinguishing characteristic across *Futureers* is their ability to turn disadvantages into advantages and to see opportunities where others see challenges, traits more often associated to entrepreneurs rather than scholars.

Discussing this point, Henry Mintzberg reminded me of how Sir Alexander Fleming (Nobel Prize in Physiology or Medicine, 1945) discovered penicillin, an excellent example of how someone saw something that many others did not: "He went back and found thirty one other studies that said things like: 'we started with the sample of twenty but mould got into six of them so we ended with fourteen.' His point was that any of the previous researchers could have done what [he] did, any one of them was faced with the same possible insight as he did. Was this great genius? [Fleming] just kind of turned it around. He said: 'hmm, the mould has killed the bacteria and may be it could be used as a treatment in the human body' ... The point he made was: 'you could say big deal-obviously it was a huge deal-but there it was — thirty one people could have done what I did and they just didn't have it or didn't do it ...'"

Harald zur Hausen's story offers a different example of how he took what he considered to be a disadvantage in his early career and realized only later what an advantage it truly had been for him: "For about three years [at the beginning of my career], it was very difficult to accomplish anything because I didn't get very much advice at all ... But retrospectively, I think this period of time was in a way quite good for me because ... I had enough time ... to think, to start some experimentations which were not really straightforward and sometimes even a little bit of nonsense. In a way it provided me with the chance to develop a little bit more my own ideas, to read more and to do it in a quiet atmosphere ... If I look back, that was a period to order [my] own ideas and ... develop [my] own way of thinking." Based on this experience, zur Hausen now sees this initial period of freedom as an important condition to recreate for young researchers so they too can have the "quiet atmosphere" they need to generate impactful ideas.

Inspiration and Encouragement from Others

Inspiration and encouragement from teachers, family members, and sometimes early career stage mentors came up in the interviews as factors that helped researchers move into their research journeys.

Not surprisingly, some of the Nobel Laureates mentioned their parents' encouragement, which was often tempered with a bit of trepidation, given the number of experiments young scientists conducted that sometimes went very wrong! Roger Y. Tsien (Nobel Prize in Chemistry, 2008) captured the uneasy feelings of many parents of future researchers when he described his early days of chemistry experiments, when he was about 10 years old: "much to the horror ... [or rather a] mixture of fear in my parents and a little bit of encouragement."[9]

Many Laureates were fortunate to encounter — some by chance — teachers and mentors in universities or research institutes that influenced their lives. Douglas D. Osheroff (Nobel Prize in Physics, 1996) had a high school teacher, William Hock, whose frequent comment to his students that science is "a way to ask nature a question" peppered a talk that Osheroff gave in 2010 to several hundred college and high school students in Boise, Idaho, where Nancy had the chance to interview him.

Some even claim to recall the *moment* when they found the field or question they were to study for the balance of their research lives. Thomas Steitz (Nobel Prize in Chemistry, 2009) credited structural biologist Max Perutz with inspiring him to pursue the field, and remembered the moment when the inspiration occurred. As Steitz said, "[Perutz] gave a lecture at Harvard in 1963. *As soon as I heard him talk*, I decided this is what I want to do."[10]

What Does It Take to Have Impact?

"... I was an avid collector of bugs, butterflies, lizards, snakes, and spiders. I remember on one of these adventures learning to be skeptical of everything one reads in books. I had read that lizards do not have teeth. I had grabbed a very big lizard and stared in disbelief as it turned its head, displayed a fine set of teeth and sank them into my thumb."[11] In this comment during an interview Lee Hartwell gave after receiving the Nobel Prize, you can find two of the characteristics most commonly identifiable among all *Futureers* I researched.

First, and by far the most common characteristic, as quoted also at the start of this chapter, is an insatiable curiosity that usually starts at an early age and that keeps on going through life. Margherita Hacks told me how "it is the curiosity that pushes you to do research, the curiosity to solve problems."

Such curiosity takes different paths, of course but, it is the driver to a life of research. Dave Ulrich is interested in "looking for situations when leaders face challenges they don't have ready or easy answers to." Philip Kotler was curious to look at something that "the marketing discipline had neglected to research [which was] the marketing of places, persons, ideas and causes." Costas Markides' curiosity on the other hand, has led him to investigate "how to use management thinking and management ideas to influence big social problems like poverty, drugs-related crime and migration to the cities and environmental disasters." For Roger Martin the curiosity to understand why some people do what they do and what better ways there are to do it pushed him to leave consulting for a role in academia.

This curiosity is strictly interconnected with the second characteristic that I could identify across the *Futureers*: a tendency to question the world around them and the facts they read or hear about. An important learning point that might seem obvious to many but that I think it is important and often understated (or not stated at all) in traditional Ph.D. training is that these people were never afraid to challenge the underlying assumptions of their fields. This is probably the single most important point I can make in this entire book.

Similar to Hartwell's desire to double check whether lizards had teeth, Jack Szostak is convinced that "original ideas ... are often orthogonal to current thinking." Markides' research, for example, shows that "the most important thing you can do to achieve change in a system is to change the purpose of the system [and ask yourself] why does the system exist? If you really want to change business you have to change this paradigm that exists, [which] says that the purpose of business is to maximise shareholder value. ... Changing the purpose of the system could have a big beneficial effect."

Is this easy? Not at all. When Harald zur Hausen contested the prevailing theory about causes of cervical cancer, his proposition was, as he said, "not very welcome, let's say it this way ... and I felt as a lonely voice."[12]

Is it worth doing it anyway? Definitely yes! The same zur Hausen found years later that his "lonely voice" research led him to be awarded the Nobel Prize!

The same applies to management research. Although it might seems impossible to compare such a complex issue like cancer with questions that a management researcher is usually faced with, Roger Martin gives us a wonderful example of how the same mentality of questioning accepted practices can yield meaningful results in our discipline as well:

"The consulting assignment that I am proudest of in my 30 years of consulting was for Procter & Gamble in 1990. And it was a study that I convinced them to do, they didn't actually ask for it … The premise of the study was … how Procter & Gamble segmented … what it calls its customers — retail trade, the Wal-Mart and Targets, Wegmans, Carrefour, and Metro. And they segmented them on the basis of: 'are they a grocery store? … a mass merchandiser? … a drug store? And they tailored their service model according to that segmentation. And for some reasons or other I didn't think that would be the most powerful way of thinking about your customers and differentiating between customers … I didn't really know why, but it just didn't seem to me very sophisticated … So I convinced them to let me do a project on that. I just started nosing around trying to understand what their sales were to their various customers, what their profitability was, what their volume growth was in the various sectors and just started messing around with the data … I came to the conclusion that, while they could tell you their exact market share of consumers, they could tell you for women 18–39 and in this demographic and urban versus rural areas what share of shampoo sales [they had], they couldn't tell what share of customer sales they had, so they couldn't tell you in a given Wegmans or Costco store, what percentage of … shampoo sales were Procter's. They just knew whether shampoo sales were higher this month than last month … I did that analysis and I found that there were very great share differences by customer, our share of customer sales, and then I started looking for patterns … and came to the conclusion that there was a huge difference in market share by merchandising philosophy. For some chains they had the merchandising strategy called EDLP — Every Day Low Prices — that didn't do promotions and just sold the product at the same price every day like Wal-Mart and a bunch of others, our market shares were dramatically higher than in what's called HiLo, which is where they sell it at a regular price for most of the time and then on a deal for the rest of the time. That's interesting for a couple of reasons; one Procter & thought that their friends were HiLo and their enemies were EDLP but, we do better in EDLP, even though we treat them in a rather nasty way, and set up all of our internal systems to make it easy for HiLo customers to deal with us. On the basis of that I concluded that and figured out in due course why our sales were higher in EDLP and that's because EDLP tends to only have the top two brands on their shelves, they get rid of brands three through seven, and because we are top or second top in every single category in which we operate EDLP essentially gets rid of a whole bunch of our competition, and so we end up with higher shares. On the basis of that, the client completely changed its merchandising philosophy, its customer philosophy, and threw out all the practices that favoured HiLo and replaced them with practices that favoured EDLP, and at that point, no other competitor understood the problem, and they got a huge jump on the competition until the competition figured it out." Although I am not one for descriptive writing, I must underline the excitement in Martin's voice when he told me this story. His passion hit me like a rock: I must have gone to the wrong conferences as I have never seen that level of passion and enthusiasm when I attended management research presentations!

Last, a third characteristic that I found across all the *Futureers* is what I call "patient-ambitious-perseverance," that is, the patience to persevere and never, ever give up on one's own ambitious journey, regardless of how many walls are put in one's way. Just before closing my interview with her, Margherita Hack made a point of how important this is for anybody aiming to have an impact: "one faces difficulties; it is not like we understand all on our first attempt. Sometimes we have to spend weeks, sometimes months to understand just one thing. Therefore [a researcher] needs perseverance, not to get discouraged easily. Often, in research, we can go down a way to just hit a wall at the end of it. [The researcher] needs to try another one. Therefore, perseverance first of all, but also the desire to succeed. In this regard, sport is very much educational. One tries to do research to win, like doing a race in a competitive sport. In addition to curiosity, there is the desire to prove oneself. ... Ambition is the spring that pushes us to persevere and do better than others."

What does it take to have impact? Curiosity, anti-dogmatism and patient-ambitious-perseverance might not get you there but they would surely give you a head start!

What Drives People to Continue Their Research Journey?

Becoming interested in research is just a first, albeit critical, step. Having the right attitude towards life in general is also essential. Then come years of work, most without any 'prize' at the end, although some people receive recognition by peers along the way.

In their book, *Renewing Research Practice*,[13] Peter Frost and Richard Staeblin acknowledged openly what many researchers may wrestle with privately: sometimes, the verve slackens. They asked highly regarded management and organisational researchers how they deal with the often frightening experience when clarity of purpose and energy falter, especially later in a career. The remarkably guileless and candid, sometimes excruciatingly so, reflections from more than 20 scholars offers a way to revive and renew and (re)take control of what can seem to be a life that others hold hostage.

The essays remind me of the unique position researchers hold. Like a marriage that may be mundane, they often need to re-ask the question "why did we get into this research business in the first place?"

So what drives exemplary researchers in the early phases of their work? And what drives them to continue no matter what in their meaningful journey? Five common themes emerged: (1) answering important and difficult questions about which little is known and; which, if possible, (2) will change and/or influence people's behavior, (3) add to the body of knowledge, (4) foster continuous discover, and (5) generate further research and thinking.

Answering Important and Difficult Questions about Which Little Is Known

For many of the characters in this book, satisfaction comes from being able to identify questions and problems that people — even those in academia or industry who are also close to the state of the art — struggle with, and then being able to find answers to those questions or a solution to those problems. Rob Goffee brought my attention on the importance of asking big questions: "I am proud and I like my sociological basics, because they produce big rich questions." And Jack Szostak gave an excellent example of what a big rich question looks like for him: "my current research is focused on the origins of life" … can't get much bigger than that, can it?

Rob Goffee points out that especially if you are a professor in an academic institution you are funded to investigate big questions. As I think back to the "Research That Matters" model I introduced earlier, and considering that universities have (or should have) a goal to create knowledge and pay professors to do so, then, I wonder: shouldn't that suffice to push us to pursue such big rich questions?

On the other hand, Henry Mintzberg is convinced that smaller questions are equally important: "we can answer all kinds of questions [and] there is no reason why people can't study little questions and do it in a meaningful way." The point is that whatever the 'size' of questions, it is critical to find ones that matter and study them in meaningful and thoughtful ways.

Some might say that seeking a cure for cancer is more important and difficult than investigating how to be a better leader. I respectfully beg to disagree. It is indeed easier to associate the concept of life changing research with research in the natural or hard-sciences than it is to associate it with research in management. After all, as Gerhard Ertl simply puts it: "the natural sciences are full of [important] open problems and new ones continuously emerge."

However, I support a comment by Professor Richard Barker, of Cambridge University's Judge Business School, who, in his *Harvard Business Review* article, "The Big Idea: No, Management Is Not a Profession"[14] argues that managers (and I would argue by extension, management researchers) are equally responsible to the well being of society.

I therefore remain of the firm opinion that any activity — research and otherwise — that might lead to improving our (usable) knowledge of the world we live in is worth pursuing, regardless its discipline or area of application.

Costas Markides's current research may help visualizing how even management research could potentially have as significant an impact as the cure for cancer. "There are a lot of ideas in management that ... [we could] apply on ... big social problems [like poverty, drugs-related crimes, the environment], yet nobody does it. You have to ask yourself: why is it that nobody does it? The ideas are there, why doesn't anybody take them and use them?"

As you consider your own research journey, I would hope that this might inspire you to think about what questions you will decide to pursue that will make a difference.

Changing and/or Influencing People's Behavior

For Rob Goffee, the word 'transform' is critical to his thinking: "John Quelch [former LBS dean, formerly at Harvard] is now the dean at the China Europe International Business School in Shanghai. He developed this logo for London Business School which was: '*Transforming futures.*' Only two words but, I liked it and I could really connect with it. In other words, I think that at their best, it's what good business schools do. They transform the futures of organisations and hopefully of individuals."

Goffee embodies the notion common to several other *Futureers*: they want to find ways to transform or change lives. Not all of them admitted to be thinking from the start about the importance of the problem they were investigating or, indeed, the impact their work might have.

Henry Mintzberg, for example, at first firmly told me that he never asks himself whether his research is going to change the way people live. And when I asked the question to Gerhard Ertl as to whether he thinks it is important to know if his research transforms the way people live, he answered a short and decisive "No." Whereas Jack Szostak surprised me by saying "I never asked whether the problems were important to anyone else, or to any organisation." Although he then added: "I chose questions that I found interesting, important, tractable, and not too competitive," showing in a way that he did after all look for important questions to answer.

For others, though, like Dave Ulrich, doing something that could influence lives is fundamental. According to Ulrich, the thought "drives almost all ... [of his] research and thinking." Philip Kotler "makes it a point to find out the results of any research and advice that [he has] given to organisations. This is the only way to assess the validity of applied theory and to become aware of larger contextual factors that might improve or inhibit performance."

Regardless of whether the potential for impact is a thought at their careers' beginnings or whether it becomes a by-product of following one's own interests and hard work, Jack Szostak typified the *Futureers*' attitude when he said "it's nice to know, in retrospect, that one's efforts have transformed a field, or even led to practical improvement in people's lives."

Even Mintzberg, perhaps feeling compelled to recognize a more modest scope for impact for management research compared to the hard-sciences, admits that "[while changing people's] life is pushing it too far, ... I think if it changes their behaviour for the better, that's what we are talking about!"

Adding to the Body of Knowledge

Where one driver for doing research is tackling difficult and unanswered questions, another is the desire of excellent researchers to advance the state of the art and add to an existing body of knowledge.

Astrophysicist Margherita Hacks explained beautifully what that means to her: "The majority of stars, in the same way as the majority of inhabitants of a country are 'normal' people, ... they behave all more or less in the same way. However, there are stars that present some irregular characteristics: either [an irregular] chemical composition, or the [irregular] presence of [specific] emissions not seen in other stars' spectra. And therefore [the objective was/is] to understand the physical explanation for such anomalies and whether such physical explanation can be linked to the age of the star, to the fact that this is a single and not double star, to the fact that the star has formed in a certain area of the milky star or in another. Therefore [the objective was/is] to try and understand the reasons for these anomalies ... It is the curiosity that pushes you to do research, the curiosity to solve problems which can also be small problems [but] which enable you to add a little piece to the puzzle of our knowledge of the universe."

This explains why all of the people I interviewed value so much studying the state of the art before deciding what to focus on. I couldn't explain it better than Costas Markides: "In my opinion [knowing the state of the art] is very important. This is what differentiates good academic research from consulting research. ... Look at the kind of research that [consultants] publish in *McKinsey Quarterly* or *HBR*. Ask yourself the question: 'what is the difference between their research and my research?' Well, like us, consultants also ask important, relevant questions. So there is no difference there. Like us, they go out and study these research questions by talking with managers and looking at 50/100 companies. So there is no difference there. Like us, they come up with interesting answers. So there is no difference there. What then is the difference? The difference is that, before I go and do my research, I always spend one year, basically, reading what everybody else has said about the question I am studying. There is nothing new under the sun. Nothing. Even when you frame the question in a totally different way from everybody else, there is still somebody out there who has written about what you are planning to study. You have to go and read it and you have to position your research relative to what is written out there ... And this is the difference between us and consultants, in my opinion."

To put it bluntly, *Futureers* do not reinvent the wheel!

Foster New Discovery

Some *Futureers* claim that it is the process of constant discovery that keeps them going. They continue to see new "mountains" and new questions, and see no reason to stop discovering. During his interview with Adam Smith, Editor-in-Chief of Nobelprize.org, Gerhard Ertl discussed what the Nobel Committee found interesting, that he "continually revisited problems, old problems," pointing out that a "scientist is never, never at the end, and when we solve a problem, five other problems develop anew."[15]

Of course, like anyone, *Futureers* are humans after all and they need periodic assurance that they've made progress in solving the big problem they are studying. Some look for those moments of clarity and resolution even as new questions that arise. As Toshihide Maskawa (Nobel Prize in Physics, 2008) says, "for a theorist, the most exciting period is after waking early one morning to discover a truth that you could not have imagined."[16]

Generating Further Research and Thinking

Spreading the word about findings, is the last driver I want to discuss. I mentioned earlier that my academic colleagues saw spreading ideas as a way to foster new research and as a source of pride and mark of research excellence. Howard Gardner confirmed that view when he stated that "the best measure of research [quality] is the influence it has on subsequent research and thinking," although he admits, hinting back at the need to be patiently-ambitiously-persistent, that "sometimes the effects are quite immediate; but other times — as in the case of pioneering geneticist Gregor Mendel — it can take decades."

I like the metaphor by Markides when he says that "academic research is like building a wall, brick by brick. You just create one brick for other people to build on. Your research can have an impact as long as other academics pick up on the idea and use it to do their own research."

Impact: Embracing Our Role and Responsibility

The importance for us management researchers to aim for *research that matters* is unquestionable and the potential benefits on society and the world as we know it immeasurable.

Many of the studies by the world's top management thinkers I interviewed have already helped public and private organisations to function better, employ more people, and up-skill society. Yet, recent events put into painful reality that management researchers have not yet fully stepped up. We have to ask ourselves: if we had tried harder to do our research matter, could have we helped avoid one of the most devastating economic phases in our lifetimes?

There is clearly no way to know now but ruling out the possibility would mean refuting the very stone upon which academia and scholarly research were first raised.

In a *Harvard Business Review*'s column by the quite self-explanatory title "The Hollow Science" Kaplan writes: "... after decades of management research and education, it's fair to say that business scholars bear some responsibility as well. We have largely failed to produce a body of knowledge that would have been relevant to valuing and managing risky financial assets."[17]

Harvard Business School Professors Rakesh Khurana and Nitin Nohria also argue that "business leaders must embrace a way of looking at their role that goes beyond their responsibility to the shareholder to include a civic and personal commitment to their duty as institutional custodians. In other words, it is time that management finally became a profession."[18]

On the same vein, I argue that it is time for management researchers to recognize and accept our duty to learn from the past, study the present and creatively shape the future of management. Our responsibility must be to create truly insightful knowledge whose adoption by further research or application in practice will allow society to better face the new challenges that the future holds.

In his 2010 *Harvard Business Review* article, Barker observed that "[business schools] have [recently] come under fire for allegedly failing in their obligation to educate socially responsible business leaders."[19] Therefore, as I move from the *Insight Generator* element to the *Insight Incubator* element in the "Research That Matters" model that I introduced earlier, I would like to pose these questions: *How early and how deeply should universities and business schools encourage young (and even older) management scholars to do research that has an impact in our profession? And should such a sense of greater responsibility become an intrinsic part of our work ethic?*

I like the ideas discussed in Barker's paper, originally put forward by Joel Podolny, former dean of the Yale School of Management, Rakesh Khurana and Nitin Nohria that managers should be trained as professionals, similar to doctors or lawyers. Likewise, I would argue that the same ideals of "serving the greater good" should be infused into the conduct of those responsible for advancing the state of the art in management, that is, us — management researchers.

Paraphrasing a statement originally written by Khurana and Nohria I end this chapter arguing that: "True professions have codes of conduct, and the meaning and consequences of those codes are taught as part of the formal education of their members. Yet, *management researchers* don't adhere to a universal and enforceable code of conduct. Maybe, they should."

CHAPTER 4

THE BIG (OR SMALL) Q: FINDING ROMANTIC PROBLEMS WORTH STUDYING

If you keep yourself in tune with world out there, you'll see managerially relevant problems all the time.

— Costa Markides

[we look for interesting questions] in our heads and in the field.

— Henry Mintzberg

What do managers do?

Why are jellyfish luminous?

How does change happen?

How do humans make and process music?

What makes good leaders?

How does the origin of life go from chemistry to biology?

How can management thinking solve big social problems like poverty and prostitution?

How can we do more *research that matters*?

These are only few questions the *Futureers* featured in this book are working on. They are simple to understand, and yet not at all simple to answer. Some are big questions, others are smaller ones, all have the "really romantic goal to investigate problems for which there are no obvious and immediate solutions" — paraphrasing Gary Hamel's thought on that we need to generate more innovation from scholarly research.

Although it is easy for all to understand that solving them would definitely have a big impact on organizations, society, and individuals, the investigative process required to tackle them and to reach the answers always demands small and cumulative steps and the ability to sense and dynamically adapt to the evolutionary journey.

As many exemplary researchers I learned from made clear, finding an important, interesting question that relates to a romantic problem is in itself a critical element of what eventually becomes *research that matters*. Although we should always keep in mind Mintzberg's remark that "the purpose of research is to come up with interesting questions," not the other way around.

At the same time, where to look for relevant problems is actually an element that is often overlooked. For most of us: as Ph.D. students or junior researchers we are assigned a topic by our supervisors or research sponsors; as research leaders, available funding programs often drive our choice of what to work on; as management practitioners, we don't look for problems but rather problems are put in our way. And yet, when I asked Henry Mintzberg what he thought were problems worth investigating these days, he told me that trying to let others tell you what to focus on with your research is self-defeating: "I think that answering that question defeats that question, in the sense that people start doing what they are supposed to be doing instead of what's really interesting."

In fact, the research behind this book has led me to believe that retrospectively understanding how to look for the 'right' research questions in the 'right place' can increase our chances to do *research that matters*.

In this chapter, therefore, the main question I contemplate is: *"where can I look for romantic problems, problems that are worth addressing?"*

Nevertheless, different grounds can be equally fertile for romantic problems. For example, Barbara Kellerman's own romantic problem is organizational leadership, which has kept her interested since her childhood years. It was during her graduate studies though that she noticed "there was no such thing then — odd as it may sound — as a leadership literature" which then led her to pioneer research in the field.

John Kotter, on the other hand, found his romantic problem in a rather different way during his undergraduate studies: "the key work for me was setting up interviews and then getting a cheap kind of second hand car and driving down to Washington DC and then to various sites in North Carolina ... and meeting people, talking to them, sitting in on meeting, watching events ..."

Regardless of what ground the *Futureers* harvest to find their problem, they are capable of generating similarly meaningful impact with their work. Based on this, I also investigate how we can develop the 'right' attitude toward searching for such problems.

Last, I discussed earlier that the underlying ethos of the system people operate from has an important bearing on whether and how much these people (and their research) will thrive in it. Therefore, the last question I look at here is how can we develop the 'right system' to foster more of the 'right attitude.'

As usual, my suggestion is that you drive along with me as I go through these questions and that you take your time to think about: where you look for your own research questions? How can you become better at identifying worthier ones? And whether your work environment or system is one that gives you freedom to pursue your grand goal to have impact with your work (or what can you do to make sure it becomes one such system).

Romantic Problems Worth Investigating

When I asked Margherita Hack what she thought defines an excellent piece of research she responded, rather tellingly, that "first of all, one needs to understand what are those problems which are worth investigating."

Before discussing where we should look for that one research problem that will (should?) keep us busy for the next many years, I thought sharing some of the research questions the *Futureers* embrace as worthy of investigation could help set the bar at the right height.

It goes without saying that I am not at all suggesting you should take these questions as your own, although I would take my hat off to you if you did. After all, we can all easily agree with Costas Markides that choosing what problems would be interesting to study today depends on our own personal biases.

On the other hand, I hope you will take these as some inspiring examples.

Costa Markides is studying how we can use the insight that we have generated in the last 50 years in business research to solve social problems. "We have big social problems right now in the world. Poverty, migration to the cities, the environment, education etc. We have got loads of big social problems all over the world; we don't have the money to solve them. So we need to think creatively about them. And we have insights and ideas from research on business organisations that we can take and use to think about these big social problems. That would be one area where I think management research ought to be focusing on."

Robert Kaplan, on the other hand, thinks that "[romantic] problems are all over the place." He mentioned C.K. Prahalad and his research tacking problems concerning the production of products that can be sold at a profit to the "bottom of the pyramid." As a matter of fact, C.K. Prahalad was mentioned several times by many of the other *Futureers* as well, who all agree that he has truly had a significant impact on the way we live and work. Observing other recent events Kaplan firmly says, "[the current global financial crisis] has made me realise that this should not have happened, we should have not had institutions like Merrill Lynch and Lehmann Brothers fail so clearly on some aspects of management practice. … That, to me, sets up a very interesting set of issues that we could explore to understand how this could happen? Why it happened? What could be done differently to prevent that from happening again?"

Another evergreen romantic problem which is still at the far front of modern management agendas today, according to Roger Martin, concerns managers having to take decisions under competition and uncertainty. "I think what has come to the fore to a greater extent is particular complicating factors in making those decisions. So [it is about understanding] how you make those decisions when you are being asked to take into account the impact on society more broadly than just your shareholders or your customers or your employees. I think it is also quite difficult to make those decisions in ways that invent new things and create things that are new to the world to solve … big problems in the world."

Targeting a different area, Philip Kotler's romantic problem relates to the level of fitness of available management principles in non-for-profit organizations: "I realised a long time ago that non-profit organizations normally do not follow the management literature and some non-profit personnel are actually anti-man-agement or anti-business. They see themselves as not after money but after doing good … I developed a research approach to learning more about how to make modern management more appealing to these organizations."

In the organizational leadership field, Dave Ulrich claims to have noticed many fascinating organizational phenomena that deserve additional study: "How to develop local leaders for global companies? How to balance the demands for global leverage and local adaptation? Which organization capabilities are most likely to help organizations succeed under different strategic conditions?"

Why and how some organizations and/or people outperform others is yet another romantic problem that has been keeping John Kotter busy since his doctoral thesis, when he first asked himself a question that he is still finding valuable elements of the answer to in this very day: "Why some do very, very well for themselves and help society, and some do poorly?"

The list could go on for many more pages (it actually does). This should suffice though to give you some ideas and also to compare your own research questions with those of people with a proven track record of *doing research that matters*.

In case you are tempted to excuse yourself by thinking that is too difficult to find something that is worthwhile investigating, keep in mind John Kotter's encouraging observation: "I think there [is much] that we don't know. Much, much, much more than we actually do know. Hence, there's plenty of room to do meaningful research."

He also restated the importance of asking the very questions you are asking yourself (clearly, since you are still reading): "An interesting question within the context of management and as you spread out to the entire university: what exactly does research means these days?"

In the end, what are these romantic problems worth investigating? "I can't give a list, if I give a list it's my list. Why should you study what I think is interesting? You should study what you think is interesting and the more variety we get, the more interesting things are going to get" (Henry Mintzberg).

Hints to Finding Romantic Problems

In this journey of mine, I have come to strongly believe that one truly can learn how to get better at doing insightful research and at generating impact. Honing our investigative skills should start with improving our ability to recognize grounds fertile for worthy problems. I used the plural for "ground" intentionally. In fact, one can find inspiration looking in the most diverse directions. In the following sections, I go through some of the most commonly cited ones.

1 — Follow Your Passion

Aniruddh Patel, Associate Professor of Psychology at Tufts University, went to Harvard for graduate school in the late 1980s and had the good fortune to study with the biologist E. O. Wilson, a world-renowned expert on ants. In the same way that Capecchi's research direction changed as a result of meeting James Watson (as we saw in Chapter 3), a chance encounter can send a young scientist's research off in an unexpected direction. Patel may have assumed that he had found a good topic, because he was lucky enough to study with the best in the field. In fact, by 1990 he was deep into the study of ants. But the story took a turn, which looking back seems to have been inevitable.

In Australia doing field research, Patel had an 'a-ha moment' that he could not ignore[1]: he realized ants were not his dream topic. Instead, he knew that he wanted to blend two fields that had fascinated him since childhood: science and music. He knew in Australia that he wanted to understand "how humans make and process music."

Wilson's response was, fortunately, understanding and positive. He told Patel to "follow his passion" and offered to help find a way to achieve it back at Harvard. And indeed, Wilson and a birdsong biologist oversaw Patel's 1996 doctoral thesis examining the relationship between language and music — a field that, according to Patel, was not at all recognized at the time. By the end of the 1990s, as the field of neuroscience began using imaging technologies, the field changed dramatically, making it feasible to study the brain while it was engaged in various activities, like processing music as opposed to processing language.

Patel's work has indeed begun to help change lives — by understanding more about the relationship between music, language, and memory — which may help with Alzheimer's and stroke patients. Further, his work is simply fun to read and hear about. He and his colleagues now work with, Snowball, the dancing cockatoo[2] to unravel whether non-human animals' brains process music similarly to humans.

Patel's story of pursuing his two strong passions, music and science, and asking questions others had not asked before, seems to be a common theme among many exemplary researchers. Once they identify a field or fields that excite them, little seems to stand in their way.

2 — Don't Resist the Unfamiliar

A common pattern for scientists and management thinkers alike is the notion of studying questions that others do not, breaking ground by simply finding 'unexplored spaces.' *Futureers* are most likely when they embrace E. O. Wilson's "consilience." Unfortunately, some of us researchers fear the unknown (or what we think will be unknown or difficult for us). I used the term "unfortunately" on purpose as, usually, it is when we stretch ourselves and our capabilities to investigate or try something we have not tried before that we grow personally and professionally.

Roger Tsien, the 2008 Chemistry Laureate, suggests that such fear may limit what topics future researchers will pursue.

He says: "That's when it's dangerous ... when students let themselves get pigeon-holed, or let their thought processes get pigeon-holed, and say 'Oh, I could never do that, that's chemistry. I don't know any chemistry'. And it's surprising how often biologists have that attitude [about chemistry] and chemists sometimes have that attitude about biology too. This instinctual fear that, 'Oh, that's a subject I can't do, and nobody should expect me to know how to do, and so I will just not pay any attention to questions that lead me in that direction'."[3]

Douglas Osheroff, the 1996 Physics Laureate, makes this point when he says that there is a tendency for people to work in established areas with which they are comfortable. Ten years ago the National Science Foundation (NSF) had a push toward greater research into nano-science.

He says: "The idea was that this was an area where we knew that things would be different, and one of the big things if you go to really tiny particles ... the surface energy completely dominates over the volume energy. So there was a good reason to expect that materials on a nanoscale would behave differently."

The NSF's decision to offer more funding to newer areas of study, rather than to give grants to people who were continuing to do more familiar work in previously explored territory on things with which they are comfortable, sent out an implicit message about the need to step into the unknown.

Moving from nano-physics to management, the idea remains that *Futureers* are not afraid to explore areas of interest that may fall beyond one's own boundaries of knowledge. Reflecting on a rather widespread tendency for universities to push students to work in relatively safe areas, Henry Mintzberg "rejects that idea that doctoral students should not bite off more than they can chew, in the sense of addressing questions that are too big."

Jack Szostak sees a world "full of interesting problems" and he focuses on ones "that aren't receiving a huge amount of attention."[4] As he began work on telomeres, the specialized DNA sequences at the tips of chromosomes, for instance, he saw and expected no application, no link to any practical results, although later there were medical implications. He actually mentions a benefit of looking at problems that are non-obvious, which could eventually lead to long-term benefit for the researcher's career as well beyond her as an individual: "the field is not hyper-competitive."

Be brave. Explore!

3 — Read Everything There Is to Read

Futureers may start exploring areas in which they have some personal experience or interest but they all at one point move on to new ground by asking relevant questions, over and over again. Some of these questions, inevitably, will have never even have occurred to others before them. That is why, as I noted earlier, *Futureers* refer to *research that matters* as being related to the fact that it generates knowledge that did not exist before it.

Budding creative writers are often told that a good way to get started is to "write about what you know." It is well-meant advice and useful up to a point. But what we do not know, and therefore need to learn, can be just as stimulating.

More often than not, good research will be a combination of the two.

So, as we look for our own romantic problem we should definitely start from what we are and what we know, but make sure that we follow Margherita Hack's suggestion that "some problems have already been studied in depth and therefore it would not make any sense [to study them] as it would be very difficult to bring something new to the body of knowledge. So, first understand what are the approachable problems."

To do that, needless to say, we should read the literature. That said, we should make a point "not to read just academic literature, but business literature, newspapers and magazines as well," suggests Robert Kaplan. Also looking across disciplines is fundamental, especially when we can't find an answer in our own field's body of knowledge. That's how, for example, in order to develop management practices fit-for-purpose in non-profit organizations, Philip Kotler "researched the literature on museums, social service organizations, associations, etc." It is also how Costas Markides is tackling his romantic problem of solving poverty and other big social problems in the world: "There are millions of articles on this topic: sociology, psychology, anthropology, you name it. People have been writing books for the last 50 years on this topic, so you have to read it all and find what is it that people have not asked that I can answer here?"

For Markides the ability to position the research problem relative to what everybody else has said about it is one of three criteria that he uses to evaluate any piece of research that he comes across. To him, positioning means, among others, being able to prove the question has not been answered already (his first criteria for excellence in research). This is a necessary step to being able to come up with a creative answer (his third and last criteria).

I know what you are thinking: "That's just common sense!" You may be right but then, how do you explain the numerous articles we read every day, most published in some of the so-called A-listed journals, that tell us nothing new and simply regurgitate what tens or hundreds of other articles have told us before, albeit (sometime) using different words? Costas Markides' experience validates this observation: "I read *McKinsey Quarterly* and *HBR* and many times you notice that these articles present their ideas as if they are brand new ideas. In fact they are not. They are ideas that somebody else has talked about, ten or twenty years ago. But of course the authors of these articles don't know this because they never bothered to do a proper survey of the literature. They therefore don't know what other people have said."

He calls it "reinventing the wheel." Margherita Hack refers to it as "reinventing the umbrella." Umbrella, wheel or otherwise, reinventing does not seem a worthwhile exercise. Most seem to agree that far too often research being published today does not get to any notable conclusions because the authors "did not read anything of what's been done before."

Interestingly, although all agree on the importance of knowing what has been studied already, some *Futureers* warn us not to focus too narrowly on the observations other people have made and suggest that "going out" looking for romantic problems is important as well.

4 — Look into Your Head and 5 — Out into the Field

This brings me to another two notable pools of worthy problems we can dip our investigative eye in: in our heads and out in the field.

Although *Futureers* are often driven by a problem or question they feel deeply passionate about, *research that matters* seems to rarely emerge when satisfying one's own interest remains the sole objective.

When I asked him where we should look for worthy research questions, Henry Mintzberg's answer, "in our heads, in the field," pointed to the need for researchers to study something of personal concern but also of concern beyond themselves. As he said: "In our heads in the sense that they are personal questions but in the field in the sense that you've got to get out of the office, get out of the university, get down to where there's real behaviour in terms of what you are studying."

4 — In Our Heads   Edmund Phelps was a *Futureer* who looked in his head at the start of the investigation that eventually led him to be awarded the Nobel Prize in Economics in 2006. He had identified a very clear topic to study: he wanted to show that allowing inflation to rise would *not,* as had been expected and predicted, lead to higher employment. He realized though that he needed to generate data to make the case that "no good would come from increasing the inflation rate to a higher level [but] there wasn't any way of really backing up [such] a policy decision."[5]

His investigations go back to 1966, when he was aware that there was no data to support such an idea and therefore no way of convincing most economists until such ideas were played out in a practical way. This occurred during the 1970s when the Federal Reserve Bank in the United States embarked on policies that led to appreciably higher rates of inflation. The thinking was that it was a way of escaping the rise in unemployment figures from earlier in the decade. The tactic was a failure.

Phelps says: "And that was probably the decisive moment for this theory. So people went from being skeptical about it to being converts."[6] He was able to take his research where others were reluctant to tread, making a point that had serious implications for future government policy.

Looking in "our head" is important also to Robert Kaplan, for whom opportunities for *doing research that matters* might emerge from "looking for areas where the current wisdom of our practice is inadequate relative to some standard you have in your own mind."

5 — Out in the Field   It is interesting to realize that looking into his own mind eventually led Robert Kaplan to go out in the field: "Certainly in the late 1970s, the early 1980s when Japanese companies came to the market they had an approach to developing products and managing production that was completely different from the Western approach. So I thought: 'Oh boy, there's something going on there that's worth learning from!' And I learned about Japanese management approaches not from other academics, but from other business people.

"They were explaining these new approaches to me and I said 'well that can't be happening'. But they persuaded me 'no this is really happening!' And I realized that the kind of academic work I had been doing prior to then would not have led me to understand the very dramatic change that Japanese management had done."

Kaplan statement raises an issue that seems to be central to many of the management thinkers and practitioners I have talked to: "the innovation that takes place in business should be continually generating new issues for us [management researchers] to be thinking about!" Or, as Robert Goffee puts it: "if you are going to do research in management, then you need to connect with the day-to-day concerns of managers."

Similar to the importance of knowing all that has been written about the topic we decide to study, being able to observe what happens in the field also has a bearing on the impact that our research might eventually generate. Dave Ulrich says it is well suggesting that "the challenge of relevant research is being aware of what is happening in and around organizations so that the theory and research offer answers to real and relevant questions."

How can we be inspired by innovation taking place in businesses and observe how things happen in the field? Simple: we've got to get out there: "You have to be out working where things are happening. Nothing happens in the University, nothing happens on the screen, unless you're studying emails. You have to go elsewhere where things are happening," says Henry Mintzberg, who certainly seems to do what he preaches and as a result has long jolted the management world.

Costas Markides is another *Futureer* who thinks finding romantic problems can be extremely easy: "you talk to managers, either directly one-to-one or through your executive education teaching. Or you read about these problems in the *FT*, *BusinessWeek* and so on. You see, if you keep yourself in tune with the world out there, you'll see managerially relevant problems all the time. And some of them strike your fancy and you say: 'This is interesting! I may as well study this one'." He concludes saying: "Everybody will tell you that." I wish that was true.

When you are out in the field, it is amazing how many problems you will come across if you keep your eyes open. You don't believe me? Dave Ulrich, just in the last few weeks before our interview, has run into research questions like: "How do we merger companies with different cultures without losing the benefit of each? How do we build next generation of leadership in a retail setting where leadership becomes critical at the front line? How do we adapt global best practices to companies in emerging markets in Africa while respecting the uniqueness of the local market? How do we communicate to investors the quality of management in organizations where they invest? How do we make the general concept of talent more specific? What choices do senior executives make to improve talent among different employee groups?" and he could add many more to the list.

6 — Look Where Others Don't Look, and See What Others Don't See

Being out in the field is not merely about finding questions to study. Field journalists live much deeper experiences than any reader of their newspaper articles could ever experience, no matter how well they write their article. In the same way for us researchers, if we are willing to work in the field we will be able to observe things and gain insight that we could never read about in books. Henry Mintzberg did find this out in his own experience when working on his legendary dissertation's question — and the first in the list at the start of this chapter — "What do managers do?" It might be a simple one but it is one that had at that time not been answered.

More often, people would try to answer it by watching and observing what managers were supposed to do, not what they actually do. He gave me an interesting example that shows both the importance of first-hand observation of the subject under study and the effective attitude of questioning the environment around us: "I went out and watched managers and I could see that they actually wanted to be interrupted. I was there and I could see: this guy is sitting in an office, which is kind of L-shaped with regards to the corridor outside. There's a door at the far end of his office that looks down the corridor with this secretary just out that door. Where does he put his desk? Right there, looking down the corridor. And he keeps his door open. Now, don't tell me he's not trying to be interrupted. If he didn't want to be interrupted, he could put his desk at the other end and close the door. So he wants to be interrupted. Ok then, why does he want to be interrupted? That's the kind of how these questions go."

Dave Ulrich, as he looks at how organizations work, considers the ways in which what they do falls short of the ideal by applying lateral thinking to everything he sees around him. He says: "I like to live in organizations, looking for situations when leaders face challenges that they don't have ready or easy answers to. This phenomenon-based experiences guide my thinking and research. I find them almost weekly in my organization travels."

For Ulrich, then, his questions chime in harmony with Costa Markides' observation about "keeping in tune with the world out there." It is precisely this outlook that enables him to come up with the "managerially relevant problems" that many say must be addressed by rigorous research.

Although some, like Mintzberg, totally reject the idea that research must solely help managers, others feel quite strongly in support of it. In fact, the desire to solve problems faced by practicing managers is what brought some people to work as researchers in the first place.

Roger Martin found his romantic problem "from watching managers deal with problems and wondering what help they could use that they didn't have currently for how to deal with those problems."

He was a strategy consultant for almost two decades before he moved to academia. In those days, working on various engagements made him curious to understand "why managers struggled with some kind of decisions, didn't seem to make other kind of decisions, got in trouble in certain ways and not other ways." At that time, he simply defined "research" as things that would help his client fix those problems that seemed to need to be dealt with but for which he could not find any 'usable' research. "What I saw was research helping researchers deal with their curiosity. That's good. You know, curious researchers are certainly good to have around, I rather them be curious than not. But I didn't see very much research on the problems that I felt were the biggest problems of my time."

To this day, his research stems from what he sees in the field as he continues to spend as much time as can with "intelligent managers" and customers to find out what concerns and interests them. Without their input, he believes, you will not have anything with real potential impact to research. "I try to keep a foot in the camp of management as much as I can, and I do spend probably a couple of days a month consulting to really interesting companies on the really interesting issues of our times. I consult with the *best* consumer products company in the world, the *best* office furniture company in the world, etc. I try to figure out what is going on in the world of business and to source ideas for what would be useful to that world."

7 — Search at the Intersections

As neuroscientist Patel found, he and others wanted to integrate fields of personal interest that had never been formally linked until they put them together. Few people would have thought there could be any benefit at the intersections of two such distant fields like science and music. In fact few people did. But Patel did, and he changed his own thinking, and increasingly that of others, about how humans and parrots and other animals learn and imitate sounds.

Former Cambridge University doctoral student and founder of the Association for Research into Crimes against Art, Noah Charney invented a new area of research — and practice — by combining knowledge in art history, criminology, psychology, and logic. The result: Charney now helps police departments worldwide find stolen art, which is a multi-billion dollar business. His interest in art history, psychology, and criminal profiling intersected with statistics, and he discovered no one else had integrated the diverse fields. So he now evaluates the types of art that have been stolen over the last several hundred years to understand what attracts criminals (and why). That gives him a sense of what motivates today's art thieves. The field he sparked, through his identifying of an anomaly others had not, brings together law enforcement experts, insurance firms, and academics in ways none of them would have considered doing before.

This skill in bringing together different worlds, as Charney did with art history, statistics and criminal profiling, or Aniruddh Patel did in linking music and the brain, helps create new fields that others can build upon. Sometimes, the newly created field generates more questions and research than the people who sparked the field might have considered possible.

Andrew Fire and Craig Mello (Nobel Prize in Physiology or Medicine, 2006) studied RNA, silencing mechanisms and genes in worms but then discovered that many more scientists wanted to pursue the topic from different angles. As Fire commented after the Nobel Prize ceremony: "It has been tremendous to watch all the different waves of people from different expertise coming to the field. First a whole bunch of biochemists and then a bunch of chemists doing the character of the RNA, and people doing genetics of it. And then suddenly you get pharmacologists, people coming in and saying how could we change this into a drug and a treatment."[7]

Craig Mello, his co-winner, talked of it in a similar fashion: "It's then just really, really exciting how many different fields, seemingly unrelated, have just merged together with the understanding of the [silencing] mechanism. As the understanding grows, we just seem to be bringing together these very distant looking-sort of unrelated looking stories [that] just keep coming together and unfolding in beautiful ways. So, there have been so many contributions from people all around the world, scientists who have been working on phenomena that we didn't know were related to the one that we discovered ... So I think that's one reason it happened so quickly. It [our piece] just was the last, but a very important piece in a puzzle that quickly fell together."[8]

As multidisciplinary and interdisciplinary research blossoms, the number of fields that seem to be blending and merging continues to expand, almost exponentially. Harvard scientist George Church, who "wants to sequence the entire genomes of 100,000 people — nearly every one of the six billion As, Cs, Gs and Ts that occur in a human,"[9] calls himself a "polyglot who believes in integration."[10] Church focuses on integrating genetics, proteomics, biocomputering, and synthetic biology in the Personal Genome Project to learn how to help people take action to prevent disease. He wants to do science that "can be used." Thus, he works with over 20 different firms in fields as diverse as biofuels to cancer to photosynthesis. Like so many of the top researchers I studied, Church's topics came from early experiences and interests. He loved computers as a child, but lacked access to one, so he built one himself.

Through his physician stepfather, Church became interested in biology. The interest in combining computers and biology continued during Church's undergraduate years when he was able to use "... math, physics, chemistry, and computers ... and robots."[11] He strives to remain open to new research directions and deliberately hires young scientists to work in his lab, because they "... indulge me in my dreams ... they don't yet think things are impossible."[12]

Some researchers bring two worlds together by making unusual and instinctive connections between their chosen areas and others. This happens in the hard-sciences, yes, but also in management, economics, political/social fields, etc.

In her interview after winning the Nobel Prize in 2009,[13] Elinor Ostrom acknowledged that her topic of political economy or "the study of social dilemmas"[14] links it directly to economic governance, or showing how individuals choose to cooperate in some settings and not others. She went on observing that this is likely to spark people's imaginations, because they can see implications for their own economic behaviors.

There is something of this free-thinking spirit in edge.org, a website that underscores the importance of — and increasingly the expectation of — blending disciplines and fields and that promotes it by fostering "Conversations on the edge of human knowledge."[15] Edge.org owes a little, too, to the spirit of C. P. Snow, the British chemist and writer best known for his *Strangers and Brothers* sequence of novels.

However, while Snow's short book *Two Cultures,*[16] based on an influential lecture he gave during the 1950s, argued that fields of art and science existed in two wildly different cultures, but should instead interact, edge.org goes further.

It seeks to create such a so-called "Third Culture" a "meeting place" for big questions that cross-discipline borders. The site invites well-known thinkers from fields as wide ranging as religion and neuroscience to art and sociology to argue and compare ideas on common themes. Each year, the founder John Brockman also poses a big question for the thinkers to weigh in on. Examples include: "What are the pressing scientific issues for the nation and the world?", "What is your question? ... Why?", "What do you believe is true even though you cannot prove it?", "What will change everything?" and so on.[17]

As was the case with many others, Brockman's 2005 question "What do you believe is true even though you cannot prove it?" became the title of an edited book, *What We Believe But Cannot Prove.* Leading thinkers from the scientific world were liberated from having to prove a belief which, in some cases, might take hundreds or even thousands of years to be shown as correct or false. The question was suggested by the thoughts of the theoretical psychologist Nicholas Humphrey who said: "Great minds can sometimes guess the truth before they have either the evidence or arguments for it. (Diderot called it having the 'esprit de divination'). What do you believe is true, even though you cannot prove it."[18]

Novelist Ian McEwan, in his introduction to the book, suggests that the writers in *What We Believe But Cannot Prove* reveal high levels of "consilience," a term coined by E. O. Wilson, the biologist who had been so encouraging to Aniruddh Patel during the 1980s. "The boundaries between different specialised subjects begin to break down when scientists find they need to draw on insights and procedures in fields of study adjacent or useful to their own."[19]

While there's an element of researchers having a bit of fun here, a 'day off,' it's the sort of thinking that can lend itself ultimately to discovering new areas of research, looking at problems that have not been solved.

That is not unlike the way that Italian astrophysicist Margherita Hack works, looking for "open spaces" or unexplored areas for research questions and problems that just have not been solved. For her, small problems and mistakes are often the triggers for big ideas and findings that may come later.

Likewise, some researchers simply 'invent' or identify areas for research that no one else has examined. Marketing expert Philip Kotler finds areas which he sees as entirely virgin territory.

It seems that scientists have started to recognize that most questions *within* their field have been addressed already or are no longer relevant; instead, the questions at the seams or borders of fields are where the action will be in the coming years.

Interestingly, while the focus of edge.org's questions is typically on science, a similar trend is emerging in the other direction as well, where fields like management and marketing have begun to reach to other disciplines as well: biophysics, neuromarketing, chemical engineering ... the combinations continue to grow. Thus, for future scientists and management researchers, staying within a single field or silo should be less attractive.

8 — Develop the 'Right' Mindset

As you may recall, I introduced earlier a model based on the assumption that *research that matters* stems from the meeting of three key elements: (1) the researcher, who does the research; (2) the system that puts in place the underlying conditions necessary to its researchers; and (3) the distributors of creative research ideas and solutions. In this section, I am going to identify what I believe are the personal characteristics that we should aim to develop in order to become better at finding and studying romantic problems.

By now, you may have fallen in the pitfall to concluding that we cannot reach a consensus as to whether or not *research that matters* should have practical application. I did it too, at first. So far, some *Futureers*, especially in the hard-sciences have told us they do not think at all about the practical application of their research. Others, especially management thinkers, have told us that we cannot hope to generate any impact with the insight we discover, unless it eventually finds its way to being adopted in the real world.

I started this research assuming that, in the case of management research in particular, it should be impossible to discern the two concepts. So much so that when Mintzberg told me he disagreed and stated firmly that good research should just be insightful, I could not understand.

I had to dig deeper into the analysis of the interviews and the material I had collected on the *Futureers* to understand that I was actually asking the wrong question.

Debating on whether your research should be applicable or not is like doing the very thing I have suggested not to do earlier in this book: it's like starting from the end, the destination. If you do that, you will miss out on the journey. And if you don't pay attention to where you are going in your research journey, you may eventually miss out on the destination you spent so much time planning for.

What I have taken from the *Futureers'* experiences is that, in reality, what you should ask yourself is whether your investigation *bears a connection* with the real world. If it does, Dave Ulrich says "reality (or Phenomenon) based research almost always have direct application."

To increase our ability to do *research that matters*, therefore, we must wire this point deep into our mindset. We must stop being introverts, we must stop sitting in an office mailing questionnaires, we must stop being afraid to get out there and we must learn to be like a "kind of voyeur ... to get close to the action to see it first-hand but not too close that you are corrupted by it" (Henry Mintzberg).

If we do that, then we have a better chance to identify where there is disconnect between what we know about a subject or event and what we observe first-hand of the same. Then, if we are courageous enough to move beyond our confidence zone, it is highly likely that the end result will generate meaningful insight.

When I stepped aside from my initial assumption, I finally realized that, in reality, all the *Futureers* talk about the importance for research that truly matters to generate meaningful insight, that is knowledge that is new and that can change the way that people think about a subject, the way they behave or the way they work.

As an example, one of the research problems Mintzberg worked on at the start of his outstanding career focused on the behavior of managers. Grossly and unjustly simplifying his contribution to knowledge and practice, Mintzberg sees his research merely concluding that: "'If you think managers plan, organise and coordinate and control ... think again! They get interrupted a lot' ... Was that applicable? No. Was it going to change people's lives? Yes."

Dave Ulrich does a wonderful job at bringing once and for all the debate to a convergence point: ultimately, *research that matters* "is mostly *theoretically rich, empirically sound*, and *managerially relevant*." To this I may add — following Mintzberg's suggestion — *insightful*.

Whereas the idea of research application might lend itself to some debate, all people I studied and talked to in my research agree that doing research for research's sake is not likely to lead to much impact. Disturbingly (but not surprisingly), all also agree that there is presently too much of this type of attitude in research and, especially, when aiming to build a career in scholarly research.

Costas Markides points out: "One of the problems is this mindset that exists in academia where people are not really interested in ideas or in solving problems but all they are interested in is publishing. Why? Because their reference point is other academics and they get promoted based on publications in the academic journals. They also develop their self worth (how important they are), not from whether they have solved problems or whether they have made a difference but whether other academics know them and know their work. They all go to conferences full of other academics and who are the stars? The stars are the people that publish a lot in the academic journals. Even though nobody knows about their work, they do publish a lot and therefore they develop this reputation. "*I am very important because all these 5000 academics in this conference know me.*" So for academics their reference point and their reference group are other academics. What you aspire to do is become famous among the 5000 other academics that are in that field rather than generating ideas that change the world or help change the world."

Markides' words might seem harsh but I am sure most of you reading this book will agree they paint a very true picture of reality.

To become better researchers, we therefore must change our mindset completely. We must forget about self-worth and peer-recognition and simply focus on the four keywords: *theoretically rich, empirically sound, managerially relevant, insightful.*

Being 'voyeurs with values,' that's what I am talking about! We must be willing to go out in the field to observe the world around us based on this strong value system, regardless of whether we are looking for a romantic problem or whether we are coming up with a creative solution to it.

Is this a guaranteed receipt for quick success? Not at all, it isn't. Many agree that generating insight and observing the expected change in reality might take time. The more novel the idea, actually, the more time it is likely required to study it and to understand how to come up with original insight about it: "since I work on quite basic scientific questions [my research ability to transform a field and to lead to practical improvements in people's lives], generally only becomes apparent after quite some time, if ever" told me Jack Szostak.

But as researchers, we can't be dismayed by this. On the contrary, Howard Gardner puts it clearly: "Of course, any researcher is interested in whether his research has effects. But researchers need to take the long view. Some of my research has had influence right away; some has had influence after decades; and some has yet to have influence, and might have influence long after I am gone."

9 — Foster the 'Right' Mindset

Many of the *Futureers* have raised the issue that the very concept of *doing research that matters* must be understood within existing constraints.

Such constraints can be tangible or intangible. As Margherita Hacks suggests, "one needs to keep into account her own possibilities and capabilities (author's note: *intangible*), and what instruments are available for her research (author's note: *tangible*). When I started, I didn't have the possibility to choose and do any research which came to mind. Especially as a fresh graduate I had to understand what research I could have done with the instruments available to me."

Tangible constraints and their impact on our research are fairly easy to identify and understand and I am not going to discuss them here. Intangible constraints, on the other hand, might be less obvious, although, I would argue, their negative impact on our research might be even more dramatic.

Futureers recognize that their environment (academic or otherwise) is a very important element of their success. In particular the culture and values of the environment we work within can be enablers or inhibitors of success. Rob Goffee notices how "in a good business school there is a culture and in that culture there is an attempt to retain good research credentials with high-levels of impact and application."

With the *Insight Incubator*-element (in reference to the model proposed in this book) playing such an important part in our chances to do *research that matters*, it is worth questioning at least whether or not we are planting our investigative seeds in the most fertile ground.

Barbara Kellerman gives an excellent example of how the underlying culture of the system (academic in this instance) might act as an intangible inhibitor since the very early stages of choosing the romantic problem we want to tackle with our research.

During the interview, she discussed how, regretfully, especially younger scholars have to be mindful in pursuing cross-disciplinary activities as they might not be supported by their universities: "in the beginning, since I wanted to get tenure and I wanted a career as an academic, I was loath to take something as highly interdisciplinary as leadership. You don't get rewarded for [interdisciplinary work] even though colleges and universities always encourage multi/interdisciplinary work. In fact the rewards structure is very traditional. So I was careful in the beginning. But once I [got tenure and therefore] could do what I wanted to do and found the way into the academy, *I never stopped studying leadership*" (paraphrased).

Going back to the positive impact that a 'good culture' might have on our research, on the other hand, when Rob Goffee was discussing how he finds his own research question, he told me that working in a good business school he can get good access to "the field" and a high level of trust that enables him to do "riskier" and "provocative" research.

An environment which values the "in our head and in the field" approach to finding relevant romantic problems to investigate also creates situations for you to mingle both with young inquisitive minds and also with practicing managers with a wealth of experience. As he says: "in a good business school you have got this great opportunity to lay your ideas in front of your consulting clients or the classes that you are teaching week by week."

There is no doubt, therefore, that your environment will influence both how you look for problems and how you come up with solutions. Markides' experience is just one more example: "I have been very lucky because first of all I have a DBA from Harvard, so my academic training is not a traditional PhD that would have put me in a very academic mindset. It's a DBA which means that I always start my research by looking at managerially relevant questions, managerial phenomena ... And then, I got doubly lucky as right after my DBA I joined London Business School, which is one of those schools where managerial relevance is encouraged. So from the very beginning, I started to look at managerially relevant problems."

An important question we should all ask ourselves, therefore, seems to me to be: "is *our system* doing enough to lessen the intangible constraints to the advantage of *research that matters?*"

At the same time, we shouldn't just assume the responsibility lies all in the system. Howard Gardner recognizes the responsibility we have as individual as well: "if I am convinced that a topic is interesting and important, it is my job to convince funders to support it, and to show that the research is important for the intended audience."

So the second important question is: "are *we* doing enough to promote the potential impact of our research within our system?"

What's New?

There appears to be a never-ending possibility of finding problems that are unexplored or have been ignored. It should perhaps be acknowledged that there is never anything entirely new under the Sun. Back in 1982, some 30 years before the time of writing this book, industrial psychologists Campbell, Daft and Hulin published a small book which could have given the title to this chapter: What to study: Generating and developing research questions.[20]

The authors examined 10 years of journal publications, surveyed members of the Industrial and Organizational Psychology division of the American Psychological Association, reviewed what questions had been researched (since the early 1970s), and what researchers saw as areas needing future investigation. In addition, they examined "significant" research projects, based upon criteria of being interesting, original, and making a contribution. Their recommendations for researchers seeking to conduct significant research could have been written today[21]:

1. Examine problems from the 'real' world of organizations.

2. Be interested, have resolve/persistence, and put in the effort.

3. Choose projects based on 'intuition' — be excited, feel 'good' about a project.

4. Be intellectually rigorous.

5. Reach out to the "uncertain world of organizations and [return] with something clear, tangible, and well understood."

6. Use or create theory.

Based on the material collected in my own research, in this chapter I have offered several ideas, some of which overlap with and some of which add to the list above. Is the insight new? I have put forward some new ideas, yes. But that is not really the point. The point is that, given that 30 years after that 1982 book was written we are still not generating nearly enough impact through our research (at least in the management field), we ought to continue asking the same question. Only if we do so, we may eventually get to the ultimate answer.

When I started putting together a list of key learning points for this conclusive section, I realized that the list's contour resembled an upward-pointing-arrow. I am not the greatest believer in destiny and divine signs but, this time, I thought it was quite a remarkable coincidence that in a book aiming to give us inspiration to do better, I would end up with an upward-pointing arrow to summarize some of its main conclusions:

Hints to finding romantic problems worth investigating.

While we may never be able to generate meaningful insight simply by searching for romantic problems, somebody once said that if we reach for Mars, we might eventually land on the Moon instead. That would not be too bad either!

CHAPTER 5

ENJOY THE RIDE

If you wish to learn from the theoretical physicist anything about the methods which he uses, I would give you the following piece of advice: Don't listen to his words, examine his achievements. For to the discoverer in that field, the constructions of his imagination appear so necessary and so natural that he is apt to treat them not as the creations of his thoughts but as given realities.

— Albert Einstein, Nobel Prize in Physics in 1921[1]

Doing good research is "hard work combined with imagination and the ability to cross borders."

— Gerhard Ertl, Nobel Prize in Chemistry in 2007

The development of a remarkable piece of art, or a novel or a musical composition is usually not an easy and straightforward undertaking. When viewed, read or heard, the end product appears remarkable and as close to perfect as the artist could make it. But it is rare for a piece of art or music, or a novel, in the first draft to look like its finished version.

Likewise, viewed as an end product, excellent research can be quite elegant, insightful, and seemingly near perfect overall. But also like art, the process behind the scene may sometimes be more like making sausage or democracy — the output can be transforming and delicious, but not always smooth going or pretty to watch during the process.

In *Outliers: The Story of Success*,[2] Malcom Gladwell suggests that to reach excellence at performing a complex task takes 10,000 hours of hard, hard work. Citing neurologist Danile Levitin, he writes: "The emerging picture ... is that the thousand hours of practice is required to achieve the level of mastery associated with being a world-class expert — in anything. In study after study, of composers, basketball players, fictions writers, ice skaters, concert pianists, chess players, master criminals, and what have you, this number comes up again and again."[3]

I think we can all agree that research, be that in management or otherwise, can be regarded as a complex task. Therefore, in our pursuit of excellence in research, we can safely assume that it is going to take a lot of time to truly generate impact through our work. 10,000 hours, to be precise.

As a matter of fact, and rather remarkably, many of the *Futureers* I studied confirmed it has taken them between 5 and 7 years to craft their research masterpiece.

Let's say: 6 years, working 220 days per year, 8 hours per day = 10,560 hours!

It can be daunting to think we have to work all those hours to have a feeble hope to achieve greatness (of meaning) with our research. And if you think that going through all that time is going to be smooth sailing across a straight course you chartered before you started your journey, think again. There is an immense number of things that can go wrong, or simply not as you expected, during 6 years.

We see this happening every day in something as common in our lives as films, where studio interference often muddies the waters and results in the release of films that are further from — rather than closer to — their directors' original intentions (sounds familiar?). Film directors, sportsmen, writers, researchers ... nobody working on a project is immune to the pressures coming from their own environment.

And yet some manage to consistently produce one outstanding achievement after the other. How do they do it? Cinema 'auteurs,' such as Woody Allen or the Coen brothers, often gain valuable insight from preliminary screenings and use that ultimately to shape the final film. Sportsmen like F1 driver Michael Schumacher and tennis all-time champion Roger Federer are well known for spending countless hours assessing retrospectively what worked and what did not work as they expected and investigating how to repeat, avoid, or adapt their performance in the future. As for writers, one of the most commonly acknowledged views is that "good writing is rewriting," as confirmed by Gore Vidal's allegedly renowned statement: "I am an obsessive rewriter, doing one draft and then another and another, usually five. In a way, I have nothing to say, but a great deal to add."

Does it exist such a thing as 'one way' to become exemplary at what we do? Be that art, music, cinema, sport, or, why not, management research? No, it does not. Each individual will bring to *it* her own influence.

John Kotter thinks that "like most things in life some people will have more natural skills than others and ... you can take somebody with some natural skills and help them develop those skills. I suspect that, as with most complex skills, the development just doesn't happen in a classroom over a year or two ... But can you start teaching the process in a formal educational program if the person has some potential? Sure. If the person has no skills, no potential, no inflammation, the wrong instincts for doing research I suspect you can put them through many classes and it's not going to help much." But you picked up this book in the first place and you are still reading it, which means you can be taught (or you anyway can learn), as I hope I can too, by people who have found the way to go about doing research that evidently works.

In Chapter 2, I attempted to translate the input from outstanding researchers into a vision for what we should strive to achieve, that is *research that matters*. Recognizing the importance of tackling romantic problems, in Chapter 4 I offered some ideas for where to look for such worthy research questions. In this chapter, I am now going to look for ideas and key elements that define the process *Futureers* adopt to do their own research, and how they may (or may not) vary across fields or disciplines.

This is not a chapter on research design and methodology as you traditionally would think about. I am not going to discuss how we should go about selecting a case study, conduct an ANOVA analysis of the data we collect, or test the validity of our conclusion by triangulation. There are plenty of other, better books available teaching those who wants to learn how to use those and other valuable instruments.

I am simply going to share with you how the exemplary researchers I have studied do their research, whether some approaches appear to work better than others, how similar concepts may be transferred across fields.

In doing so, I am also going to consider ways that research can 'go wrong,' and how we can transform such apparent negatives into something altogether more interesting and occasionally, like many *Futureers*' stories prove, arrive at the discovery of our lifetime.

Research Designed to Impress

Today, a central question in all scientific studies and in their evaluation concerns the methodology used to answer the selected research questions.

In the unlikely attempt to distil a good research process to a number of standard steps, Georgetown University adapted the Association of Colleges and Research Libraries' "Objectives for Information Literacy Instruction" and the broader "Information Literacy Competency Standards for Higher Education" to create a tutorial that would provide guidance to their students by means of "15 steps to good research."[4]

These 15 steps are as follows[5]:

1. Define and articulate a research question (formulate a research hypothesis).

2. Identify possible sources of information in many types and formats.

3. Judge the scope of the project.

4. Re-evaluate the research question based on the nature and extent of information available and the parameters of the research project.

5. Select the most appropriate investigative methods (surveys, interviews, experiments) and research tools (periodical indexes, databases, websites).

6. Plan the research project.

7. Retrieve information using a variety of methods (draw on a repertoire of skills).

8. Refine the search strategy as necessary.

9. Write and organize useful notes and keep track of sources.

10. Evaluate sources using appropriate criteria.

11. Synthesize, analyze, and integrate information sources and prior knowledge.

12. Revise hypothesis as necessary.

13. Use information effectively for a specific purpose.

14. Understand such issues as plagiarism, ownership of information (implications of copyright to some extent), and costs of information.

15. Cite properly and give credit for sources of ideas.

Seems straightforward, doesn't it? Following slight variations of the very same process, every year, more or less known researchers from all fields and disciplines conduct their research and publish their findings in thousands of articles in hundreds of scholarly journals, ranking high or low.

Like finding diamonds buried deep into the rock though, only a tiny percentage of all these articles actually presents insight that, by anybody's standard, has the potential to change people's lives.

And yet, most of the many authors follow the 15 steps to good research listed above or a similar approach anyway, giving us undeniable proof that research can be carried out ticking every box with regards to traditionally 'good' research methodology and procedure and rigor, without ultimately contributing anything of significance or importance.

How can this happen?

Costas Markides has a theory (supported by most of the *Futureers* I have studied): academics have other academics as their reference point and they get promoted based on their track record publishing in academic journals that get cited by other academics. "Our goal" he says "is not whether we find a beautiful answer to a question but 'how am I going to publish this little piece of research I am doing in an academic journal?' And to publish in academic journals you cannot have a big question, you have to have one of these stupid little questions to which most people know the answer to begin with, but you need to ask this question because this is the only way to get it published."

That is, the system placing so much importance on publishing has a negative effect on our ability to pursue romantic problems and to reach insightful solutions. "Publication for publication's sake or as something that you are coerced to do to advance your career produces questionable results," concludes John Kotter.

Designing a piece of research to impress rather than to generating insight also has an impact on what methodology we are likely to choose. "There is more pressure on juniors these days to do more sophisticated quantitative research which can be more easily published," says Rob Goffee noticing how there is an incentive these days toward getting in this "hot house," getting your head down and doing quantitative-type, publishable research. "But the danger there is that you get slightly disconnected from the field ... and that is what has happened to management research, sadly."

In fact, Roger Martin feels rather strongly that "the journals are completely methodology obsessed, and if you don't use acceptable methodologies then you just can't get published. Essentially, the acceptable methodologies are very, very restrictive." Kaplan agrees suggesting that "top ranging academic journals take a very narrow view of what is legitimate and high-quality academic research."

Note that what is being questioned here is not the importance of choosing an appropriate scientific methodology. All *Futureers* agree that rigor is an inherent requirement of good quality *research that matters*. Markides himself agrees that "There is a good way to do research and there is a bad way to do research. You have to run your regressions, you have to develop your hypotheses, you have to measure your variables etc., these are all tools of the trade. You need to have a good methodology. [You cannot do your research] just going out like a journalist, asking 100 people 'what do you think about this' and then summarising their answers and say: 'these are the findings of my research'."

No, what is being questioned here is the validity (or otherwise) of pushing researchers (or letting ourselves be pushed) to 'strategically' choose certain methodologies over others, just because these are deemed 'acceptable' by a narrow audience of other academics — academics who, by the way, use some poorly defined measures of impact that fail entirely and shamefully to generate insight and innovation (more on this in Chapter 7).

This obsession with modern social sciences methodologies, as Roger Martin calls them, is just plain wrong and should stop for the simple but grave reason that it inhibits management researchers from making insightful discoveries. Martin believes that "we are teaching researchers to be slaves to the methodology. Rather than the methodologies helping them figure stuff out, the methodologies encourage them not to figure out stuff for which their methodologies can't be rigorously applied."

"So many doctoral students call me and send me emails all the time asking methodological questions," exemplifies John Kotter. "I got to the point where I don't even know what to say because it gets to be a depressing phone call or email exchange: 'do you really want to be doing this?' and if they're honest they come back and say 'no'. 'Well, do you see the box you have got yourself in to? Do you think quality work is done by people who don't want to do what they are doing?'"

Well, do you?

I am sure you *don't want to* but quite possibly that *you have to* in order to get your promotion. As John Kotter tells his student so I say to myself: "this is profoundly depressing!"

Research Designed to Matter

There seems to be nothing wrong with Georgetown University's "15 Steps to Good Research" tutorial. As a matter of fact, many of the *Futureers* normally follow sort of the same series of steps, although they would *never* describe their approach as being such a logically structured and seemingly linear process.

When I compared the 15 steps with the experiences from my golden sample though, I identified three main differences between the way most people do their research and the way the *Futureers* go about it:

- *Futureers* have a more pragmatic, less rigid approach to investigating their problem using 'acceptable methodologies.'
- *Futureers* follow a never-ending iterative process of asking and answering questions, putting themselves in the shoes of 'the customer.'
- *Futureers* allow for creativity and creative thinking.

I have personally — and therefore arguably — interpreted such differences as being ultimately responsible for the success the *Futureers* have had in their work (for what relates to the *Insight Generator* element in my model for *doing research that matters*).

For that reason, my wholehearted suggestion is to follow their example.

1 — Take a More Pragmatic, Less Rigid Approach to Investigating a Problem

I am tempted to say that, regardless of whether *Futureers* look for a cure for cancer or for how to measure performance in businesses, they all seem to follow the same, very simple approach: (1) they learn their field's state of the art; (2) they observe the subject they want to study from out in the field; (3) they learn from other fields; (4) they take a creative jump; (5) they start again. There is clearly much more to it but those are fundamentally the five key steps all talked about with passion when I asked them how they did their research.

One thing I noticed is that, among management thinkers more than hard-scientists, a qualitative method of research seems to be predominant. Although I would not want to hazard any gross generalization in this regards. In the end, all agree that there is no 'best method' as such and the choice depends on the research question.

Henry Mintzberg is rather uncompromising about this point: "This crap of having to be quantitative, having to use statistics, or having to start with hypothesis ... it's nonsense. Of course people can do good research that way, but it's nonsense to [assume that has to be so for] every single [researcher], especially the creative ones ... the really good ones ... break away from that. They realise that they have done something or found something really interesting [and they keep going with it]."

Exemplary researchers, therefore, seem to be less concerned with sticking rigidly to a narrow set of acceptable methodologies. They basically choose a research method that fits their overarching research questions, rather than finding a research problem that fits the methodology.

Let me give you some examples.

Rob Goffee approaches his research with some loosely formed ideas and then he likes getting his hands dirty. "All the work that I have done over recent years has involved getting our hands dirty in the research process; in other words getting out there and talking to people. A lot of our work is interview based ... and the kind of work sometime referred to as grounded research, where things tends to come up along the way. So you start with a framework for sure: you don't go in with a blind mind, but stuff emerges and on-route you do a lot of trying out and testing out."

Starting from the question and designing research from the ground up is Roger Martin's preferred approach, which he says "often involves searching for the proverbial needle in the haystack. ... The research methodology is sort of floating around and I keep trying to figure out what's going on, but it's not a terribly formal kind of approach."

I took some reassurance about the validity of my own approach to this very research from my conversation with John Kotter about how he approaches his own research: "Basically what I do is pattern analysis, I do qualitative pattern analysis on relatively small samples, that's the research I do. Qualitative in the sense that very, very little of my working is grinding down data. Pattern analysis in the sense that the fundamental things I look for are patterns that relate to variables of interest, like how well an organisation actually does in serving purposes that most of us would think that organisations are designed to serve. And small samples means I do not deal with data sets that have 10,000 sites, organisations, people in them. My data gathering methodology is entirely out watching things and talking to people and it's done in as systematic a way as possible but virtually all of my research is done a long way from a library or computer. It is out watching how events unfold and talking to people about them, what they've observed about how events have unfolded. These days I don't even use questionnaires anymore, or virtually never. It's all observations and live interviews."

Looking for regularities across a sample of cases through the application of the scientific method is what Philip Kotler sees being inherent to excellent research: "When possible," he says, "experiments need to be set up with proper controls. A good case can be made for collecting a sufficient size sample of company cases and looking for regularities that might suggest hypotheses to be tested."

Large data sets are, on the other hand, the preferred instrument for Dave Ulrich whose approach we can infer from his description of some of the projects he is currently working on: "I like to observe interesting questions tied to challenges organizations and/or leaders face. Right now, we are doing three research projects. First, what makes HR professionals successful in different markets. For this research, we are creating a large data set of over 10,000 individuals who will define the competencies of HR professionals they know. ... In a second study, we are curious about how investors make decision to invest in one company over another. We are surveying a large cross section of investors to determine how much they look at industry favorableness, firm performance, or quality of leadership. We will then do focus groups to operationalize how investors can understand quality of leadership.

"Third, we have seen a lot of leadership development not last over time. We are studying leadership sustainability. ... For this research, we are reviewing how to make change last from a number of disciplines: habits, leadership development, leadership failure, making change happen, etc. We are going to do a qualitative meta-analysis of this work to define key principles for leadership sustainability. Finally, we are collecting data from over 400 companies about what makes top companies for leadership. We will work to determine what separates the best companies for leadership from the rest."

Futureers also make the same effort to keep an open mind when they scan the world for problems, as they do when they assess whether their methodology remains fit with the evolving nature of their findings.

Research methodologies may change as fashion does, when a new and better one appears. As Howard Gardner commented: "Fields develop paradigmatic ways of conducting research and these hold sway for a while. But then someone comes up with a new way of thinking, or a new methodology, and turns the field upside down — we call this a Kuhnian or paradigmatic shift."

The Austrian-born philosopher of science Paul Feyerabend warned researchers on the dangers of excessive attachment to methodology in any field of research, not just science. He believed that a single and rigid rules-based scientific method would limit the potential for significant scientific research, and therefore progress.

Dave Ulrich tries to make his own students aware of the importance of letting preconceptions on the importance of rigorous methodologies not hinder their ability to observe the phenomenon in the field: "When I taught Ph.D. students, I would require that they write a paper with no references, describing the phenomenon that they were most interested in. Some had trouble because they were more oriented to [traditional] research and theory and not to practice."

If one looks at the history of almost any discipline, several inspiring examples can be found of people who have completely disregarded what at their time seemed to be 'acceptable methodologies' to pursue what they thought was a worthy problem from one side and a fruitful investigative approach on the other.

Roger Martin cites the case of Peter Drucker and Mike Porter whom he considers two of the greatest management researchers of the last 50–75 years.

He says: "Both of them tend to be pooh-poohed completely by the rigorous researchers who say that their methodologies aren't rigorous. So Peter Drucker's got this annoying methodology which is: he thinks deeply about the way the world is working, makes a declaration about what is happening, the declaration seems preposterous in his days, but 25 years later everybody says: 'how did he figure that out, before it happened?' So he says we are going to have pension funds socialism in 1976, that there will be knowledge workers in 1958: how did he know that? and so they give him credit for being right all the time, but because he didn't have proper research methodologies he isn't beloved by the mainstream management thinkers."

The same, he says, is true of Michael Porter. His work has made him a leading authority on competitive strategy while at the same time being "pooh-poohed" for not meeting the standard of 'acceptable methodologies.' Roger Martin reminds how it wasn't until his book on competitive strategy "became the best selling business book in the history of the planet" that Harvard Business School gave him tenure.

"So I think that's one of the things that I'm in some sense freed up to do my research by not being bound to methodologies that I just think restrict our ability to understand the world rather than enhance our ability to understand the world," says Martin. Although he also mentions some of the risks for not adhering to the old men's club etiquette: "although I got appointed as full professor in a business school after 20 years in business, I will never be considered a researcher by the mainstream academics in my field but just as a business guy who teaches!"

2 — Follow a Never-Ending Iterative Research Process, Putting Yourself in the Shoes of 'The Customer'

Futureers seem to have the ability to have a big vision and also plan to reach it one step at the time. The only thing important to them is to advance their field, no matter what. As Jack Szostak says with regards to his own approach to studying the origins of life: "The question is a big one, but we are able to make steady progress by answering sub-problems. This positive feedback gives us the encouragement to continue."

This is in line with Gary Hamel's view that we ought to commit to revolutionary goals but take evolutionary steps.[6]

Costas Markides has his own way to ensure he reaches his insightful answer by putting himself in his customer's shoes and tackling one sub-problem at the time. At every step of the process he thinks of his findings as if they were definitive and then attempts to predict what question these would rise in the mind of whoever is reading his book, attending his lecture or listening to his speech. He then uses that question to engage in his next research cycle. This is how he explains it:

"Whatever I am saying [my findings are], I have to first test it on a customer (the customer being whoever is reading my book or listening my speech) and see whether they understand it and what follow-up questions they'd have for me. What is the question he is going to ask to whatever I say? And that leads me to another question. And when I find the answer to that question, it leads me to another question and you go through these questions until finally you reach a point where you say 'Ok, I now have the answers to all 20 questions that somebody might ask me about this problem'."

He puts his approach into context describing how he applied it to his latest research on solving big social problems: "The first idea was: if you want to solve poverty or if you want to solve drug-related crime, you have to look at the underlying structure of the system and change that. And then I thought, if I say that to a manager or a government official, what is the first question he or she is likely to ask me? ... He's likely to ask me: what is the structure of the system? So my next question ... is exactly that: what does the structure of the system mean? I then set about answering that question and found out that there are 10 things that make the structure of a system. And then I asked: now suppose I go to my customer (who is the manager or the government official) and I say: what you need to do is to change the underlying structure of the system and that means changing these 10 things. What is he/she likely to ask me then? He is probably going to tell me: 'these 10 things are major things: how am I supposed to change them?' So now I have to answer this question for him: is it really possible for an individual to change these 10 major components of the system? So I went back and I researched that and I came up with the answer that you don't really need to change all of them, what you need to do is, for example, to identify high leverage points in the system and then aim to influence these points. What we know is that small changes in these high leverage points can have a big effect. That is the answer. So then when I say that to my customers, what is he/she likely to say? He'll probably say: what are these high leverage points then? What are the small things that I need to do to change these high leverage points? So then I go and answer these questions. And I could go on and on."

Two elements are worth paying attention to more closely as they illustrate some key aspects of the winning characters of *Futureers* and of their proven research approach:

1. Considering that the researcher is accountable to a "client" for whatever research she is doing: This requires a sense of self-imposed responsibility and accountability.

2. Going through a never-ending iterative process of switching from questions to answers to questions to answers etc.: This shows a strong inquisitive predisposition and patience to engage in a process that could potentially take years (as it usually does).

All *Futureers*, regardless of their field, adopt the same approach, even though they might not explain it using the exact same words. "This idea of putting ourselves in the shoes of a hypothetical client of the research we are undertaking is key."

As a matter of fact, for some the client is not hypothetical at all. It is on the contrary very clear to them who might be the recipient of their insight: Kaplan, for example, suggests that "once you have made a commitment to be a scholar in a business school, you have to recognize that business is your audience."

In his inspiring response to a request from a 28-year-old doctoral graduate soliciting his advice about how to go about her forthcoming career as an academic,

Kaplan clarifies why he thinks it is important that future researchers take this view on their research.[7] He says that "[our field's] professionals are our clients. As a scholar in a professional school, you will educate current and future professionals on the field's common body of knowledge. You will learn how to dispense the existing common body of knowledge in ways that your students can put into action during their professional careers ... But also important, though less widely known, accepted, and advocated, academic scholars at a professional school should contribute to advancing the profession's body of knowledge, especially when innovation is high and major changes are occurring in the practice environment of the profession."[8]

Roger Martin as well is rather pragmatic about the fact that "if you are not in the world dealing with managers I think it's going to be hard for you to have really impactful things to say ..., you know, if you never talk to customers the likelihood that you are going to create something that they really, really, really can't live without is pretty small." It is interesting to note how Martin also sees managers as their *customers*. Even more interesting is the hidden message (or not so much hidden) that if you can't create something *really, really, really* valuable ... why bother at all?

Thinking about what our client would expect from the insight we generate is a way to hold ourselves accountable for the work we do and to make ourselves feel responsible for spending the limited time we have on this heart to do something meaningful (and to generate a return for those who have made a long-term investment in our research, which, in the case of university researchers, are the taxpayers).

The second aspect of the *Futureers*' approach is the never-ending iterative research process. John Kotter explains in plain words how this works: "Do a study that focuses on the questions raised by the last study. Do as good a job as you can at answering those questions and inevitably, as a part of the study, new questions are raised. Answer those in the next study. And it just kind of goes on like that."

The approach is common in the hard-sciences as well. Gerhard Ertl, for example, is convinced that "answering a question always triggers new ones." The same for Harald zur Hausen, for whom not even a Nobel Prize was a big enough achievement to stop him from continuing to yet another iteration of his research cycle: "At this moment, we can roughly calculate that 21% of human cancer incidents is linked to infectious events. Clearly to only those infections, which we studied. Also they count for something like 12% of all cancers in females. But for other viruses, which have been discovered and traced into bacteria and parasites linked to human cancer, the overall rate is 21%. I am firmly convinced that it is not the end of the story because all the previous findings have given some kind of epidemiological hints that there might be infectious events behind these types of cancers. There are still a couple of cancers where we believe that there is epidemiological evidence available that they could be theoretically linked to infections. And that is what we are presently working on, in particular, childhood leukemias and forms of colorectal cancers where the epidemiology provides some hints that would be worthwhile studying more intensively."

Following the hint-trail a la Indiana Jones makes the journey "endlessly interesting," to cite Barbara Kellerman. "It's almost like trying to find your way through a forest ... or a scavenger hunt: one set of clues gets you to some place and you get an answer and then it's another set of clues and you're ready to take it on, [and that] puts you on the next part of the journey," says John Kotter enthusiastically.

In a way, the same approach also stretches the length of the research journey. Many of the top-management thinkers I studied are still working to this day on a topic they approached during their graduate studies. Like for Barbara Kellerman, who claims to have said about her last several books that each was going to be her last one ever about leadership. And yet, she is writing another one as we speak — although she swears it is going to be her last one!

Or John Kotter, who explains the benefits of sticking to a research journey that has been keeping him busy for nearly 30 years: "I now understand more [about why some executives do well for themselves and for society] than I did 10 years ago. 10 years ago I used to know more than I did 20 years ago and 20 years ago I understood more than I did 30 years ago. So it's the research itself that, in a sense, raises the questions and answers the questions, not literature, it's not work done by others and then printed by others, it's my own observation of the world."

3 — Be Creative

The role of creativity in management research comes down to one key question: is management research a science or is it an art?

According to the *Encyclopaedia Britannica*, "science" is a word used to define "any system of knowledge that is concerned with the physical world and its phenomena and that entails unbiased observations and systematic experimentation. In general, a science involves a pursuit of knowledge covering general truths or the operations of fundamental laws."[9]

It follows that, based on what I discussed so far, doing research in management is definitely a science, from finding worthy romantic problems by observing the world around us to collecting data through interviews or questionnaires, to doing pattern analysis or meta-analysis of the data we have (just by means of few examples).

Peter Drucker adds an important point of further specification to this view: "Management is not a 'SCIENCE' in the way the Mathematics or Physics are. It is a PRACTICE — a DISCPLINE — similar to Medicine, to the Priesthood, to the Law.

And there, good practice is only what rests on good theory; and good theory is only what is validated in and through good practice."[10]

The same *Encyclopaedia Britannica* defines "the arts as modes of expression that use skill or imagination in the creation of aesthetic objects, environments, or experiences that can be shared with others."[11] Is management research also an art?

As I quoted at the start of this chapter, Gerhard Ertl's convinced excellent research is the product of "hard work combined with imagination and the ability to cross borders." Costas Markides as well thinks that creativity is a very important element of excellent research, and he is convinced that: "[Management] is an art, not a science." To defend his view, he cites Charles Darwin's approach. "Darwin went and looked at the birds and the bees for two years but when he came back he did not summarised what he saw. No! He looked at the data and based on that, he made this creative jump and came up with this beautiful theory called evolution."

It's interesting to note that Charles Lyell, whose *Principles of Geology* was such a huge influence on the young Darwin, went through a similar process. He noticed (this has been put down his being near-sighted) that the shape of the coastline near Norwich, in East Anglia, was gradually altering due to erosion. From this observation came his idea, and lifelong obsession, with the idea of the planet as a living and constantly changing organism. Such an idea, of course, could only be correct if the Earth was many million, rather than a few thousand, years old.

Markides says: "It requires a creativity jump to go from the data to the theory. And it takes courage to do that because there is no direct link between the data and the theory. But this is where creativity comes in. You look at the data and you make this jump into something new, something beautiful."

The view that creativity is an important element of innovation by research is supported even by the well-known "no-logical-path" argument put forward by Albert Einstein. In his 1918 address, "Principles of Research," Einstein made a point[12]:

> "The supreme task of the physicist is to arrive at those universal elementary laws from which the cosmos can be built up by pure deduction. There is no logical path to these laws; only intuition, resting on sympathetic understanding of experience, can reach them."

The field of management is filled with exemplary 'adventurers' who have made Einstein's principle one of their own and were able to take such creative non-logical step, enough to fill many books, in fact. In the field of strategy alone, Kiechel III describes the life and achievements of what he calls "the Lords of Strategy."[13] And in *What's The Big Idea*,[14] Davenport and co-authors do the same for "idea practitioners" from other areas of management, from operations to quality to leadership, etc.

According to Costas Markides, Gary Hamel is another one such creative mind who effectively went through a similar creative process at Canon. "Hamel goes and look at Canon for two years and outcomes this beautiful theory on the core competences of the corporation." He adds: "There is no direct link between the data and the theory. But then he had the courage to make this jump from the raw data to a beautiful entity, beautiful theory that caused people to think: 'Wow, I've never thought about it like that'."

And this, he concludes, is one of the most important characteristics of excellent research: "the willingness to make a creativity jump and come up with an idea that makes people say 'a-ah, I never thought of it like that'."

In conclusion, although the outcome of management research is usually not an aesthetic one as such, the process of *doing research that matters* is certainly a mode of expression that requires skills and imagination in the creation of insight that can be shared with others and influence others.

You may call it an "artistic science" or even a "scientific art." But if your aim is to do management research designed to matter, then you can't take the one ("science") away from the other ("art").

When Things Don't Go as Expected

As with most things in life so too in management research, achieving true success — in our case insight that matters — is not easy. For as much science, rigor and creativity you may be willing to put into your journey, getting to the end often involves some types of more or less planned series of trials and errors.

Very matter-of-factually, Gerhard Ertl says that "you will inevitably make errors whenever you intend to find something really new."

Is that a bad thing? "It doesn't bother me at all, I am actually happy when that happens," says Roger Martin who believes that in order to generate insightful answers one has got to have a purpose but keep flexible at the same time.

Howard Gardner, as many others, believes that "in science, the most important findings often emerge when something goes wrong or does not go according to the original plan." Albert Einstein offers a case in point. For all his undisputed brilliance as a young physicist, some claim one of his real contributions was making mistakes.[15] According to some contemporary scientists, Einstein was wrong about many aspects of physics. He miscalculated how much the sun's gravity would bend starlight. He made sure his equations for general relativity worked, even though they didn't. He refused to recognize the universe expands, but rather thought it was static.

Yet, according to theoretical physicist Fred Goldhaber of the State University of New York at Stony Brook, "Most scientists would give their eyeteeth to make even one of Einstein's mistakes."[16] That is perhaps because those mistakes allowed Einstein and subsequent physicists to learn and to see the value of intuition, the insight leaps that he made, even when "no logical path" existed.

Although this might be more evident in the hard-sciences than in management, I have observed that it is in fact as common.

Gary Hamel makes a case for the importance of experimenting with ideas as a central element to *doing research that matters* in management: "many of the most important theoretical breakthroughs came when researchers were confronted with anomalous results from experiments. They'd try something and something would happen that they didn't expect. They'd have to ask "what does this tell us?" From this process came new theoretical insights. There is a certain kind of learning and progress that you simply cannot make intellectually if you are not engaged and experimenting in the world of practice."[17]

John Kotter, for example, believes that "the research process is always fraught with the potential for not producing answers," but he thinks that there are ways to design your research to make that work to your advantage. The incremental and iterative research process I discussed earlier helps if not in avoiding problems, in enabling the alert researcher to dynamically adjust his investigative process, revise his assumptions, retune his observations.

Keeping an open mind is fundamental, suggests Rob Goffe: "There is a series of things that can go wrong. Which is why you have to keep an open mind. The scope of things that can go *badly* wrong though is limited ... I maybe have been lucky but that's not happened to me. And it's probably because our research process is incremental, gradual, and experiential and it does not involve a massive investment in a one off tested experiment. If you are more *modest, incremental,* and *iterative* and you keep your ears open and your eyes open, you won't go too far wrong."

The key to turning a perceived negative outcome into meaningful insight that you can use further is that researchers "try to explain the anomaly rather than deciding to sweep it under the rug," says Howards Gardner. To do so, it is important to be self-critical but also humble, in the sense that "it is important to realise the problem, avoid wasting time by continued fruitless efforts, and to seek outside help, training or collaboration to get past the problem," says Jack Szostak.

Turning to others for help, sharing experiences, and discussing assumptions, methods, and findings with other academics, people in the field, and even within your classroom then is a vital enabler for those of us who want to generate meaningful insight. John Kotter suggests to "look for confirmation and reconfirmation and reconfirmation ... you talk about it to other people and you listen to others."

The very process of having to share the unexpected findings with others requires hard work as it forces deeper analysis. "You have to keep talking throughout the process — and I can't stress strongly enough how important it is to stand up and share your ideas ... If you keep talking to people it really makes you work hard on this thing about keeping within the realm of impact and recognisable by the people you are working with."

And yet, the willingness to learn from mistakes, to take failure as success, is not commonly embraced with enthusiasm by many scholars these days. Research is supposed to build upon results from previous work but, often, the failures never reach broad audiences and some lessons may be lost. Some researchers do see value in mistakes, want to find ways to spread them so we can learn from them, and have sought to remove the stigma of 'failure' or 'unpromising results' from the daily grind of research.[18]

In 2002, biologist Bjørn Olsen of Harvard Medical School founded the *Journal of Negative Results in Biomedicine*, "an open access, peer-reviewed, online journal that promotes a discussion of unexpected, controversial, provocative and/or negative results in the context of current tenets."[19] For example, a recent article reported on research that examined whether computer use poses a hazard for future long-term sickness (like backache, arm pain) and absence from work.[20] The answer: no. Rather, the researchers found that being female and having low job satisfaction were more likely culprits. By 'clearing' some of the variables, researchers may be able to hone in on other possible contributors more quickly than they may have otherwise.

Even with such an outlet available, although, researchers may remain reluctant to publish their 'mistakes.' Olsen's journal seems to have a large percentage of papers coming from outside North America (Finland, Denmark, Taiwan, England, Germany), which may mean those researchers generate more 'unpromising results' or that they are more willing to share those research by seeking to publish them. When *The Journal of American Medical Informatics* sought negative result papers in 2000, only two publishable manuscripts came through the process. Yet medicine and physics may in fact be more open to publishing unpromising results than other fields. The same apply to other disciplines as well, as reported, for example, by the *New Scientist,* which in 2003 lamented the lack of articles reporting on failures in artificial intelligence research.[21]

As University of Aberdeen's Professor Ehud Reiter claims, publishing mistakes is critical as a way to improve theory. Reiter and colleagues tried to model the idea — of publishing results that did not come out as expected — and did so.[22] Their article, called "Lessons from a failure ...," epitomizes the willingness to show that we can learn from mistakes, a maxim that is embedded in many organisations that seek to improve performance, but apparently not so common among researchers.

In fact, learning organizations thrive on the notion of fast failures. The notion of using what goes wrong — early in the research and development cycle — to learn what to change has been around for years. Several experts argue for finding surprises and encouraging "things to go wrong" early in the innovation process.[23] To do so, in fact to plan for Murphy's law, could help reduce costly errors later, when they typically become more costly.

Having said that, being able to use an unexpected turn in our research journey to our advantage is as much a matter of design as it is of personal character or, as John Kotter puts it: "[when research goes wrong] that's where a combination of dedication, discipline, doggedness and skill becomes important. You got to be very disciplined and hard on yourself, you've got to constantly ask the question 'Am I fooling myself?', 'Have I really gone deep enough?' 'Have I really tested this in enough places?', 'Have I shown this to enough people?'."

Also to be noted, when research does not go as planned, *Futureers* generally react in naturally optimistic way. Just to give one example: Douglas Osheroff is often cited stating that failure is a chance to try something new, which then may even become the driving star of subsequent research efforts. He says: "when one discovers something new, one is likely to jump on it, often cutting or even dropping some of the other research subjects he or she is pursuing." *Futureers*, therefore, look positively at a new discovery, regardless of whether what they discovered is in fact what they had been looking for or not. And then, they just go on with.

In *Success Built to Last*, Porras and co-authors[24] reveal how their sample of enduringly successful people displayed the very same attitude, all agreeing on one simple but telling point: "Losers call it failure; winners call it learning ... People who have achieved enduring success drone on endlessly about learning from their mistake!"

Investing continuously in the development of that kind of attitude, some *Futureers* eventually get to the point where they do not even see how anything could go wrong at all: "I don't do the kind of research that goes wrong ... It's not as if I do an experiment which is then disconfirmed. When I find something out it is just grease for the mill. There is nothing that can go wrong!" Barbara Kellerman's confidence, as that of many other *Futureers* I have talked to, clearly comes from knowing that when your objective is to generate meaningful insight, you go after big romantic problems, you answer one small question at the time, than anything you find is worth finding *per se*.

Or, as Costas Markides told me, "If you start with the underlying purpose, that is: I don't care about publications, I care about solving a problem here, coming up with creative ideas, that is my goal, then I think that helps you stay on the right track."

Is There a 'Best' Research Methodology?

No, there is not.

When I asked Howard Gardner whether he could identify a research methodology that worked better than others, he referred to Paul Feyerabend to say that "there are no ironclad methodological approaches in science. If it works and produces interesting, replicable findings, the work gets absorbed into the scientific canon."

In a similar vein, Albert Einstein, discussing his "under-determination theory," claimed that:

> "Quite apart from the question of the superiority of one or the other, the fictitious character of fundamental principles is perfectly evident from the fact that we can point to two essentially different principles, both of which correspond with experience to a large extent."[25]

You may find proof to Einstein's point in the following two stories.

The year 2009 saw a sharp rise in the number of new enterprises formed in the United Kingdom. Similarly, Robert Reich, former Secretary of Labor under Bill Clinton from 1993–1997, said that the Kauffman Index of Entrepreneurship reported the highest number of start-ups in 14 years, even more than during the tech boom of 1999–2000.[26] But this came at point when the current global financial crisis was already getting into full swing. On the face of it, this surely has to be good news, a counterbalance to all the doom and gloom surrounding the recession.

Reich sees two ways of looking at this phenomenon. The first is that deep recession is, like necessity, the mother of invention. It is certainly true that some of the world's largest firms started in earlier recessions, among them Texas Instruments, Hewlett-Packard, United Technologies (1929–1939); Fedex, Microsoft, Apple, Genentech (1973–1976); Sun, E*Trade, Autodesk, Adobe, and Symantec (1980–1982). In the long run, this was good news. Following that argument, many would conclude (many did) that the current boom in new enterprises will lead to long-term jobs and bigger firms.

However, when Reich looked deeper, he found something rather different than what he had envisaged. Most of these entrepreneurs were not wide-eyed youngsters looking to start the next Fedex or Facebook. They were older, in some cases, much older. The bulk of new start-ups come from people 35–45 years old or over 55 years old. So what's going on? Framed another way, Reich claims this "entrepreneurship" is just another way to say "self-employed," because of job loss. Instead of building enterprises that will grow and add employment, Reich found that many of the new start-ups were people doing the type of work they had done in their former companies. They do similar work now, as contract temporary employees, but without health care, pension plans, sick leave, or paid vacation. Rather than a beacon of entrepreneurial light, Reich interpreted the data to reach a conclusion quite different than policy makers may want to hear — that the data show the result of companies trimming their payrolls (for good) and the long-term economic earthquake that comes from under or "self-employment desperation" for many as the only predictable future. It is a phenomenon that is occurring in many contracting trades and professions. As newspapers, faced with falling circulations and the growth of other news sources such as the Internet, struggle to survive, a growing number of their discarded employees are becoming freelancers. And the same happens in other industries as well, like manufacturing, retail, banking, etc.: the more companies have to file for bankruptcy or restructure, the higher the number of ex-C-level executives who, having lost their job, have to reinvent themselves as management consultants, financial advisors, and marketing specialists.

Reich took existing data, reinterpreted or reframed it and reached a conclusion which ran counter to the one that others had reached with the same question. Reich's story shows that, even with the same question, research studies can reach opposing conclusions.

Similarly, two recent studies examining attitudes of Baby Boomers in midlife did just that: one claims baby boomers are as happy as they've ever been; the other claims they are more suicidal than other age groups.[27]

A Gallup telephone poll of over 340,000 American respondents over age 50, on one day in 2008, resulted in findings that most people were much happier than at any other stage of life. The lead researcher, Arthur Stone, also suspected brain chemistry comes into play, as middle-aged adults are able to better screen negative emotions than are younger adults.

But a second study, done by the U.S. government's Centers for Disease Control and Prevention, surveyed violent deaths in 16 American states in 2007 and found something rather different: people aged 45–54 had the highest rate of suicide, overtaking the over 80 age group which traditionally had led the country. Causes tend to stem from mental illness, drug and alcohol abuse, and job or partner loss. And indeed the use of prescription painkillers has jumped, perhaps causing accidental suicides.

But some epidemiologists see another connection or possible cause: the baby boomers have tended to have (or to report) higher incidents of depression than earlier generations, which may link to suicide. Still other reviewers of the data suggest that the cohort of baby boomers is "large enough" to contain both ends of the "happiness" continuum — people who are quite positive and those who are the opposite.

One of those same researchers, Dr. Eric C. Caine of the Center for the Study and Prevention of Suicide at the University of Rochester Medical Center (New York), also makes the point that there simply is not enough information to yield conclusions. Since the previous decades of suicide research have focused more on the young (teenagers) and the very old (over 80), little attention has come to the middle age groups.

The point here is not to decide who is right and who is wrong, which methodology works best or worst. As a matter of fact, the next time you find yourself arguing your method is better than another (or criticize somebody else's method), I would like you to keep in mind and learn from John Kotter's exemplary display of self-awareness and modesty; he asks himself: "Is [mine] the best way to study the subjects that I'm interested in? It's too easy to rationalise that what you're doing is the best for everything. So clearly, I can make the argument why mine is the best way to study any person or any source associated with business and managerial behaviour and organisational behaviour these days. But I would also admit that even if I made that argument, I'm not sure how much of that is a piece of my brain just trying to justify that what I'm doing is indeed perfect for everyone."

Rather, the point is to bring your attention onto the importance of focusing on designing our research to matter, since the start; to keep an open mind as to what new information, new instruments, new observations might impact our assumptions; to be willing to go deeper and deeper by continuously and repeatedly asking ourselves sequential questions; and to be willing to fail but not to look at it as failure, just learning.

My own conclusion is that if we design our research *to matter*, rather than *to impress*, and we follow the examples and ideas that I have shared in this chapter, we are not going to eliminate entirely the possibility to hit a wall or reach an unexpected conclusion, but we are certainly limiting the risk of not being able to turn each and every experience into an insightful one, not just for us but, sometimes, for humankind.

Are You Prepared for What Might Come?

Susan Clancy didn't set out to make enemies. She wanted to better understand what happens to victims of childhood abuse, particularly sexual abuse.[28] But her resulting research and book, *The Trauma Myth,* put her in direct conflict with ideas held by professionals and the public alike about what happens to children after abuse. Clancy challenged that the "trauma model," which argues that abuse is always done against a child's wishes, is traumatic, and damages the child. Clancy, an expert in memory research with a Ph.D. from Harvard University, says that many child victims did not see the experience as traumatic at the time, because they knew the abuser and had little understanding of what was happening. Rather, the feelings of fright or trauma came later, along with guilt that they "agreed to" the abuse.[29] In a review of the book in *Science,* Loftus and Frenda, two researchers at the University of California, Irvine, note the paradox in the reactions to Clancy's findings that go against popular thinking.[30] As they note, social workers and other professionals have sought to increase awareness of childhood sexual abuse and have stressed that the victim is not the guilty party. Yet for so many years the expectation was that victims would feel trauma, and as a result, many (once they were older) reinterpreted the experiences to be so. Thus, although Clancy (re)confirmed that many victims indeed do not feel guilty or experience trauma at the time of the incident, but only later learned — from the public discussion about abuse — they were supposed to have felt those emotions. Since they had not, the victims felt they were abnormal. In a way, Clancy suggests that pressure from without has affected the victims who were relatively unaffected until they learned they 'should' feel trauma. That was a message few professionals in the field wanted to hear.

Challengers to long-standing research may find that more is at stake than just ideas. Clancy's shake up of the underpinnings of the last several decades' work on childhood sexual abuse has had unexpected and unwanted repercussions for her personal life as well. She has been accused of "being a paedophile apologist"[31]; she has received numerous hate mail, and colleagues often avoid her.[32] In the 2003 *The New York Times* article, A bad trip down memory lane, Grierson recounts how Clancy was once invited to give a lecture at Cambridge Hospital just to find out that many had protested her appearance to the hospital chairman, and how her Harvard pedigree would have not been enough to help her save her self-destroyed academic career.[33]

Yet, she played a role that is critical to advancement in knowledge. Regardless of how controversial Clancy's point of view is, her experience has implications for science more broadly and "No matter how strongly a theory has been embedded in the cultural zeitgeist (as the trauma model certainly has), we should always be prepared to discard it on the basis of persuasive evidence."[34]

Loftus and Frenda also raise the point that researchers and professionals can become quite emotional when someone attacks their theories, views of the world, or reputations (which is essentially what the attacks to theories and worldviews become). And some simply go too far.

Similarly, not long after she published *Coming of Age in Samoa*,[35] Margaret Mead faced controversy and attacks from colleagues unwilling to believe some of her claims, especially the most startling about sexuality and incest in Samoa. Over the years, questions about the accuracy of her research — whether she was duped by her own naïveté, whether she coaxed Samoans to tell untruths — gained ground. Five years following her death, a New Zealand anthropologist Derek Freeman did his best to smash whatever vestige of reputation Mead held.[36] He claimed to have re-interviewed some of the remaining islanders, who said they were joking or told Mead what they thought she wanted to hear. She challenged earlier theories about "native peoples," and was in turn challenged right back. Freeman's vituperative attacks left Mead's reputation in tatters for years.

But sometimes, the challenged have angels. University of Colorado anthropologist and expert on Samoa and Polynesia Paul Shankman found Freeman's assertions a little too assertive. In his book *The Trashing of Margaret Mead*,[37] Shankman relooked at Freeman's work and found it lacking, just as Freeman had claimed Mead's to be. Shankman declares that Freeman made inaccurate claims to exaggerate his attack, including that Mead ignored biology (not true, according to Shankman). Interestingly, Shankman says that Mead's early conclusions were in fact correct, even if some of the facts may not have been entirely as expected.

The moral of this last story, perhaps, is that, in the end, good researchers with sound integrity, strong values, no fear of swimming counter-current, and with the objective of *doing research that matters* will always have the last word.

CHAPTER 6

TRAVELLING SOLO, OR IN GROUPS?

No man is an Island, entire of itself; every man is a piece of the Continent, a part of the main.

— John Donne

When individuals with distinct competence share a common goal, more innovative and productive work follows. I can't underestimate the need to collaborate.

— Dave Ulrich

Jack Szostak and Elizabeth H. Blackburn both regard their chance meeting at a conference as a crucial moment in their life and their research journey. The two scientists, together with Carol W. Greider, won the Nobel Prize in Physiology or Medicine in 2009. Thinking about their chance encounter, Elizabeth H. Blackburn says: "That's the way science happens. It's a lot of meetings of minds."[1] Jack Szostak explains what that meant in practice: "We dreamed up an experiment that neither of us could have done easily alone, but by combining resources we were able to solve a major puzzle."

Similarly, Robert Kaplan's experience developing some of the greatest management breakthroughs of our times, such as activity-based costing and the balance scorecard, give clear examples that "two [partners] working together achieve something that's better than either one of [them] could have done."

Francoise Barre-Sanoussi, joint winner of the 2008 Nobel Prize in Physiology or Medicine with Luc Motagnier and Harald zur Hausen, thinks that the success in the discovery of the AIDS virus "is really a success of a world team with different expertise. And I think, for the future, it's also important, especially when working on infectious disease, to have a world network of clinicians, virologists, and microbiologists working in the hospitals and basic sciences. This was really essential for me in the discovery of the AIDS virus. And I think it's essential also for tomorrow for discovering new, emerging, or re-emerging agents responsible for infectious disease."[2]

Collaboration doesn't always work out that way, however, for any number of reasons. Fiascos can happen for as simple a thing as a clash of egos, or the feeling that not everybody is pulling in the same direction or pulling their weight, especially if the aggrieved party or parties feel they were in some way the prime movers of the research. Or, as in my own experience working with Nancy Napier, my original research partner on this project, simply because of life events and differing priorities.

As it is easy to see even in everyday life, the higher the number of collaborators the more challenging the process of working together and coordinating everybody's input. As the old proverb goes: too many cooks may spoil the broth.

But failure to bring out the benefits of collaboration can come also down to more complex issues that are not directly under the individual's control. This returns us again to Alexander Fleming who suggested that his curiosity regarding moulds and antiseptics was piqued for the very reason he was working in a different sphere. Had he been a member of the original team working on the topic he would probably not have pursued the subject. As Fleming himself said during his Nobel banquet speech: "I was working on a subject having no relation to moulds or antiseptics and if I had been a member of a team engaged on this subject it is likely that I would have had to neglect the accidental happening and work for the team with the result that penicillin would not then have been described."[3]

Here the danger is not so much that too many cooks may spoil the broth as they create a stew of limited palate. In other words, everybody looking in the same place and failing to spot something remarkable, as the outsider Fleming did. Perhaps the overriding lesson is that multiple perspectives can be fine when a project works but the involvement of too many people is dangerous when it does not. As usual, hindsight is a wonderful thing.

As a rule of thumb, though, collaborative working is not going to cancel out the solo moments of inspiration that can get things moving or put the final piece in a jigsaw.

Scholars at Indiana University and the University of North Carolina studied collaboration and the factors that affect the probability for a collaborating team to succeed.[4] They offer many definitions of collaboration that all basically evolve around few common elements: a team interacting by sharing complementary skills, resources, power, authority and knowledge to reach a common goal that could not be accomplished by the individuals alone. They observe: "In reviewing these definitions of collaboration, two common elements emerge: working together for a common goal and sharing of knowledge. Unfortunately, working together is not a simple task, nor is the development of a common goal or vision. Sharing meaning, knowledge, resources, responsibility and/or power often involves building social capital and taking risks and trusting others, which can be difficult to do when careers, reputations or other valued assets are at stake. ... In short, collaboration is neither easily achieved nor guaranteed to succeed."[5]

Yet, Eleanor Josaitis, co-founder of Project HOPE, a human rights and training organization, is convinced that "anything worth doing can't be done alone."[6]

As researchers seeking to generate meaningful insight we must acknowledge Josaitis' true point, regardless of whether we like to work with others or not. We must acknowledge the benefits of collaborating, seek out opportunities to engage in such relationships, and, most importantly, we must do all that is in our power to make collaboration work. The question is: *how*?

That is what I look at in this chapter. In my research, I have so far reached the conclusion that collaboration goes far beyond merely sharing goals or resources and it is not to be approached lightly.

As you seek out your own collaborative opportunity, you may — or may not — consider my own findings so far: to me, smaller teams seem to work better than larger ones as they allow for more fruitful brainstorming and co-generation of ideas; also, intellectual alignment's bearing on your potential to succeed in your collaborative effort is not nearly as important as the following three elements: *sharing values*, *compatibility of personalities*, and, finally, *complementarity of skills*.

Collaboration in Relation to *Research That Matters*

There exist hundreds of interesting articles exploring the issue of research collaboration, what it means, how to make it work, etc. I do not intend to summarize here the topic's state of the art and the different perspectives on the subject.

On the other hand, I want to clarify the perspective I take in my research: I look at it from the point of view of trying to understand what type of collaboration is more conducive to *doing research that matters*. The central idea of this chapter is, therefore, to share insight on those elements that have come up more often during my interviews and studies and that I believe we should pay attention to in order to increase our chances to generate meaningful insight.

It makes sense at this point to remind you of my assumption and the central idea behind the "Research that Matters" model to generate meaningful insight, there must be collaboration not just between individuals, but also between the individuals and their system and between them and the distributors of research. That is, between the *Insight Generators*, the *Insight Incubators*, and the *Insight Distributors*.

To understand my perspective on collaboration in this context, you may think of it this way: even when you go on the road-trip of your life, riding alone on your

Harley Davidson, your experience will inevitably be influenced and, more importantly, enhanced (or otherwise) by the people you will meet, the places you will see, the hotels you will be sleeping at, etc. While "action" might be singular, "success" is definitely plural.

Mintzberg's comment that "even when you're working on your own you're getting help from other people in all kinds of ways" is central to the meaning — and importance — I give to the term collaboration in this book.

Investing in Collaboration

Collaboration is very important in science for a variety of reasons. Markides suggests that "it allows you to think about the different issues from different angles. It allows you to be creative. It shares the load and allows you to do better research. … I always try to find collaborators, who could be other academics or non-academics, who share the same goals and aspirations about research as I do. And also, bring a different perspective into their research so that you learn as much from them as you learn from doing the research."

Let's have a look at some of these perspectives that could be brought to a joint project and how they would add to its value.

"Collaboration with the Future Generations" Perspective

The idea of mutual learning is a central element to collaboration and acts both as a driver and an enabler. Howard Gardner, who often works with students and research assistants, says: "I hope that we both learn from the process."

It's a view endorsed heartily by Gerhard Ertl who adds another facet to the view of collaboration as he explains how he feels a responsibility toward his research partners: "My research has been largely based on collaboration with students and other scientists. You must continuously motivate them and, on the other hand, provide them with freedom."

Ertl's perspective, then, is that these students will be tomorrow's researchers and that his approach will provide them with the opportunity to learn and to establish their credentials in a way that helps to secure their future.

Younger career stage academics also have concerns about whether, with whom, and how to collaborate. Tynan and Garbett, for example, examined the experiences of young and also of female academics to understand more what they feel they need to become better researchers. The requirements are not unusual or unexpected: "more time, less teaching and administration, ... funding; ... access to mentoring and team research projects, ... supportive collegial networks within which our confidence is fostered through genuine exchanges."[7]

But they go further and comment that collaboration has benefits that allow for some reduction in "academic competition" but also brings up usually unspoken and unacknowledged concerns that younger researchers have. Yet the undercover wariness has also led them to feel they may have more 'power' than they had realized.

One young academic observed: "*We are still wary of our more experienced colleagues who seek recognition for our research ...* We need to understand and play the political game so that we may attest to our ability to contribute. Some might argue that we should accept our position as we will eventually have access to resources as we become more established and learn the ropes. This is why we feel our collaboration has been successful. It has spurred us on. We may not be as powerless as we thought. We have, in using our voices here, challenged the order of the way things are done. On one level we have entered the system, recognised the game for what it has to offer, but have refused to lose ourselves within it. We have realised that we want more than a step up the ladder and, certainly, more than a list of research outputs."

"Collaboration between Geographies" Perspective

Be that with peers, mentors, or associates, collaboration just happens more often these days because we can do it more easily (e.g., technology helps communication, access to data, and reduces geographic obstacles).

A way by which collaboration helps widening the debate in a field is by bringing in perspectives from geographically different locations. Technology such as the Internet and social media, for example, make it 'easier' or at least a way to start discussions that might have otherwise never taken place.

Often researchers interested in common themes may not meet, sometimes ever or for years, and still be able to collaborate successfully through email, web conferences, common electronic worksites, wikis, and document sharing. Although Henry Mintzberg seems to be one of the few people sounding a note of alarm in relation to this technological brave new world. Would Szostak, Blackburn, and Greider have brainstormed their way to their great breakthrough if they had been on separate continents and only connecting electronically? Mintzberg would probably say not. "I think one of the big dangers of the Internet is not brainstorming anymore, they just think it comes automatically," he says.

Globalization as well has created opportunities for extending collaboration to many who have been traditionally closed out of the research academy in the past, such as people who wish to study interesting problems in remote locations (e.g., non-Western, emerging economies).[8]

That also widens the net in bringing in a wider group of people of different cultures and backgrounds, all of whom might bring insights and different ways of approaching issues which were not possible before. In the management field, for years the prevailing theories and research findings reported in publications had a similarly narrow perspective. The publications of note and 'importance' came mostly from English-speaking industrialized countries, primarily North America and the United Kingdom.

As more academics (from Western and increasingly from developing countries) questioned whether the results applied outside of the industrialized West, the need for research and insights became clear. Collaborations with or by indigenous researchers about their local situations began to increase. In addition, as researchers from developing economies such as China have received their doctorates (often at those Western institutions that had led the research), they learned how to carry out research and publish it in the journals that had before closed them out.

"Collaboration between Genders" Perspective

The American-based physicist Alma Norovsky has a sharp sense of humor that has served her well in the hard-sciences world, which is still very male dominated.

She recalls a story about an incident while attending a conference: "I was standing with a group of physicists, all men, and I was introduced to a new member of the group. He said: 'You're the first good-looking physicist I've ever met'. I casually indicated the man standing beside me and said: 'Oh, that's not true. You know Richard here. He's good looking and he's a physicist'."[9]

If certain fields of activity choose to ignore women, then 50 per cent of the human species' brainpower is not being tapped.[10] The direct consequences of this thinking are obvious, but there can also be indirect ones associated with this mindset. For example, for years any person who had heart disease received information, prescriptions, and advice based on the research available to date. But the advice did not always seem to help women patients; at last, of course, researchers started to note that the findings were based upon studies of male subjects, only, and that no one had considered men and women might differ on heart disease. The reason that the advice was less effective for women was based upon a methodology that ignored a key subject group.

"Collaboration Inter-Disciplines" Perspective

Craig Mello (Nobel Prize in Physiology or Medicine, 2006), believes that there is a cumulative effect in research which means that collaboration is an intrinsic part of the process, as one group of people build on work done by others. It's what he calls an "invisible" collaboration.

Mello and Andrew Fire received the award for their work in RNA interference, the process within living cells that moderates the activity of their genes. He says that there is still much we do not understand about the mechanism and adds: "And it's then just really, really exciting how many different fields, seemingly unrelated, have just merged together with the understanding of the mechanism. As the understanding grows we just seem to be bringing together these very distant looking-sort of unrelated looking stories that just keep coming together and unfolding in beautiful ways.

"So, there have been so many contributions from people all around the world, scientists who have been working on phenomena that we didn't know were related to the one that we discovered. And all of their work has really helped to make this something that has been so widely recognized as a fundamental discovery, because lots of work was already being done. So I think that's one reason it happened so quickly. It just was the last, but a very important piece in a puzzle that quickly fell together."[11]

Fire also acknowledges the importance of earlier work done elsewhere and says that the two of them were "led to it pretty much by our experimental noses."[12]

One, Few, or Many?

The idea that collaboration widens the debate on a particular topic adding various perspectives to it applies equally to both the world of business and that of scholarly research. Dave Ulrich is convinced that "collaboration brings individuals together with different skills and focuses them on a common goal ... The same holds true in companies when people with differing talents collaborate to accomplish a shared outcome. When individuals with distinct competence share a common goal, more innovative and productive work follows. I can't underestimate the need to collaborate."

Of course, the idea that collaboration in science and research more generally is good for innovation does not exactly qualify as 'breaking news.' National, international, and cross-national funding institutions continuously support collaboration among individual researchers and among research institutes, favoring research across disciplines, sectors, and geographies.

At the same time, an old Italian proverb about business partnership goes something like this: "partnerships in business work extremely well when the number of partners is an odd number greater than 0 and smaller than 3." I am not sure how scientifically valid this is, but I have certainly lived through many situations where I could see its merit.

But does it translate to research? Keeping in mind our aim to generate meaningful insight is research more productive (toward our goal) if carried out individually? Or is collaborative research more productive? And in the latter case, does it work better to have a team of two, few, or many?

As you might expect, and as Margherita Hack simply puts it: "naturally, you can't define a general rule."

Solo work in its purest form is very rare indeed. Even people who instinctively prefer the idea of working alone acknowledge that they are highly unlikely to work in total isolation at all times. To what extent collaboration will be kept at as low a level as possible depends on individual preferences. Margherita Hack admits, "There are those who like it better to study and to reason in a group and those who would rather be on their own."

In her subject, astrophysics, research is normally done by individuals in isolation. But she says that in particle physics, work in groups is more common because of the instruments they use, although she also realizes that the increasing complexity of instruments in general has led to collaboration becoming more mainstream in her field as well.

Her observation does reinforce the point about no man being an island, as even the astrophysicists who are working in splendid isolation admit they need input and support from other sources.

It might be suitable to think of an analogy to the business world: although someone might describe himself as a 'self-made man,' his journey to the top, assisted by staff, clients, suppliers, lawyers, accountants, etc. will never have been made alone.

Collaboration among researchers varies across fields. You can find dramatic examples of large numbers of co-authors and collaborators in some fields, while in others it is difficult to find any co-authored publications at all. Publications such as *Science* or *Nature* publish scientific articles that routinely carry co-authorship ranging from 2 to as many as 20 people.

Also, large research teams are nowadays not anymore exclusive to large-scale experimental-type research common in the hard sciences. Even though tradition-ally it was rarely the case in the management field, now it is not uncommon. In Europe, just to mention an example, EU-funded research often involves two/three-digit large research teams involving several universities, researchers, and test companies.

In some fields, the norm appears to be single authorship in published articles, but multiple authorship in books. Some, like Crafton (2004),[13] have gone as far as to attempt to surmise some general conclusions but have soon raised a number of opponents. Among them, Professor Neil Sinyard, formerly head of film studies at Hull University, UK, observed: "I can't see any basis for that generalization about publications in cinema studies. Although there are many co-authored books, I certainly wouldn't say it's anything like 'the norm'; and co-authored articles on film studies are, I would think, proportionately about the same as co-authored books. I couldn't quantify this with any certainty: two out of 25 of my books are co-authored; and maybe three out of 100 or so articles, and my feeling is that a more widespread survey wouldn't reveal a lot of difference between those percentages."

While at a macro level it appears that more co-authored research is happening generally within management disciplines, the question as to whether small-groups collaborating work better than large ones appears less clear.

Markides thinks collaboration is absolutely vital for doing research but he also thinks that one cannot spend their whole academic career doing research always with somebody else: "Sometimes you have to do it on your own. If only to prove to people that you can do something on your own." Henry Mintzberg as well, who though admits to have not thought about this issue in any systematic way, sees the importance of doing both solo and collaborative work: "in the last 20, 30 years ... I probably wrote half my articles with co-authors. So I collaborate a lot ... but I also do a lot of stuff on my own."

Expectations might vary depending upon career stages as well. In management, an inverse U-shaped curve seem to be quite common: researchers show at least some ability to publish alone in the early career stages, then conduct work jointly to enhance the quantity and range of publications and, finally, go back to more solitary work or anyway to collaborating within smaller teams once they get tenure.

Donald Crafton again suggests that the most critical reason is to allow individuals to leverage their ability to publish if they have several projects and work with a number of collaborators going on. In addition, he argues, universities are beginning to recognize a need for undergraduates (who may never become researchers) to learn how to collaborate for the benefit of their future careers. If they do choose to move forward in research careers, of course, they'll have that history and ability to work in teams, which may lead to more natural and easy collaboration on publications.[14]

Conversely, sociologist Barbara Lovitts raises the concern held by many educators of graduate students that they may be incapable to transition from being a successful "course-taker to independent scholar/researcher" and thus many fail in their early graduate school years in learning how to conduct independent research.[15]

That is not necessarily a reason to shut them out. It must be difficult if not impossible to know who will make the grade. But it is interesting to note that this concern is a two-way street.

In any case, it does not look possible to me, nor plausible, to infer a general rule (or anyway any one rule that would make any sense) based on statistical analysis of bibliographic references. Different people have different views and preferences. Besides, my objective is not to understand common practices in scientific publishing: although I accept that many see the published research as the tangible and most easily recognizable outcome of the research process, I will discuss later how co-authored research does not always imply that the same research was done collaboratively between the authors.

My objective is to understand what seems to be working better for exemplary researchers. To do that, I must go back to my data set, what I have personally observed and what I have personally experienced. And when I do that, I see two clear patterns emerge.

The first one, significantly less important, widely known within the academic community, but still worth putting in writing and in the public domain: non-exemplary researchers generally tend to seek membership in larger groups not because that might lead to more insightful research but rather because it almost certainly will lead to increased number of publications. I like the way Croton puts it: "We are familiar with the strings of names at the beginning of articles, as well as with the importance of (and the squabbles over) the hierarchy of these author listings."[16] And just in case you are about to criticize me for such grossly generic statement: no, I am not claiming this to be a scientifically inferred conclusion but merely a personal observation from having spent over a decade out there in *that* field.

The second one, significantly more important, and which I am going to discuss here, remains stable across the disciplines I investigated: working in small groups just seems to function better and to better serve the purpose of *doing research that matters*. It is truly rather remarkably clear.

None of the *Futureers* I have interviewed thinks their approach works better than others. Margherita Hack says that she has always studied on her own but immediately and strongly underlines the fact "that is *strictly* a matter of personal preference."

Rob Goffee also admits that there might be approaches to research where "there is basically a big team and it is a bit like a manufacturing process and it can often be rather efficient and rather effective. But I have never done research like that ... I have always been slightly weary of the transactional research relationships, which explains why I have never got involved with them … You might find that other people who have had a high impact have been able to make that stuff work, but it's not being good for me." Although he is reluctant to generalize on the subject of when and how well collaboration works, indeed he is uncertain as to whether generalizations can be made at all.

I, though, am going to make such risky generalization based on the following.

Harald zur Hausen claims that throughout his whole career, he has always worked, as far as his personal research problem was concerned, in relatively small groups usually of 6–8 people at most. He says, "I found this quite profitable … I never worked in very large networks. I know it is quite popular today and everywhere networking is almost fashionable … but I feel that at least for the project that we were following up, small groups were more helpful, we could discuss in small circles, we could quickly devise experiments among ourselves and perform them. So I was certainly in favour of it." And, having been appointed as Scientific Director of the Deutsches Krebsforschungszentrum (German Cancer Research Center) in Heidelberg for about 20 years (1983–2003), he was certainly no stranger to larger-type collaborations (the institute employs around 2,500 employees): "Obviously, I had to deal with a number of other problems not only administratively but also as far as scientific advice and so on was concerned."

Jack Szostak's research group, the larger in my observations for sure, is 15-people strong, including a mix of students and postdocs: "we talk frequently and have group meetings to share ideas within the lab."

In the management field the ideal team size seems to reduce further.

John Kotter has written 18 books. Of those, seven were done with other people. "And in those [collaborative] cases, mostly it was with just one other person. Only a couple of times did we have two other people."

Philip Kotler enjoys working with other experts, especially from other fields. When he cites his latest collaboration, the book *Social Marketing to Protect the Environment: What Works*, he says: "Four experts (psychology, environmental science, marketing and social marketing) looked for the best cases demonstrating the power of social marketing to improve the environment (reduce waste, use water more efficiently, reduce pollution, etc.)."

For Rob Goffee, "deep relationships with a limited number of co-authors have been good and enjoyable." He says to have never worked in larger teams and is another supporter of the 'team of two' model. He has actually been part of one for over 30 years: "I have tended throughout my career to work with two co-authors. One with whom I have worked with for about 15 years and another one with whom I have worked for another 15 years. The first one was the supervisor of my doctoral research and he thought me as an undergraduate. And the second, Gareth Jones, who I have worked with for the last 15 years. He and I were at university together doing our doctorate."

Last but not least, Robert Kaplan, who has had "many, many different collaborations," claims: "it's typically working with one other person and maybe some of my articles have had a few more people but most of it has been a bilateral relationship."

Literature on management gurus and Nobel Laureates alike illustrate other several examples of how small teams of just a few people have been effective in generating meaningful insight. That is in striking contrast with the incredibly high number of articles published these days that usually have a string of authors so long it could be mistaken for the abstract itself.

So, although I am sure that there are many instances where collaboration among large teams works perfectly, allow me to mimic Harald zur Hausen who, toward the end of the interview, made a point of repeating to me firmly: "Let me re-emphasise this again: as far as the research I have done and I still do to these days, I always rely on small groups."

Making Collaboration Work: Be Choosy about Who You're Going to Work With

The literature on collaboration gone wrong generally identifies many possible causes of failure, such as differences in levels of time and effort put into a project, different views about the goals of the research, problems in ensuring standardization and rigor of the data collection, and communication.[17]

How to build more effective teams also have been studied and written about for years. Often the assumption is that building a good research team is similar to building a good team within an organization, but in many ways, scholarly collaboration and business collaboration vary quite dramatically. Typically, the team leader in an organization has rewards and sanctions available depending upon team member behavior. The academic research team leader or colleague may have fewer options and more challenging human relationship dynamics to deal with. The psychology of collaboration is not easy to understand in fact, but zur Hausen is convinced that practice and experience will eventually make it easier.

Discussing the human aspect of collaboration, Barbara Kellerman raises an interesting point as she takes the example of editing a volume and suggests that "you have to use maximum personal and interpersonal skills in order to get people to collaborate," also offering a word of warning based on experience that "it is not uncommon for one or two to really let you down in terms of the quality of the product, the timetable."

She makes a point that an additional complicating factor can be traced back into the leadership preferences — if we may call them so — of the typical scholar: "Academics like to follow their own lead and not the lead of others but, if you have a collaborator, then obviously you actually have to cooperate as opposed to getting your own way all the time."

John Kotter is one who admits to there maybe being an issue relating to control that might influence his preferences in terms of collaboration. 18 out of the 18 books he has written, he points out, carry his names as the first author which is a good proof that he likes to ultimately take control of the project (although, as he says, this could say more about his psychology than about his research).

Listening to John Kotter rating his overall satisfaction from collaborating with others, I started to think that making collaboration succeed can be a matter of design: "I have found collaboration, under the right circumstances, with the right person, on the right topic, both useful and fun." It seems excusable to read a message between the lines that collaboration is something to be approached with extreme caution. In fact, talking with the *Futureers*, I get the feeling that they are very guarded about starting collaborations and very selective about their travel companions, that is, their research partners.

That is understandable, as collaborative relationships often fail for many reasons. Howard Gardner is studying this very topic within the context of education and he says that "collaboration with peers, with equals, is often important but very difficult to do successfully ... and it is already clear that the failures outnumber the successes." Wanting to give us an example of what might cause such failure, he says culture might play an important role: "I think that collaboration is particularly difficult for Americans because we are such an individually-oriented society. I would guess that collaboration is less problematic in Japan or Sweden," although he admits that his experience is primarily U.S.-centric. Based my own experience, on Gardner's point about some cultures being more open to collaboration than others, I would suggest that cultural differences *between* members of the same team also play a significant role in deeming a collaborative effort more or less successful. I have worked on numerous joint projects that involved, in particular, Norwegian, British, Italian, American, Chinese, and Vietnamese nationals. In all these, I could observe clearly that: (a) team members sharing a similar cultural background tended to work better together, and (b) to make inter-cultural collaboration work there needs to be a high-level awareness — on both sides — of the key differences between one and another culture. This might seem to many as common sense but, if it were really, there wouldn't be so many failures.

Ultimately though, Barbara Kellerman is convinced that collaborations fail primarily for reasons that are usually traceable back to the relationship, not the work itself.

Stories of collaboration gone right, like good news, may be less frequent. Still, some researchers have examined factors that contribute to the success of collaboration. Scholars at Indiana University and the University of North Carolina, for example, identified "four key factors that impacted collaboration in the context of the research setting: personal compatibility, research work connections, incentives, and socio-technical infrastructure."[18]

My own research confirms those findings as all of the four factors can be easily identified when studying the life stories of the exemplary researchers featured in this book, or listening to them speak about their collaborative efforts.

However, curiously, three themes seem to stand out in particular that define the drivers of value that the *Futureers* both seek to generate and reap out from collaboration: (1) shared values, (2) compatibility of personalities, and (3) complementarity of competences.

Shared Values

Despite the mainstream definition of the term "collaboration," in reality, collaboration goes far beyond two or more people sharing resources to reach a common goal.

While most might find it logical to assume a common intellectual interest is key to the outcome of the relationship, sharing the same set of values actually seems to be much more important than intellectual similarity.

First, sharing values inevitably leads to trust, which Rob Goffee keeps in high regards: "To do research you need a high level of trust and for me that's always been a bit of an insurance policy."

Second, it aligns intentions. Think of a collaboration between one of these *Futureers* with your average impact-factor-driven researcher: how long do you think it would take for the collaboration to fail?

Third, having shared values just make it easier to work with others. Barbara Kellerman explains it: "it can be maddening if one partner is quite traditional and has the old fashion virtues such as punctuality and reliability and the partner is not. So I would say that shared values, shared sense of what they want to accomplish by when and the sense that both parties, or three, or whatever it is, will meet those — then that is more important than any intellectual alignment."

Rob Goffee summarizes the three points when he describes how he works with his two long-time research partners: "We have common intellectual origins and probably, common types of obsession maybe beyond the intellectual origins and these people are as much friends as colleagues."

Compatibility of Personalities

Following on from the importance of having shared values, compatibility of personalities as enabler of collaboration implies that the collaborators' way of thinking, feeling, and behaving must fit, rather than coincide.

Mintzberg thinks making collaboration work is "a question of the meeting of personalities, it doesn't mean you think exactly alike, you've got to be sufficiently similar but then you've got to kind of play back and forth a lot, have a lot of discussions and, for me, brainstorming is key."

A shared set of values and an alignment of personalities are more important than a shared point of view on something. Martin agrees that he is looking for somebody who is capable of questioning his point of view constructively, and he explains why: "I do some collaboration but not a whole lot. I am just really picky, because I have to be able to have really fundamental conceptual discussions if not arguments with my collaborator ... I do need somebody who is not fearful, who is kind of fearless and doesn't spend their time trying to convince me to ordinarily look more within one field."

Complementarity of Competences

In their study of scientific collaboration, the team at Indiana University and the University of North Carolina observed that "No individual scientist can possess all of the knowledge, skills or time required to make theoretical or applied contributions in more than a very narrow area of research."[19]

To widen the potential "impact area," Kaplan looks for someone who generally has something in their capabilities that are different from and complement his.

"It is important to have this complementarity [of expertise], otherwise the collaboration may degenerate into a competition," says Jack Szostak talking about his team's approach to collaborating with other outside groups.

Kaplan's examples of how he developed his research on some of the concepts that have made him one of our era's global top-management thinkers and for which he will be remember long after he is gone are illustrative and are worth reading just as he recounted them during our interview:

"I've had many, many different collaborations. In activity based costing, I started out with Robin Cooper, who was assistant professor here and Robin had much more experience in how cost systems actually worked in practice than I did. I had only an academic view of it and he had actually experienced it in practice and he was also very creative and he was a very good case writer so he had a whole bunch of skills that I didn't have. It turned out I had more perhaps more analytic skills, writing skills and so it was a very good match.

"On the Balanced scorecard, I worked with Dave Norton. He's a doctorate from the Harvard Business School so clearly he is very well trained but he has never worked as a professor, he was always a practitioner. That's been the most successful collaboration because he directly and then subsequently with his organisation were actually putting our ideas into practice. David and his consultants could actually implement the ideas and then I would get access and write cases about it. Also, as we wrote up our work into articles and books, so we had particular cognitive skills that were different but complementary that enabled us to work together.

"I collaborated with Bob Merton, who was a Noble Prize winner in Economics, to do some writing on stock options and more recently on fair value. It turned out these kind of issues require expertise in finance and expertise in accounting. A finance scholar couldn't have done it by himself and an accounting person couldn't have done by himself but when the two of us analyzed a phenomena together we drew upon our relevant expertise to produce something that's much more powerful, I believe than either one of us could have done alone.

"Currently with regards to the hospital costing work, I'm collaborating with Michael Porter. Michael has been working on healthcare for some time and he's been working on measuring outcomes, how do you measure the outcomes when someone is treated in a facility. He came to me and said 'I can measure the outcomes but I can't measure what it costs to get to those outcomes' and I said 'I know how to do that' and he said 'well good, why don't we work on these sites together and introduce both the outcome measurement as well as the cost measurement'. This is an area you couldn't succeed in measuring only outcomes or only costs. It needed both of us working together to help transform the economics of health care delivery."

Similarly, recognizing the central part that his co-authors have on his learning, Dave Ulrich selects those whom he wants to work with based on "whose ideas I admire the most."

As technological capability and complexity increase, the need for a wider range of technical competences become an equally important driver (and enabler) of collaboration, as Margherita Hack explains: "The technology we use now requires various competences, e.g. electronic engineers, computer scientists, theorists."

Finally, in the attempt to identify the 'ideal collaborator,' Roger Martin identifies three types: "one is protégés, people who I develop and end up being able to extend my thinking back and forth ... Then there are colleagues from the same field who are willing to be bold and brave — but I don't have many like that. And then, occasionally, there are people from other fields, like some of the earlier stuff I did on governance and stock based compensation which I did in conjunction with Canada's number one corporate lawyer of his generation, a guy named Jim Baillie, who achieved his prominence by being bold and different and so we wrote very well together."

With collaboration playing such a central role to generating meaningful insight and at the same time being so difficult to make it work, it might be helpful to read how, in his role as a research leader, Jack Szostak makes sure the three elements discussed above co-exist in his research lab. He explains how once he sets the general goals for the lab — for example, at present the goal is to create life from chemicals — he then tries to find the most talented people he can who are willing to join in the team effort to solve the problem. He encourages initiative and creativity that, as I discussed earlier, are two fundamental enablers of *research that matters*. "My favourite students" he says "are those who, after I tell them their idea will never work, go back to the lab, make their idea work, and then show me I was wrong. Many new ideas, either new questions or new approaches, arise from individual or small group discussions. So it's important for people to talk, exchange ideas, and work together."

Think about How Your System Affects You

The Israeli chemist Ada Yonath (Nobel Prize in Chemistry, 2009) tells a nice story about the reason she started to think about polar bears and about the research that would eventually make her a Nobel Laureate. "Why the hell did she start with such a project?" she was asked, to which she replied: "I had a brain concussion!"[20]

The spare time she had as a result of her concussion, following a bicycle accident, provided plenty of opportunities for reading books, and she became intrigued by what she read about polar bears and what happens to them when they hibernate.

Together with Thomas Steitz and Venkatraman Ramakrishnan, Yonath worked on one of life's core processes, the ribosome's translation of DNA information into life. Ribosomes produce proteins which control the chemistry in all living organisms, and Yonath had realized that in some way the polar bears were preserving their active ribosomes during hibernation: without them they could not survive after waking. The trio showed what the ribosome looks like, and how it functions at an atomic level. Their use of X-ray crystallography mapped out the position for all the hundreds and thousands of atoms that make up the ribosome.

Ramakrishnan, talking about his work at Cambridge's Laboratory of Molecular Biology, home of many great ideas, said: "I think it's the ability to tackle difficult problems in a sort of stable and supportive environment. I think that's the real key to it."[21]

The partnership of William S. Boyle and George E. Smith as well was rewarded with a Nobel Prize for Physics in 2009, and their lab work was equally harmonious. Boyle says: "I think the atmosphere set up by the management was very conducive to people being creative."[22]

In this context, Boyle makes an illuminating comment about a famous brainstorming session with Smith during which the charge-coupled device (CCD) was conceived. Asked if they were under a directive to come up with something, conjuring up images of a desperate attempt to come up with ideas, followed by a Hollywood-style "Eureka" as the "baddies" are about to enter the building, he say quite emphatically that this was not the case. Despite the two men's different levels in the hierarchy (Boyle was laboratory director and Smith department head), no one was ever leaned on. "We had total freedom to do what we wanted to do," says Boyle.[23]

Their invention, the imaging semi-conductor CCD, was to provide the basis for digital imaging in everything from the smallest objects such as pocket cameras to the Hubble telescope.

The environment within which we work influence us, undoubtedly.

Jack Szostak gives another example to illustrate the importance of ensuring successful collaboration among all elements (as opposed to just between team members) as an enabler of *research that matters*: "With regards to research in general, there are two levels of management that concern me: first, the organisation of a research enterprise, e.g. a laboratory or institute; and second, research management from the point of view of funding agencies. In the latter case, there is a clear problem, which is the funding decisions become more conservative when funding is limited. The quality of research declines, even though everyone involved is trying their best to support the best work. In my opinion, one solution to this problem is to support people, not projects, allowing individuals to pursue their own best ideas."

And again, in Harald zur Hausen's research experiences, collaborating with the system meant, for example, being "dependent on getting clinical materials from hospitals and the collaboration of some physicians who were interested in the phenomena we were investigating."

Interestingly, a number of research studies have examined what leads to another type of collaboration, i.e. industry–academic partnerships, with the primary viewpoint of the industrial organization or the academic departmental unit, rather than that of the individual researchers and why and to what degree they engage in such collaborative partnerships. It would appear that the level of involvement stems from both characteristics of the individual researcher as well as the institutions involved.

How Not to Collaborate?

I said it many times before: this is not a 'how-to' book. That still leaves me freedom to discuss 'how-*not*-to' do something, in this case, how not to collaborate. I mentioned earlier in this chapter how most people look at a published piece of research as the most easily identifiable outcome of a research initiative. It follows that many, when discussing collaboration, refer to co-authored articles as examples of tangible outputs from collaborative research. There are some inherent risks in doing so although that are, ashamedly, related to behaviors by some researchers who falter under the pressure of the "publish or perish" mentality predominant these days in academia (or who, deplorably, thrive in it).

In their 2007 article by the title "The Trend Towards Multiple Authorship in Business Journals,"[24] Manton and English argue that the number of multiple authorship publications among the top English-speaking management journals over a 30-year period from 1970 to 1972 to 2000 to 2002 has skyrocketed, as *The Academy of Management Journal* percentage of single authored articles has fallen from 63.5 per cent to 21.4 per cent with the largest growth being in three-person authored publications (from 5.9 per cent to 27 per cent). The pattern holds as well for other disciplines (e.g., *The Accounting Review*, *Management Science*, *Journal of Marketing*, and *The Journal of Finance*).

The pressure for publishing in order to get tenure as well as journal accreditation has no doubt pushed researchers to co-author more often, but the issue of collaboration in relation to such pressure takes a questionable meaning. Some of the co-authorships are likely to be so called "gift authorships" where one or more of the co-authors does little on a project and still ends up as an author on a publication.[25]

I myself have very often sat in meetings or been part to conversations at conferences with other academics where strategies were being defined to 'trick the system' with the objective to increase the number of articles these academics could add to their list of publications (*I put your name on my paper, you put my name on yours*-type of strategy!).

When I was researching material for this section, I took a close look at the list of publications of many colleagues from various universities from around Europe. Again, I did not do any statistically valid analysis but, as I was going through these lists, I started asking myself the question: "how can one publish 10 articles in one year, all in A- or B-level journals, discussing 10 different research problems (often very distant from one another), with the same 10 authors (switching places, of course, in one or another article's long string of authorship)?" More importantly, what value does this approach generate? None, in fact. None for the body of knowledge. None for management practice. And certainly none at all for society.

Unfortunately though, this type of ill-intended collaboration is indeed predominant. In one of my earlier working experiences, I was hired to foster collaboration between industry and academia in a specific area of application, which I thought was kind of a dream job at the time I accepted it. Unfortunately, the truly grand opportunity got polluted by the immense pressure we were all under to generate publications — at the time created by the up-coming so-called research assessment exercise (RAE).[26]

Because of RAE-driven pressure to publish, the many times an industry partner came forward with an interesting project proposal, this was usually met by the then senior researchers' and professors' foremost concerns: "Can we write an article about this? Who is going to be first-author? What journal should we publish for?" And this was before the project even started (and hence before any value whatsoever had been created)!?

The point here is not to point fingers and find winners or losers. It is simply to share an experience where the wrong focus never led to anything good. There was no winner at all in fact: the government funded a project that never reached its aim; the university team never managed to generate any meaningful research from the project; and the industry never benefited from what could have been meaningful, transformative, insight.

My experience is not isolated. In fact, it is far too common. Henry Mintzberg, discussing how a similar type approach takes junior scholars' focus away from the real value-adding side of research, says: "I call this [publishing articles before you finish your thesis], writing the overture before you write the opera."

It is for this reason that I find a very valuable suggestion in Roger Martin's approach to choosing his research collaborators: when I interviewed him he was keen to underline that "if I meet somebody whose primary concerns is 'can we get it written even though we haven't really resolved this important issue?', [my answer is:] 'Thanks but no thanks. I don't play that game!'."

Well, what would your answer be?

Making Collaboration Work for Yourself

The researcher's journey to insight involves collaboration at one point or another. Be that with a fellow colleague to jointly carry out an experiment; or with her institution or company to be given the tangible and intangible support she needs to achieve her objective; or with the journal editor who might have to courageously accept her article even though reviewers rejected it because it goes against mainstream assumptions of the field (references/warnings to myself are purely coincidental!).

So, understanding how to make it work is fundamental.

As I was going through the stories of these exemplary researchers, I realized that part of the *Futureers'* success in collaborating with others is that they look at collaboration as a way to do *more* work, *better* work, *more* comprehensive work, *more* meaningful work.

For as simple as that might sound, looking retrospectively at my own personal experience as a Ph.D. student, supervisor, co-author, co-investigator, and research associate, I couldn't but be slightly surprised and ashamed of myself to realize that the concept of collaboration in the many groups I had been part of had followed an entirely different path, one that focused on merely splitting tasks as a way to minimize input, rather than optimize output. A path where *more* had inexcusably become *less*.

On that basis, I want to close this chapter with two more suggestions, that I personally intend to treasure in my journey to become a better management researcher.

First, one by Goffee on how to build successful collaborations: "Things have not tended to go wrong and maybe I have just been lucky but *I have conservatively invested in a small number of relationships* rather than lots of different ones."

Then, one by Kaplan on how to make sure these collaborations multiply insight rather than simply divide tasks: "I don't delegate things, *I actually do the work myself*, I want to get my hands close to the data, I want to feel the phenomena and that's why it helps to give me more insight into what I am studying."

CHAPTER 7

SHARE THE EXPERIENCE TO MAKE IT MORE VALUABLE (TO YOU AND OTHERS)

We are way more conservative and incremental than it is sensible.
— Roger Martin

Not everything that can be counted counts, and not everything that counts can be counted.
— Albert Einstein, Nobel Prize in Physics in 1921

John Kotter, Professor at Harvard Business School, has written many books and shows no signs of slowing down. Many are big sellers, particularly *Leading Change*.[1] Here, his chief concern is with transformation and the book examines the efforts of more than 100 companies to become better competitors. So why does he continue to publish? What drives him to disseminate the outcome of his work?

For John Kotter the answer is disarmingly simple and yet incredibly noble: "I want to make a difference ... no matter how small to the close to the seven billion people that live in this little rock called Earth."

As a professor and management consultant, Dave Ulrich is similarly concerned with getting the message out there, using as many pathways as possible, and making a difference. The outcome he seeks is "impact" and he observes: "Since most of the research starts with application in mind, I like to share the insights through speeches, articles, consulting, workshops, and other forums."

Futureers may choose different means to spread the world about their research findings, but the objective remains the same. Those who do *research that matters* and generate meaningful insight want others to know about it and to use it. As a matter of fact, they see these elements — dissemination, testing trough adoption (not to be read restrictively as application) and feedback — as pieces of the same complex puzzle that is meaningful research.

Costas Markides claims that dissemination is one of the five most important factors that influence whether an innovation, idea, or product will catch on and, eventually, generate impact. So, the drive and objective to 'get the word out' would seem straightforward.

Still all acknowledge, in one form or another, that most researchers — in management and other fields alike — these days are negatively distracted by the enormous pressure coming from the prevalent culture in academia that has transformed publishing in a mere instrument to gain promotions, status, and peer recognition.

Dave Ulrich quotes Peter Lorange, the Norwegian economist, on the problem he sees with mainstream approach to measuring research quality. Lorange worries about the extent to which academics measure research in terms of publication in lead journals. He concludes that it is not the ideas *per se* that are important, it is the impact of those ideas that should concern us.

What pushes most scholars to publish these days is as far from Kotter's noble aim as Earth is from Mars. As long as these questionable measures of research quality and impact remain mainstream, management research will continue to be neither an art nor a science but merely a commodity mass-produced by thousands of uninspired mercenaries.

In this chapter, I aim to understand whether and how we can go back to being scientific artists and use dissemination as an enhancer, rather than an inhibitor, of impact.

To do that, I first look at what traditionally drives us to disseminate our findings; I then ponder on how that compares to what *Futureers* do; finally, I try to extract some ideas for how we could improve our effectiveness (in spreading our ideas for the right reasons, that is).

What the Hell Is Wrong with us?

A few years ago, I remember sitting in a seminar and being captivated by Bernard Marr's keynote speech on performance management. Marr is a world-renowned authority, best-selling author on organizational performance and proclaimed one of today's leading business brains by the *CEO Journal*. His speech thesis, rather well known to experts in the field and outsiders alike, was that the wrong measures drive the wrong behavior. He gave two examples that I thought were rather entertaining:

The first was about how when Mumbai was faced with an increasing rat problem in some of their slum areas of the town. The town officials promoted a reward program offering a 1$ reward for each dead rat that citizens would turn in. What was the result? The number of rats increased, rather than decreasing as expected. Why? Simple: people started breeding rats to collect the 1$ rewards.

His second example was about performance measurement in airport logistics. He spoke of an airport management effort to increase customer satisfaction of the baggage collection part of their airport experience. To improve service levels, the operations management team started measuring the time it used to take for the first bag to reach the collection conveyor belt. They also created a reward program linking the baggage handlers' financial bonuses to improvement of this particular indicator. The measure itself started showing significant improvements in a short space of time. Yet, passengers' complaints increased as well. Why? A closer look revealed that in each team, one baggage handler would take one bag from the airplane and dash to put it on the conveyor belt, while the rest of the team continued to perform the same task the same old way.

What do these two examples have in common with *doing research that matters*? To understand that, we must take a look at how the academe measures research impact, an issue that could in itself fill many books. I start from the assumption that if it is true that the wrong measures drive the wrong behavior, if we use the wrong measures to assess the impact of research, then it is likely that we are going to drive the wrong behavior in those doing the research whose impact is being measured.

Based on the model I am using in this book, then, I am going to look at the measures used by, and the behavior they drive at: the *Insight Generator*'s; the *Insight Incubator*'s; and the *Insight Distributor*'s level.

Research Impact — the Insight Incubator's Perspective

The original noble purpose of universities was to conduct research that would contribute to advancing societal understanding and well-being.[2] Within that context, back in 1990 Ernest L. Boyer noted how the term 'scholarship' originally referred to "a variety of creative work carried on in a variety of places, and its integrity was measured by the ability to think, communicate, and learn."[3] In an analysis of relevance, rigor, and reach in business research, Professor Pramodita Sharma from the John Molson School of Business at Montreal's Concordia University observes how things have changed significantly over the years to the point that "today, the word 'scholarship' evokes thoughts of academic articles published in peer reviewed journals, most frequently written by individuals holding academic ranks in colleges or universities."[4]

The main reason for such infamous evolution of the term (as well as of the behavior and profession it is used to describe) can be found in the way universities are measured for — and consequently measure — research impact. In his 2007 article by the title "Making Sense of Research Quality Assessment," Emeritus Professor Peter Lansley from the School of Construction and Engineering at the University of Reading in the United Kingdom noted how "in the UK, the nature, orientation and quality of academic research is overwhelmingly determined by considerations of how that work will be graded in research assessment exercises (RAEs). The grades awarded to work in a particular subject area can have a considerable impact on the individual and their university."[5] RAEs and the measures used to assess research quality and impact have become quite standardized across the globe.

Two of the most frequently used metrics for assessing and ranking the significance of management research are the number of publications in top-tier journals and citations.[6] The first part of the first indicator, i.e. the number of publications, and the second indicator, i.e. number of citations, are straightforward counting activities, of articles published by the same author and of the number of times those articles are cited by other articles, respectively.

The second part of the first indicator though, i.e. "in top-tier journals," is less straightforward as there are numerous so-called lists ranking journals based on different and more or less rigorous, more or less publicly declared, more or less quantitative methods of computation. I will get back to this part later, when discussing the *Insight Distributor*'s perspective.

The point is that RAEs measure universities' research quality on the basis of their ability to produce quality research whose impact is assessed using, primarily, measures of quantity (of articles and citations). In turn, universities have created reward and career advancement systems based on the idea that the better research you produce, that is, the more articles you produce and the more citations to those articles you manage to generate, the more likely it is that you will advance in the system and, eventually, get tenure.

So, what behavior do these measures drive at the Insight Incubator's level? One that has now become so mainstream to have even gained its very own name, that is, the so-called "publish or perish" mentality. Costas Markides agrees that "we have become so dominated by this 'publish or perish' attitude." And for Henry Mintzberg, "the five-year tenure review [in academic institutions] is completely crazy ... it puts everybody on a treadmill." This is even more so for junior scholars, for whom, in the words of Barbara Kellerman, "the reward system is very much still in traditional departments. Most young scholars do find that they have to satisfy ... senior professors, many of whom tend to be very traditional in what they consider good enough work to get tenure and that obviously depends a lot on publishing."

Howard Gardner observes that although "publish or perish" sounds harsh it is the reality in the sciences and in scholarship in general. "If you want to investigate something as an amateur or as an eccentric and do so, that is fine. But if you want to be part of the scientific/scholarly community, there is no choice but to publish in the best possible places." The point of view within the academy is matched by outsiders as well: back in 2009, when John Peters was still president of Emerald Publishing Inc., based in Boston, Massachusetts, and CEO of Emerald Group Publishing Limited, based in Bingley, England, he wrote an article by the rather telling headline "The Modern-Day Men's Club" in which he argued: "Institutions rely on this productivity count to help them decide which scholars to recruit and retain, and which professors are making progress toward fulfilling tenure requirements."[7] But he had grave reservations about a system which is focused too much on "discipline-based scholarship defined by the rigor of the research. Such a system cannot provide the relevant research the world needs today."[8]

Peters' conclusion has been supported by many others, like Concordia University's professor Sharma who observes: "With the publish or perish dogma dominating the academic career progression, it is no wonder that scholars choose to focus on research questions that may be of most interest to journals with a high impact factor (IF) by which their performance is calibrated."[9]

Ultimately, he adds, the widespread agreement is that the contemporary academic assessment and reward systems "in the field of management may have fallen into the folly of rewarding A [top journal publications], while hoping for B [relevant research]."

Research Impact — the Insight Generator's Perspective

Citing earlier studies, some have also noted that "considering that the objective of scholarly research should be to influence the thinking of other scholars and — in the aggregate — the field, citing a given article provides a public acknowledgment of an influence whereas the other possible influences cannot be objectively verified."[10] On this basis, counting articles and citations might seem a proper way to measure (and therefore foster) research impact. Or is it?

To the untrained eye, measuring these indicators might seem straightforward. However, as most academics would know, it is not at all an easy exercise. There exist many measures, some have been used for long and more appears as technology develops further, for example, Google Scholar based measures. In fact, there are so many measures that a number of software tools have emerged that support academics in conducting citation analysis. Anne-Wil Harzing, Professor in International Management and Associate Dean Research at the University of Melbourne, Australia developed one such software tool that, coincidently, is called the "publish or perish" software. In her book, *The Publish or Perish Book: Your Guide to Effective and Responsible Citation Analysis*, Professor Harzing presents a list of impact measures which makes for an insightful reading. The experienced academics among you are surely aware of all the available measures. However, for the benefit of the non-academic readers, allow me to offer just a few examples:[11]

The Hirsch's h-index provides a single-number metric of an academic's impact, based on a combination of quality and quantity. The Egghe's g-index builds on the h-index but gives more weight to highly cited articles. The contemporary h-index also builds on the h-index but gives more weight to recent articles. The age-weighted citation rate (AWCR) measures the average number of citations to an entire body of work, adjusted for the age of each individual paper. The individual h-index (original) divides the standard h-index by the average number of authors in the articles that contribute to the h-index in order to reduce the effects of co-authorship. The multi-authored h-index uses fractional paper counts instead of reduced citation counts to account for shared authorship of papers, and then determines the multi-authored h_m-index based on the resulting effective rank of the papers using undiluted citation counts.

The list (unfortunately) goes on.

Using one, more or all of these measures (?!), the 'best scholars' are considered by the academe and within the scientific community as those who have published the most or have generated the most citations for their published articles.

Therefore, assuming that the objective of *doing research that matters* is to influence behaviors in industry, government, and society, the 'best scholars,' that is those who produce the most and are most cited, should be those who also have the greatest influence. But, are they?

Thankfully, there are a few researchers who have looked into it. Peng and Zhou, from the University of Texas and Ohio State University, respectively, studied citations in global strategy research to ascertain the impact and influence of the most frequently cited research in the field. Their conclusions? "While a high number of publications in top journals indicate that a scholar has been prolific and successful in generating high visibility output, such a number, which would earn a scholar a position in the lists of top contributors based on publication counts, gives us no information about whether this output has a significant impact."[12]

The same authors point out: "Sometimes, certain works are cited not because of their direct intellectual influence but because of the legitimacy they provide to certain topics. One may call this the 'herd effect'. Consequently, some high quality articles are not widely cited, whereas many relatively low quality articles may be extensively cited. Also, theoretical, conceptual, and review articles tend to receive more citations than do empirical articles. In addition, there are incidences of significant mis-citations."[13]

Barbara Kellerman saw this lack of influence in her own discipline as well: "In my discipline, for example, the *American Political Science Review*, which is the journal of the discipline — and God knows it follows rigorous research — it is not touched, not read ever or virtually ever by people who actually practice politics."

That is not limited to the *American Political Science Review*, by any means. Worryingly, even if we were to accept citations as a measure of influence, Concordia University's Professor Sharma's research concluded that "based on the joint probability of having a paper accepted in a top journal (roughly 20%) and generating over 100 citations ..., 99.26% of our research efforts do not have a major impact on the field and it is very difficult for authors to predict when major impact may occur."[14]

So, what behavior do these measures of research impact drive at the Insight Generator level? There is no better way to answer this question than to cite Bruno S. Frey, Professor of Economics at the Institute for Empirical Economic Research in Zurich, Switzerland: "career success for academics depends on their *intellectual prostitution*."[15]

Research Quality — the Insight Distributor's Perspective

According to a recent report by London School of Economics, when compared to books, magazines, newspaper articles, etc., journal articles generate the majority of citations.[16] This, and the fact that citations are used as a measure of influence, implies that the responsibility for journal editors and publishers as distributors of *research that matters*, is significant. And yet, many agree with Mintzberg that "journals are full of a lot of marginally interesting stuff." Why is it so?

To understand that, we must understand what the term 'quality journal' means and the role these so-called A-Journal play in giving one piece of research the traditional mark of high quality or high impact. Although the quality of journals has been evaluated for many years, it has recently become possible to actually 'measure it.' An essay by Thomson Reuters[17] explains that the creation of citation indexes made it possible to do computer-compiled statistical analysis of both number of articles published and number of citations generated, which we have seen are the two main measures of research impact in use. In the 1960s, Thomson Reuters created the so called 'journal impact factor,' which they define as "a measure of the frequency with which the 'average article' in a journal has been cited in a particular year or period." This impact factor is calculated mathematically as a "ratio between citations and recent citable items published."

The essay goes on concluding: "Thus, the impact factor of a journal is calculated by dividing the number of current year citations to the source items published in that journal during the previous two years."

And there lies the heart of the problem: the more citations those articles that are published by one journal attract, the higher the impact factor of that journal is going to be. The higher the impact factor of that journal, the more articles submissions that journal will attract. The more these articles are authored by authors with a high-citation index, the more citations those articles (and therefore the journal that publish them) will attract.

This is an issue that has been examined very elegantly and scientifically by Stuart MacDonald and Jacqueline Kam of the British Universities of Sheffield and Bristol, respectively. They note how this circular nature to the way that the world of scientific publication works might seem to outsiders like a fiendish version of Catch 22. It goes along the lines of: Why are quality journals regarded so highly? Because they publish quality papers. How do we know that they are quality papers? Because they are in quality journals.[18] Other indicators of quality in journals include the high number of rejection rates, circulation age, the institution with which they are affiliated. But the way that Management Studies departments tackle the issue of quality lists returns us to another variation on the Catch 22 theme. MacDonald and Kam cite research that suggests management studies departments compile their lists from other management studies departments, which in turn have adapted their lists. This leads to an even more dangerous version of what Harald zur Hausen describes as 'scientific in-breeding': "At the moment, one major problem is that you are forced already as a graduate student or as a young post-doc to publish early and in very good journals. This forces you to sit in very good groups, they perform very well and they also achieve a lot. But in a way it leads in many of these cases to a continuation of the aim or the goals of that particular group into what I would consider a kind of scientific in-breeding. Topics which are selected become relatively narrow in the end and while what you select might be interesting and produce good results it effects in a way the broadness of approaches and narrows it substantially."

Journals' impact measurement contributes to making a bad situation worst and John Peters concludes that "publications are racing each other to reach greater levels of introspection, narrowness of view, and obscurity of content."[19]

The corollary is that a journal on one list will make its way on to another, while unlisted journals remain out in the cold. As editor of a journal myself, I have witnessed an inverse trend between the increasing pressure to publish on A-listed journals and the number of submission we receive. In that sense, I am a victim of the very same Catch-22 described above: since the journal I edit was only recently founded (in 2008), it does not have an Impact Factor; since it does not have an Impact Factor, it is not on any list; since it is not on any list, articles published by it are not likely to receive many citations; since the articles are not going to be cited, Thomson Reuters is not going to give the journal an Impact Factor (and, even if it did, it would be very low). Rewind and replay all over again.

Those who defend journal publishing refer to the peer review argument as the most legitimate way of ensuring that credible findings make their way to the public realm. Douglas Osheroff says: "It's important, I think, that if you have an exciting result, it should go through peer review and be subjected to scrutiny by one's peers. Because otherwise you're going to get all sorts of misleading erroneous results published, either by charlatans or fools or even by professors who have relied too heavily on their graduate students to carefully scrutinize the results of their research and the conclusions they have drawn from it."

But even that is coming under fire in terms of the inside track that some scholars may have and the value of knowing and understanding the system of publishing. In fact, there is no good reason to be complacent about the peer-review system at all. The notion that its very existence is a mark of quality is dubious to say the least. And the problem can work both ways, MacDonald and Kam argue, with good research falling foul of referees and poor research getting the go-ahead.

In addition, some submissions are reviewed by editors without going to referees: "so, rigorous refereeing is an indicator of journal quality, but pressure to publish in high quality journals means that refereeing is not always rigorous. Logic dictates that the higher the rejection rate of a journal, the less likely that submissions will be refereed at all."[20]

The (rhetorical) question is: does publication in prestigious A-listed journals really tell us much about the quality of the research or its impact and influence? In fact, as we saw earlier and as most players in this game know full too well, it does not.

Sometimes the 'best' journals may not publish the 'best' articles at all. Trying to understand how much better are the most prestigious journal, William Starbuck, Professor of Creative Management at the Stern School of Business in New York, found that the criteria and approach used for editorial selection of articles to publish and for assessing value of scientific articles showed "considerable randomness," revealing that reviewers' judgments "correlate weakly with manuscripts' true values."[21] He discovered that the most prestigious journals often publish low value articles and low prestige journals publish some very high-value articles. Based on his findings, he questioned whether universities make decisions regarding rewards and promotions using enough and reliable data.

More importantly, however, Starbuck's discussion raises the question of whether the long-held assumption that low prestige journals do not publish high-value articles (and hence, fewer people may read, learn from, and use them) could mean that new knowledge is not as widely spread.

So, what type of behavior do these measures of research impact drive at the Insight Distributor level? MacDonald and Kam suggest that an intensely cynical world operates where gaming the system has become mainstream in the academy. The citation game is played by many people, they say. Editors can do it by cultivating "a cadre of authors who will boost the measured quality of his journal"; authors who cite one another's paper to increase the impact factor of the journal where their paper is published — thereby making it more likely that it will get cited itself; and authors "whose work is so anodyne and so generic that it can be cited anywhere."[22] The authors describe these tactics as gamesmanship and, while suggesting there never was a golden age when "academics published largely to improve the lot of mankind,"[23] the current system encourages this unethical behavior more than ever before.

Their remedy comes from J. M. Barrie: a "Tinkerbell Solution." In Barrie's "Peter Pan," Tinkerbell is saved when children clap their hands to show that they believe in fairies. If the uncritical clapping stops, to be replaced by laughter, some sanity could be returned to the world of management studies.[24]

Let's begin to laugh, please.

The "Publish or Perish" Madness

The OBJECTIVE SCIENCE ("Quantifying objectivity in the natural and social sciences") project funded under the People Specific Programme of the Seventh Framework Programme (FP7) demonstrated that the ever-growing pressure to produce publishable results can adversely impact the quality of scientific research. "Scientists face an increasing conflict of interest, torn between the need to be accurate and objective and the need to keep their careers alive," explains Dr. Fanelli, a Marie Curie Intra-European Fellows working on the project. The conclusions of the study are staggeringly worrying: "Academic competition for funding and positions is increasing everywhere ... policies that rely too much on cold measures of productivity might be lowering the quality of science itself."[25]

In the field of international business and international management research, a recent working paper published by Michigan State University concluded that even the 'best scholars' in the field (as traditionally defined, that is, most prolific) thought that most of the latest research and additions to the body of knowledge were basically an extension or a replication of previous work.[26]

To which John Peters adds an important observations about the role scholarly journals play in hindering the spreading of research insight (hence limiting its influence): "the top journals may have a two or three-year lag time between acceptance and publication. Therefore, papers that appear in them may have taken a year or two to research; spent a year or two being shuttled among editor, author, and referees; and then spent another two years waiting their turns to be set in print. Because of this system, scholarly publications with the greatest prestige tend to reject any form of research except the highly conceptual — otherwise, the publications would be hopelessly out of date."[27]

In an article that appeared on *The New York Times* on January 17, 2012 by the headline "Cracking Open the Scientific Process," Thomas Lin summarized the effectiveness of using scholarly journals to disseminate research harshly but accurately: "Peer review can take months, journal subscriptions can be prohibitively costly, and a handful of gatekeepers limit the flow of information. It is an ideal system for sharing knowledge, said the quantum physicist Michael Nielsen, only 'if you're stuck with 17th-century technology'."[28]

In conclusion, in the words of Stanford University Professor Jeffrey Pfeffer: "The structure and processes governing both the careers of academics and the prepublication review of their work limit the influence of management research on practice, social policy, and even the terms of public discourse about organizational issues."[29]

Since none of this is exactly 'breaking news' and everybody — at least in the academe — is actually aware of the situation, I wonder: WHAT THE HELL ARE WE DOING? (and, in case you're wondering, yes ... I am shouting!)

What Can We Do About It?

This is a question that Harald zur Hausen admits torments him. "I think it is really one I constantly am thinking about: how can we change this aspect? And I must admit that I cannot find an easy solution." After agreeing that there is indeed a problem, also Kotter concludes, with a tone of disappointment in his voice: "No, I don't have a solution for that one."

Costas Markides has a proposal though that makes an enormous amount of sense to me.

When studying how he could solve big social problems, Markides realized that 50 years of research in social psychology agreed that 70% of the variance in our behavior is determined by the underlying environment. He says: "This is one of the most fundamentals findings in social psychology. We always think that what determines how we behave is our own personality but this is not the case. Only 30% of our behaviour is determined by us, 70% is the situation/environment you put people in. Academics call this the structure of the system you put people in."

He concludes then that to revert this dominant trend toward incrementalism in research, we must change the underlying structure of academia: "The first step in my opinion to generate more innovation in academic research is to change the purpose of the paradigm, which says that our goal is to publish or perish. It is not! Our goal is to generate ideas that help change the world, that create value. And if you don't develop a new paradigm and use new mindsets you are never going to have progress in academia."

How do we do that in practice? I am not sure I have an answer to that yet but I think that by first adopting MacDonald and Kam's Tinker Bell solutions (i.e., laughing at traditional measures of impact and at those who enforce them) and then trying to understand the real motives that push *Futureers* to disseminate their research, and emulating them, we might be able to start a movement that will, eventually, lead to a solution.

Below, my effort to share what I have learnt about the real motives pushing *Futureers* to disseminate (next session's title is rather telling in this regards).

Making Worthy Ideas Spread Like Viruses

The clear indication that emerged from all my conversations with *Futureers*, which is also an important part of the learning from my journey, is that for an idea to have impact it needs to spread as much as possible. Spreading results in adoption. Adoption results in testing. Testing results in richer observations. Richer observations result in further insight.

Dissemination through *Insight Distributors* therefore is necessary "to have impact in a widest sense," clarifies Rob Goffee for whom this truly the only driver behind disseminating his research: "I think that anybody working in management that does not have that kind of interest in a wider impact frankly shouldn't be in a management or business school. Having said that, I realise that there are people who are just driven by narrow publications."

Spreading, or dissemination, of an idea, therefore, affects three stakeholder groups: (1) the scientific community; (2) the public; (3) the support system.

Ideally, each stakeholder group plays a specific role and each provides a different type of feedback to the researcher doing the research. Each, therefore, needs to be fed certain information using a specific medium, or *Insight Distributor*. I use the term "ideally" on purpose to remind you that here I am once again de-composing the *Futureers'* experiences to identify key 'ideal' enablers of the process of doing meaningful research.

According to Szostak, "there are many factors. We want people to know about the progress we have made. Publication also establishes priority. Education of the public is also important. Finally, publications etc. are critical for continued funding. We publish papers in peer reviewed journals, write technical and popular reviews and I give many talks at Universities and conferences."

Scientific Community — Dissemination as Scientific Validation

The role of the scientific community is one of insight validation. Normally, this takes place in two ways: (1) feedback on the idea; (2) up-take of the idea.

Harald zur Hausen, for example, says that "you should like to disseminate your ideas among the scientific community and among your peers to get a critical statement back, some feedback and to see whether you are right or not right. I think it is quite important, which I've learnt of course particularly during our study of the papilloma viruses, that you get some kind of acceptance of the scientific community of what you contribute to your field."

The same works in management research where, according to Costas Markides: "90% of the time we spend it on explaining how we did the research. Not the idea, but how we did the research. Because you have to convince the academics that you did the research in a rigorous manner ... so that nobody is going to stand up and way 'your research is wrong'."

The second way an idea gets validated within the scientific community is indirect as opposed to direct feedback. Indirect validation happens when an idea is picked up by fellow scholars and further developed. As I mentioned in an earlier chapter, *Futureers* see *doing research that matters* as building a wall brick by brick. In line with Henry Mintzberg's rejection of the idea that research insight must be usable by managers, Markides underlines: "Impact is not just what managers do [with your idea] and what they think [about it]. It's also what other academics do with your research. You incrementally build a body of work in a research topic/subject and you can only do that if you can get enough academics out there to do research on that topic."

A good example of this — although there are many — comes from Elinor Ostrom who, together with Oliver Williamson, won the 2009 Nobel Prize in Economic Sciences for their separate work on economic governance. Ostrom acknowledges the significance of an understanding of Game Theory, the study of strategic decision-making developed by German economist Reinhard Selten, to their work. She says: "We've been able to take game-theoretic models and put them in the lab and test them. And thus my early exposure in the 1980s to the work of Reinhardt Selten, who is himself a Nobel Laureate, was a very, very important step in my training."[30]

Can you imagine what would have happened if Selten had not spread his ideas?

Regardless of whether one seeks validation through direct feedback or through up-take by further research, it is important to reach the widest academic audience. Needless to say, the *Insight Distributor* of choice for disseminating research insight within the scientific community is scholarly journals. There are some obvious benefits, especially when the journals are edited seriously. Margherita Hack explains that the review process can often yield meaningful feedback and ideas by experts in many and varied fields, not just a positive or negative evaluation: "Therefore [in these cases] it also becomes a collaboration."

Nevertheless, for the many reasons I discussed earlier in this chapter, although journals are given such an important role in determining who is going to become a star and who will be doomed to a life of anonymity, they are by no means the best way to reach the widest audience — not just the widest audience in general, but even the widest audience of fellow academics.

Markides has a point when he says that "not many people read the academic journals, even the academics don't read the academic journals … People are more likely to listen to a 20 minutes presentation than to read an article." Whereas many agree that more effective ways to disseminate research ideas include seminars and conferences.

The Public — Dissemination as a 'Members' Test'

The role of the public is also one of validation, albeit a different type of validation from the one I discussed above. As I mentioned earlier, Rob Goffee tests his own ideas using the 'members' test,' a tool used in sociology to try out ideas with the members of the community that the idea applies to (or concerns anyway).

Broadly speaking, the community that might be influenced directly by ideas and insight generated through management research is made up of practicing managers. It is worth clarifying that, throughout this book, I use the terms 'public,' 'client,' and 'community' interchangeably to refer to same group of people whose behavior might be influenced by the research insight.

Dissemination, then, is often used as an instrument to seek out opportunities to influence practicing managers and observe how their behavior changes as a result of being influenced by the research insight one generates.

The aim in disseminating insight to the public is the same as in the case of dissemination within the scientific community, that is, gaining feedback and validation (or otherwise). And also the strategy does not vary, that is, reaching the widest possible audience. The medium though is almost certainly going to be different.

To reach their audience, besides going to conferences, most of the management thinkers I have talked to primarily use the following *Insight Distributors* (ranked from most to less often mentioned): (a) consulting; (b) executive education; (c) books; (d) managerial oriented journals; (e) the press; (f) the media.

Consulting is certainly the most common tool used to develop, test, and spread management research ideas and insight. A lot could be said about this and the infamous reputation management consultants have within academic circles — more on this later.

John Kotter is almost evangelistic about the work of Kotter International, the consulting company he has co-founded with an ex-Microsoft executive. He says: "We've got a million projects so the new [dissemination] vehicle besides just the traditional ones is this company. The company is now also a research vehicle for me because anything it does with clients, I'm watching as carefully as I can to see what else I can learn." Roger Martin also claims that consulting with the very best companies in the world give him a chance to test out new ideas and, for that reason, he aims to spend at least a couple of days a month doing it.

On the other hand, Rob Gofees' experience working at London Business School shows how well consulting and executive education works for validating research impact: "working at a top level business school which does a lot of executive education I have been involved in company interventions which lasted for 5 to 8 years and in effect have been a mixture of consulting and teaching or development. When you have dealt with, as we did, literally the top couple of thousands executives over a 4/5 year period, you can get to a stage where you feel that you have collectively had some kind of impact." Similarly, Robert Kaplan exploits Harvard alumni reunions and executive education to run the members' test within his own community.

Books are also often cited as a powerful method of dissemination that usually reaches a large audience. Granted, it takes longer to produce a book than it does to produce an article or a seminar presentation, but that is not relevant. Roger Martin writes "readable books," for 'the public' and academic books as well, "much harder to read and orientated to a more academic audience." He's also got 15 *Harvard Business Review* articles and probably since becoming Dean some 300 popular articles in newspapers, magazines, and the likes. As he says, "writing makes me happy." And John Kotter as well has traditionally tried to spread the word through books (in addition to the usual consulting and teaching).

In terms of managerially oriented journals like *Harvard Business Review*, *Sloan Management Review* or *The California Management Review*, Costas Markides explains why he thinks these are important avenues for an idea to spread: "Because 300,000 people subscribe to *Harvard Business Review*, I don't expect all of them to read my article but even if just 10% bother to look at the article, that is 30,000 people which is many more than the few academics who are going to read my academic articles."

Of course, being able (and supported) to disseminate through these non-academic outlets pretty much depends on the *Insight Incubator* within which the *Insight*

Generator works. Some institutions reward researchers for spreading their ideas (and their university's and school's brand) to broad audiences, often beyond the organizational constituents that may be the primary focus. They are rarer, for sure, and it seems the list includes all of the usual suspect (London Business School and Harvard Business School firsts among all). For the rest, those working in more traditional *Insight Incubators*, the focus remains depressingly strong on traditional scientific journals, which means, clearly, that most researchers miss out entirely on an important stakeholder group.

As for press and media, again, if your system supports it, dissemination through these outlets helps spreading the idea even further, into the domain of wider society. Speeches, television, and radio appearances all seek to reach an audience beyond academic colleagues and peers as well as beyond the professional community of those who may be likely to adopt and use the research findings.

Barbara Kellerman, Harvard University, says that the Kennedy School "places quite a high value on reaching a larger public, much more than a conventional political science department would. So I happen now to be in a situation where there is a high value placed on everything from a TV appearance to an op ed to a blog so forth and so on."

Costas Markides talks with newspaper reporters, such as those from *The Financial Times,* in the hope that they will pick up on his ideas and help to publicize them.

Paul Krugman's story gives a good illustration of how powerful media and PR can be as *Insight Distributors*. In the United States, the economist Paul Krugman of Princeton University is a high-profile name. Krugman won the Nobel Prize in 2008 for his work on, among other economic issues, New Trade Theory. He is probably best known to the general American public for his journalism but does not see the two words as being unrelated.

He says[31]: "I do believe that the task of boiling down an intellectual problem to its essence, which is a lot of what's involved in [economic] modelling, and the task of figuring out how to talk about some fairly complex problem in fairly simple natural language, are related.

"I always felt that what I do when I try to explain, let's say explain the financial crisis in 800 words, and what I do when I try to model the financial crisis in a half-dozen equations, are very much the same kind of effort. That said, I was doing a fair bit of that kind of translation before I went to work for *The New York Times*, and that continues to be one of the things I do at *The Times*. I had not anticipated that I would end up in such a politically charged environment, where I feel I need to do more than explain, but it did seem natural."

Krugman would doubtlessly agree wholeheartedly with Einstein's contention that you shouldn't be working in a specialist field if you cannot explain to your tobacconist what you are doing. The Nobel Prize therefore makes Krugman's journalism more rather than less important, as a means of enabling him to get across the issues that concern him, because the accompanying media interest has drawn ever more attention to them.

Finally, there is a timid attempt by most toward using the Internet and social media tools like Twitter, LinkedIn and Facebook to reach the more 'modernized' part of their community. Philip Kotler acknowledges this trend when he says: "We make increased use of social media such as Twitter, Linkedin™, Facebook, etc., to inform more persons about our results."

The Support System — Dissemination to Raise Support

The role of the support system is to provide the *Insight Generators* with what they need for them to do their research. Support systems include, for example, funding bodies whose role is to provide financial support, but also *Insight Incubators* and *Distributors* more widely, whose responsibility is to provide 'cultural' support. The latter is the focus of this entire book and, therefore, I am not going to discuss them here.

The role of funding in research is pretty simple to understand: if there is no funding, there is no research. As simple as that. The availability of funding, therefore, may influence the focus of one's research. Howard Gardner has been conducting psychological and social scientific research for over 40 years. He has written hundreds of articles and dozens of books. He says he is always impelled by two factors: (1) What is he really interested in? (2) What can he raise funds to study? "I have been successful at fund raising and have been able to use funds, eventually, to investigate issues in which I am interested. I also have had many students who have carried the work further. As long as I have curiosity and funding, I will continue to conduct research."

Dissemination, therefore, plays a role in feeding the right information to funding organizations to influence funding decision-making. Gardner thinks the researcher's role in influencing funding decisions is central to its ability to do *research that matters*: "If I am convinced at saying that a topic is interesting and important, it is my job to convince funders to support it and to show that the research is important for the intended audience. That may or may not be an organization. It could be other scholars, the general public, or even an unexpected audience — say the groups that I am studying or the groups that are annoyed (or relieved) that they were not studied."

Create Your Own Dissemination Strategy

Dissemination is not an easy task, regardless of whether one chooses to disseminate her idea in peer-refereed journals, in highly rated practitioner journals, in books, or through speeches.

Finding a good and worthy problem, collecting and analyzing appropriate information, having the discipline to write and do it well, persevering through (if one is lucky) multiple revisions of a manuscript, and having the patience, sometimes years, to wait before those precious words may appear in print is not a sprint, it's a marathon. On top of that 'normal' process, some people seek to build in other challenges for themselves. Robert Goffee, for example, seeks increasingly to write for organizational members who he hopes will use some of his ideas to change their behaviors or their organizations.

But to reach them requires writing in ways that they will read what he does. That has become a personal challenge — to "write differently." He wonders whether academics who stay just within the peer-review academic journal universe understand the challenges associated with the type of writing he tries to do.

He says: "… those who start with academic journals probably don't appreciate the kind of traits of application-type literature. And it is not that easy to produce. It's got its own types of challenges and it forces you to put your ideas in a language which a large number of people might be able to connect with."

For that reason, and that reason alone, most try to reach as wide an audience as possible. "My passion for some years in fact has been to reach the widest possible audience. So, for virtually really my entire academic career I write in plain English jargon-free hopefully accessible to the widest possible audience."

When your objective for disseminating an idea to the widest possible audience is to generate the widest possible impact then, clearly, using journals' impact factor as a decision criterion for choosing the best *Insight Distributor* is not going to be enough.

Futureers know that having a creative idea is not enough. You need a real strategy, a plan of attack that usually involves considering five variables. Markides explains how it works:

"There are 5 different variables that we know influence whether an idea or a product will catch on or not: one is what I would call the seller, i.e. who is the person who is pushing for the idea or the innovation? Some people are better at pushing for the idea than others. Secondly, what is the idea/innovation? Some ideas are simply better than others and therefore are more likely to catch on given everything else constant. The third is the buyer: who is the buyer and why would he buy this idea and/or how do you overcome their resistance? The fourth is: how do you sell the idea? What tactics and what methods do you use? And the fifth is the context in which you sell your idea (for example, the timing that you choose to sell). ... These 5 variables are all important and you as the innovator have the potential to influence all these 5 variables to sell your idea/product innovation.

"The same with academic ideas. It's not enough to just come up with a wonderful creative idea ... You have to think first of all: why would anybody buy anything from me? Who am I? Am I credible? Am I a well-known academic? Secondly: Have I positioned the idea in a way that people look at it and say '*Yes, that is a good idea*'? In other words, a lot depends on how you frame the idea. It might be a good idea but if you don't position it and frame it really well, nobody is going to buy into it. Third, who are you selling the idea to? Is it other academics? Is it a journalist? Is it managers? You have to think about this and for each audience you are selling to you have to think about how you are going to position your idea so that they are going to more likely buy into it. If the idea is for academics, you write it up and talk about it in a totally different way than if the idea is for managers. Four, how do you sell it? People think that the best way to sell it is by publishing it. No!!! The problem is that nobody reads anymore! So, the question is: if nobody reads what you publish, how are you going to spread the word about your idea? You have to start thinking about other tactics ... And then you have to think about timing. Some ideas die because timing wise they are positioned at the wrong time."

When was the last time you made a conscious effort to plan in this much detail how you would disseminate your idea?

Short-Term Focus on Bogus Quality versus Long-Term Focus on Meaning

So far, I have learned that the journey to meaningful insight and impact involves finding romantic problems worthy of investigation; collecting data and observations; finding the right partner who shares the same values, is compatible and complementary; going through the creative process with him or her; stumble across and learn from the unexpected; and start all over again. That is an extremely laborious process and we couldn't expect otherwise, given its grand aim.

Coming up with our idea, our meaningful insight is not the end of the road either. Not at all. As I have discussed in this chapter, the idea needs to spread through the best *Insight Distributors* to become popular before we can start to see *if* and *how* it influences people's behavior. And that requires additional time, sometime a very long time.

It seems that, in the very same way that only longevity can ensure the place of great art and literature in the canon, it is only the passing of time that can ultimately reveal the real significance and impact of one's research.

Just how long though does it take to actually do *research that matters*? Is it possible to estimate the length of time it normally takes to "kick the ball in the net" to use Mintzberg's analogy?

As you might expect, most of the people to whom I asked thought it was a preposterous idea. However, when *Futureers* talked about the time it has taken them to achieve their objectives, I could see remarkable similarities. In fact, as I mentioned in Chapter 6, *Futureers* seem to take between 5 and 7 years to craft their masterpiece.

For Roger Martin, "the gestation period is sometimes long, I would argue that I started thinking about integrative thinking challenges in 1991, and I wrote my book on it in 2007, so that took a long time. But my thinking on design was more like five years of work rather than fifteen." Martin recalls how he wrote an article later published by *Harvard Business Review* — which is notoriously extremely selective — in matters of hours during a lecture that did not interest him a great deal (to be honest, he said the lecture disgusted him so much that it gave him the idea for the article — another wonderful example of how *Futureers* have a habit to turn negatives into positives).

Although, in a similar vein to Gladwell's thesis in *Outliers* that behind an over-night success there is always a great deal of hard work, tears, and sweat, Martin admits that "sometimes it just flows out of your head, but that's probably because you've been thinking about it in the back of your mind for a long time and something clicks. Other times its very long and arduous work."

Harald zur Hausen says that "in the early days of the papilloma virus, [peer] acceptance was remarkably low and it changed only after we finally were able to isolate those respective virus … But this took quite a long time." Similarly, Jack Szostak thinks that because original ideas are often orthogonal to current thinking, "it is often hard to tell whether a new line of research will open doors or just lead to a blind alley — sometimes it takes decades for the implications of a new idea to become apparent," not just for the idea to become apparent but also for the idea to gain the recognition it deserves. For Szostak, the Nobel Prize was awarded 20 years after he had stopped his research in that field.

This also brings light onto another facet of timing which is fundamental to ensuring the idea catches on: it is important to ask yourself whether the intended audience is ready for the idea. Costas Markides is convinced that "some ideas die because timing wise they are positioned at the wrong time." This actually applies across all four stakeholder groups I discussed earlier, as sometime, you may craft the most beautiful article, or book, or presentation, but, says Martin, "the world [might not be] ready for what you want to say!"

He gives an example of one of his upcoming books, the idea for which he came up with in 2003. At that time, he says, "absolutely nobody paid attention to it." He first wrote a back page editorial for Barron's, which is an important outlet, but that generated no reaction whatsoever. "I wrote the same article virtually in 2009 for the *Financial Times*, and there was just a firestorm of reactions. It got published a bunch of times, it got quoted in *The Economist* and others. And there is nothing different. I probably should have cited the previous article because there was so much overlap, but you don't say those things in *Financial Times* articles. So the world changed, and now what I'm saying seems more consequential to people and so they pay attention to it."

Paul Krugman's experience also illustrates well this idea that timing plays an important role in making a piece of research matter. Speaking about how his ideas were being perceived by the public reading about these in his columns, he says[32]: "My views as a columnist are less controversial than they were a few years ago. Not because I've changed, but because a lot of, certainly of the United States, has come around to my way of thinking.

"So, when I was being critical of Bush and he had an 80 per cent approval rating, there might have been an enormous firestorm about all of this, but now that, I'm still critical of Bush but now he has a 22 per cent approval rating, I don't think it's going to be as much of an issue. I think it may surprise some people who know me only as a columnist."

In management, Peter Drucker probably serves as the best example of somebody whose ideas were so advanced that the world struggled to recognize their value. Roger Martin thinks that "virtually everything that Peter [Drucker] ever said during [his] career, people disdained as a weird and probably stupid idea. And then 25 years later everybody just says 'oh yeah, management by objectives that's what you have got to do'. 'The emergence of the knowledge worker, yeah it's obvious'. For the first ten years though they were all saying 'Peter [Drucker's] saying another stupid thing'."

In conclusion, I found that *Futureers* are aware that to achieve great things normally requires a great amount of time, but they are simply not concerned about it and they don't let the short-termism driven by the current system affect their integrity toward their key objective, which is, and always will be, to do *research that matters*.

To close this chapter, I would like once again to set two challenges, to you (and to myself).

The first one concerns deciding what we want to adopt as our own drivers for the dissemination of our research (and, consequently, for the choice of the most appropriate *Insight Distributor*). Roger Martin told me that his aspiration is "to be a voice that would be missed." Should he ever stop writing, I am sure he would be quite pleased if his authors' epitaph (if there is such a thing) would say something along the lines of: "he had interesting things to say on interesting subjects and now he's not saying them anymore. And that is just sad."

What would you (I) want your (my) authors' epitaph to say?

The second one concerns deciding how much we want to blend in the current system of *intellectual prostitution*. John Kotter, referring to those who play that game, told me: "Well, they make their life choices, I make my life choices!"

What is your (my) life choice going to be?

EPILOGUE — SHAPING THE FUTURE OF MANAGEMENT (RESEARCH)

What does it take to have impact? Curiosity, anti-dogmatism, and patient-ambitious-perseverance might not get you there but they would surely give you a head start!

— Chapter 3

We need for management research what Impressionism has been for painting and music in the late 19th and early 20th century.

— Epilogue

At last, I am coming to the end of my journey. Or, I should say, to the end of its first leg: what I have discovered to date is only the initial clues and, borrowing John Kotter's words once again, these clues are only going to push me toward searching for new ones.

I have undoubtedly answered some questions — at least to my mind — with regards to how I can do more research that matters more and, hopefully, give my contribution to shaping the future of management. At the same time though, as I am writing this conclusive chapter, I have the strong feeling that I have just opened a Pandora's box and these answers are nothing more than new questions needing further investigation. There will be a time for that, I am sure.

Now though, I have to bring all the best pictures from the journey into an album of the most memorable moments.

Based on the evidence available, only the minor part of which I've discussed throughout this book, it is safe to argue that today the very community who should be leading the race to innovation has by and large given up. Regardless of what some might say, the very fact the scientific community is dominated by (and supports) the "publish or perish" culture is proof to such statement.

Ashamedly, the focus has been brought on meaningless measures of alleged research impact rather than on doing insightful research. The goal is not anymore to do research to better understand and consequently influence the way we live, work, and manage. It is merely to flood the literature with meaningless reports that, at best, incrementally add to what we already know on subjects on phenomena that we have already studied or observed.

This is all due to the fact that research output is measured in quantitative terms (i.e., number of articles and citations) rather than real impact or influence terms. That's like playing football aiming for newspaper headlines or TV appearances rather than for having the game of your life! Can you imagine Al Pacino in *Any Given Sunday* pushing his team to aim for 10 first-page headlines? I doubt he would have had the same motivational effect as he had with his unforgettable half-time speech.

We are teaching and learning how to trick the system of management research in order to make our work fit within a rotten framework, rather than spending time and energy on what really matters.

As with all complex issues, this is not an easy problem to solve. Although, I do wonder if (and indeed propose that) we should start measuring and investing in *inputs*, rather than *outputs*. If we do that, then we would maybe start asking important questions such as: How well are we teaching and mentoring younger scholars to study the romantic problems of their choice with perseverance and ambition? Are we creating an environment whose culture rewards responsible use of public and private funding to generate meaningful insight? How widely are we spreading such meaningful insight? How well are we championing those who are willing to try and fail and who always keep themselves accountable for what they do?

We need to go back to fostering 'scholarship' as originally defined: creative work whose integrity is measured by the ability to *think*, *communicate*, and *learn*. By measuring our ability to create the underlying conditions for *doing research that matters*, rather than focusing on the outcome, we might be able to shift from a reactive short-term attitude to a proactive long-term vision.

I am convinced that if we approach a journey by looking only at how good the final destination is, we are going to lose the opportunity to learn, influence, and just enjoy the very journey that is going to take us there.

We have little chances to influence people into buying into our insight, but we sure as hell *can* and *should* influence what *we* can do to ensure that our insight is meaningful.

In this book, I have argued that there are three key components to *doing research that matters*: the *Insight Generator* (responsible for creating), the *Insight Incubator* (responsible for enabling), and the *Insight Distributor* (responsible for spreading). These three elements do not inhabit entirely separate worlds. On the contrary, for research to matter there must be an alignment of values among the three.

In the same way as excellent research is collaborative, every element in the model can and should influence the values and cultures of the others. In the wrong, unsupportive environment, even the brightest of talents might not flourish. And in the right environment, where some excellent research is done, all the good work could amount to very little if the distribution end did not go on to play its part in spreading the message.

As promised, I am going to collate as much of the insight I have gathered in the research behind this book as possible into this final chapter, using the "Research That Matters" model as a container for that insight.

The Ideal *Insight Generator*

For as long as I can remember since I started my career in research, I have tried to understand the difference between management researchers and management consultants. As a matter of fact, I must have asked this question to hundreds of colleagues and people I have met at conferences or working on projects. Generally, I have received many variations of the same answer, over and over again. Academic researchers talk poorly of management consultants for their mere attempt to transfer 'known' best practices from one project or company to another; conversely, management consultants condemn the work of academic researchers for being too theoretical, behind the trend, and non-usable.

In my attempt to profiling the typical *Futureer*, that is, the ideal *Insight Generator*, I asked some of the *Futureers* what they thought characterizes one and another professional role.

As you should expect by now, they did not focus on the limitations of the two, but rather pointed to what we could take from either to build our ideal *Insight Generator*. Most agreed with Henry Mintzberg, who would accept "a merger of ... two dysfunctional ways of training the world."

Roger Martin also sees a convergence of the two worlds, where "you have management researchers who care about problems that management has and try to come up with new knowledge on those and you have strategy consultants who recognise that you can't solve every problem by benchmarking it to practices when there is no practice, and there is nobody solving the problem at hand, and you have to come up with innovative ways to think through new problems. So, there is a meeting in the middle between the *very very best* of management researchers and the *very very best* of strategy consultants."

So that is it! That is what *Futureers* are! And that is what management researchers who aim to do *research that matters* should aim to become: the *very, very best* of one world blending with the *very, very best* of the other. Like Hamel's practice-oriented theoreticians blending with theory-oriented practitioners.

But defining *Futureers* simply by looking at what they *do* would be too restrictive. Through the information and the many excerpts from the interviews reported in the preceding pages, it is clear that *Futureers* can also be described for what they *are*.

Why do I think it is important to do so? Because I agree with John Kotter that if somebody has got some "inflammation" for *doing research that matters*, most of whatever else is needed in terms of skills and attitude can be learnt or developed. So, it makes sense to have a look at some of the key facets of the *Futureers'* character that have emerged.

Futureers are definitely curious, anti-dogmatic, patient, ambitious, and perseverant.

In fact, curiosity and a willingness to explore new territories appear to be key characteristics that come up again and again. Answering difficult questions about which little is known was regularly cited by the Nobel laureates and management gurus alike as one of the main drivers for what they do. Costa Markides observed that, before any intellectual or analytical rigor is brought to bear, researchers should ask themselves whether work has a fresh feel about it. It's the "a-ah, I have never thought about it like that" factor, says Markides, which makes the researcher think instinctively that they should pursue the topic. And Kaplan suggested: "looking for areas where the current wisdom of our practice is inadequate relative to some standard you have in your mind."

Curiosity also often comes from the keenness to follow one's interests even if these very interests took you down a very different path than the one on which you had set out. Interests can change, of course, as can inclinations depending on where people's talents lie, a serendipitous encounter, inspiration, or encouragement by a colleague or a friend.

As we have learned, John Kotter's start in Physics owed everything to the United States wanting to win the space race against the USSR. But Kotter realized that he would never be a great Physicist. In looking for a different area where he could make a real contribution he hit upon Electrical Engineering at the Massachusetts Institute of Technology, and it was that path that led him finally to his interest in organizations and leadership. Similarly, Kaplan started doing operations research using mathematics to study stylized problems drawn from the real world to then move into accountancy by a serendipitous request by his employer to teach a class for which they did not have a lecturer.

Chemist Venkatraman Ramakrishnan, who shared the 2009 Nobel Prize in Chemistry with Thomas A. Steitz and Ada E. Yonath, for studies of the structure and function of the ribosome, started out as a Theoretical Physicist. He admits[1]: "My PhD work was on a problem that was not particularly interesting to me at the time. And I used to subscribe to *Scientific American* and I found that there were all these wonderful discoveries happening in biology and I also knew that a number of physicists had gone into biology and been successful. So, I decided to switch."

His work on ribosomes goes back to 1978. He says: "It was just a fundamental [and not at the time solvable] problem in biology. And we felt, no matter, anything we do to chip away at the problem would be useful. So it was more that that attracted me. And I think the fact that it was large and kind of difficult to come to grips with, yes, it was attractive. Really what was attractive was that it was a fundamental problem."[2]

To solve such fundamental problems, *Futureers* are not afraid to propose research outputs in direct opposition to the mainstream paradigm or to the field's beliefs. Henry Mintzberg, for example, studying what managers actually do from out in the field, as opposed to studying what they should do from the University library, suggested that managers actually want to be interrupted. And that observation guided all his ground-breaking future research. Roger Martin as well taking the risky step to recommend that P&G switch its strategy from favoring retailers who followed a HiLo merchandising strategy to those following an EDLP strategy.

Allied to this is the resilience and perseverance required to keep going when others lack faith. Mario Capecchi discovered a way to create mice in which a specific gene was turned off. But, when initial experiments were followed by a long battle for funding, he needed the resilience of someone who had come through a tough war-time childhood.

He says: "Our first grant was actually refused with respect to that project, mainly because they didn't think it was possible. The probability that an exogenous piece of DNA would be able to find the cognate sequence in 33 base pairs was thought to be not a significant possibility. So I think that was the resistance, and I think we just had the feeling that if we could make the assay sensitive enough, we knew it was going to be a rare event, but if we could make the assay sensitive enough then we knew we might be able to detect it."[3]

Of course, it takes time to develop the right attitude, not just to do the research. As John Kotter says, "how much time you put into it makes a difference and how intense you work on it makes a difference."

In this regard, *Futureers* are also *Outliers*, that is "men and women who, for one reason or another, are so accomplished and so extraordinary and so outside of ordinary experience that they are as puzzling to the rest of us as a cold day in August."[4] Put simply, they are just prepared to put in the hours.

The truly dedicated will pursue their lines of inquiry indefatigably, often in the face of overwhelming odds, or when others are saying they are looking in the wrong place.

In this regard, *Futureers* are also *Enduringly Successful People* or *Builders*, that is, "people whose beginnings may be inauspicious but who eventually become defined by their creativity. At some point in their lives, [they] feel compelled to create something new or better that will endure throughout their lifetime and flourish well beyond."[5]

Ada E. Yonath admits that the worries she nursed affected her more than she had expected. In fact, she goes further, she was plagued by doubts throughout the entire process. She says: "I had doubts all the time ... there were lots of them." The way she described her research to somebody who was not a scientist is rather telling; "we felt ... that we are climbing mountains in order to reach the climax — and these mountains are like the Everest, the biggest most difficult to climb — only to find out that there is another mountain waiting behind it to be climbed afterwards.

"So every climbing was an achievement but there was a bigger problem behind it or above it. I had lots of [moments] that I didn't expect, but I thought science in general and this science particularly is worth the effort — even if we would never get the ultimate result."

The journey is ultimately worth it because the destination is so worthwhile (and vice versa): the impact that the research will have, even if, metaphorically, it demands that the travelers reach the Earth's highest peak, then descend and repeat the feat elsewhere. And that point about the journey also holds true whether it involves life-changing discoveries or it leads to a greater understanding of the world around us, and the way it operates — or perhaps the way it should operate.

This is what Rob Goffee was alluding to when he talked about the need for research to have an impact — no impact, he is saying, ultimately means no value of any great significance. Roger Martin's quest for "knowledge for action" is another interesting and important common across the *Futureers*.

Making a difference, no matter how big or how small, through their actions and the knowledge they generate is, ultimately, what drives *Futureers*.

Besides these key characteristics, many more have emerged, which I have collected in the word diagram below. The list is in no particular order whatsoever as there is not one attitude or facet of a *Futureers*' character that is more important than another. Going through the list (this one as well as the others I am about to introduce), you should simply be glad to find some that match your character and be keen to develop those which you don't recognize having.

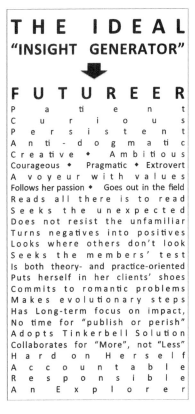

Recognizing the ideal Insight Generator.

The Ideal *Insight Incubator*

The *Insight Incubator* is the place of work of the *Insight Generator*, which can be a university, a research lab, or a company. Its role is simply but importantly to provide a controlled environment for 'hatching' and caring excellent researchers capable of *doing research that matters.*

In other words, the ideal *Insight Incubator* has the typical incubator's mentality. That is, it creates those ideal conditions for *Futureers* to thrive. If you accept the profile of the ideal *Insight Generator* that I presented above, then you should also accept that the ideal *Insight Incubator* invests long-term in hatching *Futureers* who can transform futures, while rewarding in the short-term those who commit to the same vision.

In practical terms, this means developing a culture based on a set of very distinct values, and creating rewards and promotion mechanisms in line with those values. From one side, the ideal *Insight Incubator* needs to be hands-off enough to let the researcher follow his or her true path while being controlling enough to make sure only the very best researchers can thrive and to weed out improper behaviors.

First, it creates opportunities for its researchers to formulate their own interests and research ideas, especially at the early stages of their career. Rather than pressing people to "publish or perish," the ideal *Insight Incubator* follows Harald zur Hausen's suggestion to create a relaxed environment where researchers have the freedom to find their romantic problems, experience various methods and find initial solutions, both of which might be imperfect.

At the same time, it also creates opportunities for researchers to go out in the field looking for real romantic problems. As all of the *Futureers* featured in the book have pointed out, very little happens in a university library and it is important for researchers to be out in the field, mingling with managers and observing the romantic problems they want to investigate in their natural environment. Some *Incubators* push their researchers to engage with consultancy activities, others favor executive education-type activities. As Rob Goffee says, in an ideal *Insight Incubator*, "it's quite difficult to separate out 'research' from a lot of other areas of work. The boundaries become blurred."

Furthermore, it should create opportunities for researchers to try out their ideas seeking both scientific and impact validation. As Markides suggested, a good researcher should be able to defend his own ideas in front of other academics, in particular for the rigor of the research process. Nonetheless, a good piece of research should also pass the member's test, as sociologists put it.

Harvard Business School, for example, creates such opportunities organizing reunions for MBA and executive program alumni. Robert Kaplan explained: "Every three or every five years the alumni come back to campus for two and a half days and during one of the days they have the talks by the faculty members, where the faculty members are talking about their research ... and actually talking to our alumni who are leaders and managers about what we're working on, what are the insights we have and how these might apply."

He adds: "I think [that] if you can get that group of people saying 'I'm glad you're working on that problem, I can see why that's an interesting problem and I'd be interested in the solution to that problem' [then] that's the definition to me of impact."

Finally, the ideal *Insight Incubator* should also cooperate with *Insight Distributors* to ensure that only the very best research insight spread, and it should reward those researchers who are either capable to generate it or fail to generate it while trying.

Defining and rigorously implementing a culture based on these values is also conducive to a better, more collaborative process. Good research collaboration, as we saw earlier, is not dependent on two people working in perfect harmony or even being in total agreement about beliefs and goals. It is about shared values, compatibility of personality, and complementarity of competences.

Universities and research environments that support the "publish or perish" mindset are clearly at the antithesis of this, because they have become concerned above all with mere quantity, not real influence (and therefore don't deserve to be called *Insight Incubators*). As soon as this becomes the ultimate objective, the whole focus changes and the range of inquiry becomes narrow and even banal, because, as Costa Markides pointed out, those who become too focused on short-term goals are more likely to ask uninteresting questions and, consequently, find uninteresting solutions. These can be satisfied with easy (and perhaps already known) answers.

Answering tough and truly demanding questions take rather longer. That is why the ideal *Insight Generator* as well as the ideal *Insight Incubator* have a long-term focus.

As Dave Ulrich points out, there are further lessons which academia and business can learn from one another in a changing world, and which have implications for management research. He says: "In universities, tenure was the ultimate mark of performance, which assured one the capacity to create outside traditional boundaries. But, just as tenure is losing its lustre, so is guaranteed employment. In a world of competitiveness, transparency, and accountability, individuals who perform well will be duly rewarded and those who don't must face equally severe consequences.

"It is more difficult than ever to feather-bed employees. This means that leaders must constantly be challenging employees to learn and grow and that employees must realize that what they have done counts, but not as much as what they still can do."

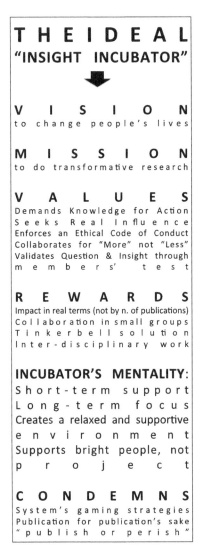

Recognizing the ideal Insight Incubator.

The Ideal *Insight Distributor*

Distribution is the third and last fundamental enabler for *doing research that matters*. The ideal *Insight Distributor* is a channel built to spread meaningful insight as widely as possible so that it can be validated in the scientific community, adopted and consequently tested in the community it might eventually influence, refined and further developed by the research it originates, and supported by funders who believe in it. It must enable the *Insight Generator* to communicate their message to different audiences using ad-hoc strategies.

It is also a channel whose culture and values are aligned with those I summarized above for the *Insight Generator* and *Incubator*, of course.

Scholarly journals, as they have become these days, are just not fit for purpose. All *Futureers* have underlined that they are *full of marginally interesting stuff*, they *make researchers slave of methodologies* and they *foster a continuously more inward looking approach to research* in each field. Academic publishing hinders the impact of potentially meaningful insight also by delaying its spreading because of the long and less than perfect review process, which means that months (at least) or years (more likely) go by before an idea reaches its target community.

Academic publishing must catch up with the 21st century to continue being a player in the *doing research that matters* game. Doing that is the responsibility of publishers, editors, authors, readers, and *Insight Incubators*. All must shift from focusing on quantity to focusing on the ability to generate real impact and true influence.

This means *Insight Distributors* as well need to be courageous: supporting *research that matters* means going against the mainstream, which is the "publish or perish" mentality, again. But, as it should be rather clear by now, you don't get to be part of success by staying in the mainstream. Not in the world of management research and management innovation, you don't.

Granted, *Insight Distributors* are for the most commercial entities for which the profit model is based on selling more of what buyers buy. As I was discussing this point with a colleague working in publishing, she sent me an email asking point blank: "how do you propose publishers can continue to make money if they stop selling ISI journals when ISI journals are what University libraries want to buy?" That's a fair point. As I was thinking about my reply, I realized that the answer might lie in changing the revenue model, that is, to stop trying to sell the wrong product to the wrong crowd. Rather than selling thousands of meaningless articles to university libraries for a few thousand pounds per volume, why not trying to sell meaningful insight to those who are going to use it for the real value it generates or even for a portion of the benefit they may accrue by acting on it? This might translate into executive education products, professional magazines-type products or even facilitating the distribution of ideas through matching communities with those who study and generate innovation for those communities.

This might be too far-fetched an idea, and I am not claiming to have found the answer to the problem. On the contrary, the thesis I am defending in this book is that to change the system of management research we must see a parallel change in the three key areas of insight incubation, generation, and distribution, and that such change must start at the individual level, where few individuals operating in each of these three areas can find the courage to initiate the change.

Talking about academic publishers as *Insight Distributors*, laudable is the example set by some CEOs of publishing companies, like former Emerald's CEO, John Peters, who pointed out the deficiencies of their element in the system and tried to do something about it.

At the same time, the type of cultural shift we are talking about here might also require that outlets other than (and more effective than) academic journals should gain more recognition within the scientific community.

There is a lot of merit to Robert Kaplan's notion of creating publications where younger researchers can have more freedom to do "ground, descriptive research, work at the problem level, give us some insights based on small samples and write it in ways that are rigorous and that people will accept," rather than being side-tracked by pressure to conform.

Along these lines, Roger Martin points out an initiative by Michael C. Jensen, former Professor at Harvard Business School and co-author together with William H. Meckling of the *Theory of the Firm: Managerial Behavior, Agency Costs and Ownership Structure*, published in the *Journal of Financial Economics*."[6] It is worth noting that their paper has gone on to become the most-cited academic business article of all times.[7] According to Martin, "[Jensen] is of the view that the current journals are devoid of new ideas and he is in the process of launching a series of management journals that are all for new ideas ..."

Jensen founded the Social Science Research Network (SSRN) in 1994 and he is currently SSRN Chairman and Integrity Officer. The SSRN vision was and still is "to enable scholars to share and distribute their research worldwide, long before their papers work their way through the multi-year journal refereeing and publication process. ... at the lowest cost possible for authors and readers."[8]

The importance of having some type of refereeing system that acts as a distribution filter is not in question. However, it is not easy to identify what type exactly works. But, once again, starting from the well-known fact that what we have today does not work and trying to do something differently is better than to sit and do nothing.

As Roger Martin himself observes: "How do you referee those [open access journals] so that they are rigorous is of course a challenge. It's not an easy question. But I do think [it is important] ... that several people who have got together and said we are going to have a journal that says, across the field of management, that we're going to break out new ideas, that [these ideas] will be measured on the basis of how different they are, even if they are not yet ... rigorously [developed] from a methodological standpoint, ... that will probably be the best [that we can do to solve the current problem we have in scientific publishing]."

Journals and academic publishing are not the only distribution channel available though. As *Insight Generators* and *Incubators* we must recognize that there exist other *Insight Distributors* like, for example, cutting-edge consulting companies such as Kotter International (and I would humbly include my own, Carisma RCT). History of management innovation shows us that consulting is certainly effective in distributing a worthy idea and gaining supporters for further spreading.

Books as well, and not necessarily academic books, are widely acknowledged to be excellent distributors of meaningful insight as they allow researchers to creatively generate and communicate insight at the same time.

Needless to say, and in line with this idea that for management research to be insightful it must connect with the real world of management in one way or another, managerially relevant journals should be given more importance as they do undoubtedly allow insight to spread like wildfire.

Paul Krugman, with his newspaper columns and twitter feeds, gives us another excellent example of how we should make better use of the media to reach parts of the community which we would never reach through more common scientific or industrial publishing.

Last, we can't ignore the power of technology-enabled distribution and networking in reaching an even wider population.

In conclusion, the ideal *Insight Distributor* also continuously studies ways to integrate all channels available, including print, digital, media, etc. so as to guarantee the widest possible reach of the insight it spreads.

T H E I D E A L
"INSIGHT DISTRIBUTOR"

Enables MAXIMUM spreading
Pioneer ◆ Courageous
Anti-dogmatic ◆ Open
Facilitates up-take ◆ Facilitates validation
Adopts Tinkerbell Solution
Cares for younger scholars
Invites all forms of research
Focuses on quality, not quantity
Facilitates more conducive language
Stops gaming of an imperfect system
Facilitates spreading of meaningful insight
Acts as a filter for non-meaningful insight
Welcomes paradigm shifting contributions
Aims for a balance of rigor, relevance,
creativity ◆ Integrates all distribution channels

Recognizing the ideal Insight Distributor.

The Ultimate Destination: *Research That Matters*

Assuming *Incubators* develop the right incubator's mentality, they will then be able to hatch *Futureers* who will keenly commit to tackle romantic problems and put in the hard work it's required to solve them. And assuming we all contribute to creating distribution channels that ensure the maximum spreading of these solutions, then, and only then, we will end up truly with *research that matters*.

Rather than repeating what I have said so far, I am going to try to list in the word diagram below some of the key words that I would use to describe the characteristics of *research that matters*, as I have learned from this journey.

Pioneer
Creative
It is used
Rewarding
Initiates further research
Challenges the underlying assumptions
Orthogonal to current thinking, anti-dogmatic
IT TACKLES A ROMANTIC PROBLEM
THEORETICALLY REACH, EMPIRICALLY SOUND, MANAGERIALLY RELEVANT, INSIGHTFUL
Generates knowledge we do not already have
Connected with the real world
Passes the members' test
Influences behaviour
Makes you proud
Challenging
Rigorous
Timely
Fun

Recognizing Research That Matters.

The only point worth repeating in this conclusive chapter is about this idea that management research has to be useful to matter. In management research, the worlds of theoretical and practical research are inextricably bound up with one another. When talking about his field, Edmund Phelps, who was awarded the 2006 Nobel Memorial Prize in Economic Sciences, summarizes extremely well what in this book I have argued are the pillars of *research that matters* to the management field[9]:

> "… there is sometimes a sense that the concepts are not clear, that the questions being asked are not clear, and so you have to dig deeper. So that kind of basic [theoretical] research has to always be a part of our portfolio of research activities.

"But at the same time applied research is necessary too because if we don't do any applied research we may miss learning that some of our models have implications that appear to be contrary to the data, appear to be counter-factual, not empirically borne out. A healthy economics has got to have both conceptual, theoretical research and applied, empirical research. Well, I think of myself as a theorist, so I think of myself at the conceptual end, but I would like to say, modestly if possible, that I have paid pretty close attention to questions of whether the data are consistent with what my models say."

A Matter of Ethical Responsibility

I started this book by stating my assumption that, as management researchers, a commitment to generating meaningful insight should be part of our ethical conduct. As I was evaluating how this idea fits within the bigger context of research quality, I found a report published in 2005 by The Swedish Research Council's expert group on ethics,[10] by the title *Good Research Practice*. In the report, the authors investigate the relationship between good scientific quality and good research ethics. In particular, they ask whether there might be conflicts between the natural requirement for research to be ethical and the requirement for research to be of good scientific quality.

Gustafsson, Hermerén, and Pettersson identify two types of such potential conflicts: (1) certain ethical criteria make it harder to reach new and valuable knowledge, and (2) certain ethical criteria make it impossible to reach new and valuable knowledge.

Although their discussion focuses more on ethical issues such as the need to get research participant consent and be academically honest, their conclusion is applicable to the context of *research that matters* as well. As a matter of fact, their definition of poor research ethics is in line with the one adopted here (although, once again, we can see here the association of 'research outcome' with 'publication', which I have argued is not ideal): "a research report exhibits poor research ethics if it contains scientific shortcomings in the precision of its questions, uses incorrect methods (or uses established methods incorrectly), systematically excludes observations that do not support the author's hypothesis, handles the problem of dropout in a statistically unacceptable way, or uses a study design that does not allow for the research question to be answered."

Therefore, if *doing research that matters* were an ethical responsibility of the management researcher and, consequently, a criterion we should use to evaluate research, could there be a conflict of interest between the requirement for research to matter and for it to be ethical?

"The criteria for good scientific quality" the Swedish authors say "can have both broad and narrow interpretations. In a narrow interpretation these criteria are met by research that provides new knowledge, reveals conditions not previously known or sheds new light on previously known phenomena and relationships ... With this narrow interpretation, the content of the criteria for good scientific quality is not completely unequivocal, as research can meet many of these criteria to higher and lower degrees ... Nevertheless, it is important to remember that the concept of scientific quality is used in a broader sense as well. In such cases this entails an overall judgment from which it is not possible to single out individual criteria. When the total quality of the research is evaluated, no single quality can be ignored. The quality is evaluated based on the collective qualities of originality, external and internal validity, precision and ethics. The requirement of good research ethics is thus included here."

Their conclusion is unequivocal: "there can be no conflict between the demands for good research ethics and good scientific quality ... Against this background it is reasonable to regard work to improve the ethical aspects of the research as a quality issue."

So, if you agree with (a) my assumption that doing research that does not matter is unethical, and (b) the definition of *research that matters* and its fundamental characteristics that I have outlined in this book, then you should agree with me that the quality of management research should inherently be measured by whether or not the insight it generates is *theoretically reach, empirically sound, managerially relevant, and insightful.*

Just Talking the Talk, or Also Walking the Walk?

As I have come to the end of the road, I wonder whether the research I have done and discussed in this book meets the criteria of *research that matters.* The honest answer is: I am still a long way away from rightfully claiming that it does, but I feel it's a good start.

As I compare my personal characteristics (i.e., *Insight Generator*), those of my company (i.e., *Insight Incubator*) and those of my publisher (i.e., *Insight Distributor*) to those I have summarized in the three elements of the model, I must admit that the underlying conditions for this research to eventually matter are undoubtedly there.

If I use the same model to compare my research output against benchmarks of excellence as defined here, I can also see where it fell off the mark.

If you agree with my conclusions, then consider the model validated and feel free to start spreading the word.

Self-assessment: does my research matter?

In the end, I might just have to work harder, and I will. But, for now, I return to Dr. Milton Chen to underline that "the point of doing rather than trying is to make no mistake about your intention. Your effort must be an intentional one, filled with sincerity and emotional commitment rather than half-hearted compromise."[11]

I can wholeheartedly confirm that my effort has been just that!

From Incrementalism to Impressionism[12]

I am 100% convinced that Costas Markides' suggestion to change the underlying purpose of the system of management research from publishing to solving romantic problems is the only way we have to foster more management-research-led innovation.

As we were discussing the "publish or perish" culture promoted from within the scientific community, Roger Martin observed: "We have gotten into the mode of honouring incrementalism and being extremely harsh on new thinking. If people on the outside knew how incredibly conservative the world of academia is, there would be a firestorm of protest. People on the other side think that the academic world is full of creativity and great new ideas but if they knew how conservative it is, they would hesitate seriously ... because ..., it's so incremental, so methodologically driven ... It makes it harder for new ideas to flourish. We are way more conservative and incremental than it is sensible."

This absurd "publish or perish" mentality is like a disease that has spread deep into the tissues of the international scholarly system causing the impoverishment of innovation (in management and beyond). I do wonder whether it has now gone so deep that it has become incurable. That might very well be but we must try anyway to do what we can to revert this trend at all costs.

No revolution has ever been easy. This one wouldn't either.

We need for management innovation and management research what Impressionism has been for painting and music in the late 19th and early 20th century.

This is not the place for a comprehensive historical overview of the Impressionism movement and I am neither a historian nor an art authority. So I hope you will be lenient with me for the elementary attempt I am about to make to illustrate why I believe impressionists should serve as examples for management innovators today.

Impressionism originated out of the dissatisfaction of a group of French painters in the late 19th century with the conventional emphasis that academic teaching used to give onto a specific mode of painting. By ways of comparison, a group of management researchers, that is those who can rightfully call themselves *Futureers*, are clearly dissatisfied with today's conventional emphasis the academic system places on quantity rather than quality and real influence. The conditions are there for a new movement to emerge led by few brave management researchers who believe in the importance of *doing research that matters* more than they are afraid of never making it and, consequently, of living a life of anonymity.

Back to the Impressionists: led by Manet they radically changed the concept of aesthetic, in which the importance of the traditional subject matter was demoted and attention was shifted to the artist's manipulation of color, tone, and texture as ends in themselves. Similarly, we need management researchers to let go of the current approach to measuring impact by counting publications and to start shifting their attention to the intent for doing research and the research journey as the ends in themselves.

Back to the Impressionists: they also adopted Boudin's practice of painting entirely outdoors while looking at the actual scene, instead of painting from sketches in the studio, as was the conventional practice. Here again the similarities with the world of management research are striking: management researchers should conduct their research mostly out in the field, while looking at the actual phenomenon they want to study or the behavior they want to represent, rather than sit in their offices or university libraries.

Back to Impressionists: they abandoned traditional formal compositions in favor of a more casual and less artificial disposition of objects within the picture frame. And so should management researchers do: abandon "publish or perish" imposed methodologies and favor a more open-minded approach to doing research, which allows for a multitude set of methodologies used to enhance our understanding of the world, rather than restrict it.

In conclusion, where Impressionists embraced the principles of freedom of technique, *Futureers* will embrace freedom of methodology; where impressionists took a personal approach to the subject, *Futureers* will have the courage to propose ideas that are anti-dogmatic; where Impressionists sought the truthful reproduction of nature, *Futureers* will seek to observe first-hand the phenomena they are studying.

What should we expect if we start such an Impressionist movement in management research?

Well, Impressionists had to organize their first show in 1874 independently from the official Salon of the French Academy as this last had consistently rejected most of their works. They were publicly humiliated by 'the system': journalist Louis Leroy derided Monet's *Impression: Sunrise* (1872; Musée Marmottan, Paris) in the satirical magazine Le Charivari in 1874.

But they persevered against all odds, they held seven more shows, and, more importantly, they accomplished a revolution in the history of art, providing a technical starting point for the Post-impressionist artists and freeing all Western painting that followed from traditional techniques.

So if the parallel holds, then we, management researchers and innovators, can expect to suffer much ridicule and face many hurdles, probably. Getting promoted and making a name for ourselves is not going to be easy. Our manuscripts might get rejected a few (or many) times. But if we manage to stick to our objective to influence people's lives and if we keep being guided by the right values, we can expect everlasting legacy in the long term. We should only hope to be able to revolutionize the approach to management research, to shape the future of management, and to provide a technical starting point for future generations, who will not be slaves of traditional methodologies and approaches to measuring research quality.

That might be a grand aim, but if you have gotten thus far in the book, you and me both share the desire to change the world and this is as good a starting point as any.

Besides, as Theodore Roosevelt famously said during his *The Strenuous Life* speech before the Hamilton club in Chicago in 1899:

> "Far better it is to dare mighty things, to win glorious triumphs, even though checkered by failure, than to take rank with those poor spirits who neither enjoy much nor suffer much, because they live in the gray twilight that knows not victory nor defeat."[13]

In line with the approach I have adopted for this book, I would like to conclude borrowing yet again the words of one of the *Futureers* who have made this journey possible, Harvard Business School's Emeritus Professor John Kotter: "I think the questions you've asked are interesting questions and there are lots more obviously [that] you could add to your list ..."

"Do I have anything to add? No. Nothing that could be said simply."

ENDNOTES

PROLOGUE

1. Stein, G. (2010). *Managing people and organizations: Peter Drucker's legacy.* Bingley, UK: Emerald.
2. Bisoux, T. (2008). The innovation generation. BizEd, September/October 2008, 18–25.
3. *ibid.*
4. Gross, R. (1993). *The independent scholar's handbook.* Berkeley, CA: Ten Speed Press.
5. Shapiro, G. (2004). Oh, to freely pursue the scholarly life! *The New York Sun,* October 15, "Knickerbocker" column, p. 16.
6. Retrieved from www.thinkers50.com/about. Accessed regularly throughout 2009, 2010, 2011, and 2012.
7. Retrieved from www.nobelprize.org/nobel_prizes/economics. Accessed regularly throughout 2009, 2010, 2011, and 2012.
8. Bisoux, T. (2008). The innovation generation. *BizEd,* September/October 2008, 18–25.
9. Davenport, T. H., Prusak, L., & Wilson, H. J. (2003). *What's the big idea, creating and capitalizing on the best management thinking.* Boston, MA: Harvard Business School Press.
10. Kiechel III, W. (2010). *The lords of strategy: The secret intellectual history of the new corporate world.* New York, NY: Harvard Business School Press.
11. Porras, J., Emery, S., & Thompson, M. (2007). *Success built to last* (p. 131). Upper Saddle River, NJ: Wharton School Publishing.

INTRODUCTION

1. Based on information collated from http://www.nobelprize.org, accessed on October 6, 2012; http://www.chemistryviews.org, accessed on October 6, 2012; http://www.nndb.com/people/969/000163480/, accessed on October 5, 2012; http://www.research-in-germany.de/main/researcher-portraits/nobel-laureates/73028/gerhard-ertl.html, accessed on October 6, 2012; Superstars of Science

website, http://superstarsofscience.com/scientist/gerhard-ertl, accessed on October 6, 2012.

2. Retrieved from http://superstarsofscience.com/. Accessed on October 6, 2012.

3. Based on information collated from http://www.whyshouldanyonebeledbyyou.com/, accessed on October 6, 2012; http://www.london.edu, accessed on October 6, 2012; Thinkers50's website, http://www.thinkers50.com/biographies/72, accessed on October 6, 2012.

4. Based on information collated from http://erewhon.ticonuno.it/2002/scienza/hack/bio.htm, accessed on October 6, 2012; http://www.leggo.it/, Pascucci Interview with Margherita Hack published May 7, 2012 and accessed on October 6, 2012.

5. Based on information collated from http://www.hbs.edu/faculty/Pages/profile.aspx?facId=6487, accessed on October 5, 2012; http://fisher.osu.edu/departments/accounting-and-mis/the-accounting-hall-of-fame/membership-in-hall/robert-samuel-kaplan, accessed on October 5, 2012; Thinkers50's website http://www.thinkers50.com/biographies/16, accessed on October 6, 2012.

6. Based on information collated from http://barbarakellerman.com/, accessed on October 5, 2012; Thinkers50's website http://www.thinkers50.com/biographies/100, accessed on October 5, 2012 and http://www.hks.harvard.edu/fs/bkeller/, accessed on October 6, 2012.

7. Based on information collated from http://www.kotlermarketing.com/, accessed on October 6, 2012; Thinkers50's website http://www.thinkers50.com/biographies/11, accessed on October 6, 2012 and http://www.kellogg.northwestern.edu/faculty/directory/kotler_philip.aspx, accessed on October 6, 2012.

8. Based on information collated from http://www.hbs.edu/faculty/Pages/profile.aspx?facId=6495, accessed on October 5, 2012; Thinkers50's website http://www.thinkers50.com/biographies/41, accessed on October 5, 2012 and http://www.speakersbulgaria.com/ on October 6, 2012.

9. Based on information collated from http://howardgardner.com, accessed on October 5, 2012; http://www.infed.org/thinkers/gardner.htm, accessed on October 5, 2012; Thinkers50's website http://www.thinkers50.com/biographies/83, accessed on October 5, 2012.

10. Based on information collated from http://www.businessweek.com/authors/3521-costas_markides, accessed on October 6, 2012; http://www.london.edu/facultyandresearch/faculty/search.do?uid=cmarkides, accessed on October 6, 2012; Thinkers50's website http://www.thinkers50.com/biographies/74, accessed on October 6, 2012.

11. Based on information collated from http://rogerlmartin.com, accessed on October 5, 2012; Thinkers50's website http://www.thinkers50.com/biographies/95, accessed on October 5, 2012.

12. Based on information collated from http://www.mintzberg.org/; Bradshaw, D. (2006). Henry Mintzberg: Biography. Published October 23, 2006 on www.ft.com, UK; the Strategic Management Society's website http://strategicmanagement.net/bio.php?u=5283, accessed on October 5, 2012; Thinkers50's website http://www.thinkers50.com/biographies/8, accessed on October 5, 2012.

13. Based on information collated from http://www.nobelprize.org, accessed on October 6, 2012; https://physics.stanford.edu/people/faculty/douglas-osheroff, accessed on October 6, 2012; http://www.jewishvirtuallibrary.org/jsource/biography/osheroff.html, accessed on October 5, 2012.

14. Based on information collated from http://www.nobelprize.org, accessed on October 15, 2012; http://newsinfo.iu.edu/news/page/normal/22577.html, accessed on October 15, 2012; http://www.nytimes.com/2012/06/13/business/elinor-ostrom-winner-of-nobel-in-economics-dies-at-78.html, accessed on October 12, 2012; http://www.economist.com/node/21557717, accessed on October 15, 2012.

15. Based on information collated from http://www.nobelprize.org, accessed on October 5, 2012; http://ccib.mgh.harvard.edu/, accessed on October 5, 2012; http://www.hms.harvard.edu/, accessed on October 5, 2012.

16. Based on information collated from http://daveulrich.com/, accessed on October 6, 2012; http://execed.bus.umich.edu/Faculty/FacultyBio.aspx?id=000120058, accessed on October 6, 2012; Thinkers50's website http://www.thinkers50.com/biographies/85, accessed on October 5, 2012.

17. Based on information collated from http://www.nndb.com/people/305/000176774/, accessed on October 6, 2012; http://www.nobelprize.org, accessed on October 6, 2012; http://www.dkfz.de/en/zurhausen/index.html, accessed on October 6, 2012.

Chapter 1

1. Bisoux, T. (2008). The innovation generation. *BizEd*, September/October 2008, pp. 18–25.

2. *ibid*.

3. Schiller, B. (2011). Academia strives for relevance. *Financial Times*, 25 April, p. 11. Retrieved from http://www.ft.com/cms/s/2/4eeab7d4-6c37-11e0-a049-00144feab49a.html#axzz2Bvf5YChO.

4. AACSB. (2007). Final report of the AACSB international: Impact of Research.

5. *ibid*, p. 10.

6. See for example: Goldman, 1977 Toward more meaningful research. *The Personnel and Guidance Journal*, 55(6), 363–368; Boyer, E. L. (1982). Scholarship reconsidered: Priorities of the professoriate. *Issues in Accounting Education*, 7(1); Beer, M. (2001). Why management research findings are unimplementable: An action science perspective. *Reflections, 2*(3), 58–65; Salmon, P. (2003). How do we recognize good research? *The Psychologist, 16*(1); Kieser, A., & Nicolai, A. T. (2005). Success factor research: Overcoming the trade-off between rigor and relevance? *Journal of Management Inquiry, 14*(3), 275–279; Mentzer, J. T., & Schumann, D. W. (2006). The theoretical and practical implications of marketing scholarship. *Journal of Marketing Theory and Practice, 14*(3), 179–190; Pfeffer, J., & Sutton, R. I. (2006). *Hard facts, half-truths, and total nonsense: Profitting from evidence-based management*. Boston, MA: Harvard

Business School Press; Van de Ven, A. H., & Johnson, P. E. (2006). Knowledge for theory and practice. *Academy of Management Review, 31*(4), 802–821; Lawrence, P. A. (2008). Lost in publication: How measurement harms science. *Ethics in Science and Environmental Politics, 8,* 9–11; Lorsch, J. W. (2009). Regaining lost relevance. *Journal of Management Inquiry, 18*(2), 108–117.

7. Goldman, L. (1977). Toward more meaningful research. *The Personnel and Guidance Journal, 55*(6), 363–368.

8. *Ibid,* p. 365.

9. See for example: Mintzberg, H. (2005). Developing theory about the development of theory. In K. G. Smith, & M. A. Hitt (Eds), *Great minds in management: The process of theory development* (pp. 355–372). Oxford: Oxford University Press; or Kaplan, R. (1998). Innovation action research: Creating new management theory and practice. *Journal of Management Accounting Research, 10,* ABI/INFORM Global, pp. 89–118

10. Starbuck, W. H. (2004). Why I stopped trying to understand the real world. *Organization Studies, 25*(7), 1233–1254.

11. Starbuck, W. H. (2007). Why researchers should sometimes seek out opportunities to cooperate with managers. (A contribution to "On the relationship between research and practice: Debate and reflections" by James P. Walsh, Michael L. Tushman, John R. Kimberly, Bill Starbuck, and Susan Ashford.) *Journal of Management Inquiry, 16,* 128–154.

12. Stone, D. L. (2010). Creating knowledge that makes important contributions to society. *Journal of Managerial Psychology, 25*(3), 192–200.

13. Lee, T. W. (2009). The management professor. *Academy of Management Review, 34*(2), 196–199.

14. Busi, M., & McIvor, R. (2008). Setting the outsourcing research agenda: The top-10 most urgent outsourcing areas. *Strategic Outsourcing: An International Journal, 1*(3), 185–197.

15. Bisoux, T. (2008). The innovation generation. *BizEd,* September/October 2008, pp. 18–25.

16. *ibid.*

17. Kaplan, R. (1998). Innovation action research: Creating new management theory and practice. *Journal of Management Accounting Research, 10,* ABI/INFORM Global, pp. 89–118.

18. Kaplan, R. (2010). Accounting scholarship that advances professional knowledge and practice. *The Accounting Review, American Accounting Association, 86*(2), 367–383.

19. *Journal of Management Inquiry, 18*(4), December 2009, 263–264.

20. Miller, D., Greenwood, R., & Prakash, R. (2009). What happened to organization theory? Journal of Management Inquiry, 18(4), 273–279.

21. Palmer, D., Dick, B., & Freiburger, N. (2009). Rigor and relevance in organization studies. *Journal of Management Inquiry, 18*(4), 265–272.

22. Murray, D. S. (1971). That's interesting: Towards a phenomenology of sociology and a sociology of phenomenology. *Philosophy of the Social Sciences, 1*(4), 309.

23. Cooper, W. C., & McAllister, L. (1999). Can research be basic and applied? You bet. It better be for B-schools! *Socio-Economic Planning Sciences, 33*(4), 257–276.
24. Beer, M. (2001). Why management research findings are unimplementable: An action science perspective. *Reflections, 2*(3), 58–65.
25. Adler, N. J., & Harzing, A. W. (2009). When knowledge wins: Transcending the sense and nonsense of academic rankings. *Academy of Management Learning & Education, 8*(1), 72–95.
26. Starbuck, W. H. (2005). How much better are the most-prestigious journals? The statistics of academic publication. *Organization Studies, 16*(2), 180–200.
27. Worrell, D. L. (2009). Assessing business scholarship: The difficulties in moving beyond the rigor-relevance paradigm trap. *Academy of Management Learning & Education, 8*(1), 127–130.
28. Bennis, W. G., & O'Toole, J. (2005). How business schools lost their way. *Harvard Business Review, 83*(5), 96–104.
29. Polzer, J. T., Gulati, R., Khurana, R., & Tushman, M. L. (2009). Crossing boundaries to increase relevance in organizational research. *Journal of Management Inquiry, 18*(4), 280–286.
30. Hughes, T., O'Regan, N., & Wornham, D. (2009). Let's talk: Getting business and academia to collaborate. *Journal of Business Strategy, 30*(5), 49–56.
31. Markides, C. (2011). Crossing the chasm: How to convert relevant research into managerially useful research. *The Journal of Applied Behavioral Science, 47*(1), 121–134.
32. Bartunek, J. M., & Rynes, S. L. (2010). The construction and contributions of "implications for practice:" What's in them and what might they offer? *Academy of Management Learning & Education, 8*(1), 100–117.

CHAPTER 2

1. Bisoux, T. (2008). The innovation generation. *BizEd*, September/October 2008, pp. 18–25.
2. Davenport, T. H., Prusak, L., & Wilson, H. J., (2003). *What's the big idea, creating and capitalizing on the best management thinking.* Boston, MA: Harvard Business School Press.
3. "Apple's 'Get a Mac,' the Complete Campaign." Adweek. 13.04.2011, Retrieved 02.06.2012.
4. Woodell, V. (2003). An interview with Chris Argyris. *Organization Development Journal, 21*(2), 67–70.
5. Bornmann, L. (2012). The Hawthorne effect in journal peer review. *Scientometrics, 91*, 857–862.
6. Bunting, C. (2005). Early careers spent grinding teeth, not cutting them. *The Times Higher, 25* February 2005. Retrieved from http://www.timeshigher education.co.uk/story.asp?storyCode=194364&sectioncode=26. Accessed on October 10, 2012.

7. Macdonald, S., & Kam, J. (2007, June). Ring a ring o' roses: Quality journals and gamesmanship in management studies, *Journal of Management Studies*, *44*(4), pp. 640–655.

CHAPTER 3

1. Fox, K. C., & Keck, A. (2004). *Einstein, A to Z*. Hoboken, NJ: John Wiley & Sons Inc.
2. http://www.nobelprize.org/nobel_prizes/chemistry/laureates/2007/ertl-telephone.html?print=1
3. See for example: Pina e Cunha, M., Clegg, S. R., & Mendoça, S. (2010). On serendipity and organizing. *European Journal of Management, 28*, October 10, pp. 319–330.
4. Lee, H. Hartwell's autobiography. Retrieved from http://www.nobelprize.org/nobel_prizes/medicine/laureates/2001/hartwell.html?print=1. Accessed on June 5, 2011.
5. Telephone interview with Professor Mario R. Capecchi immediately following the announcement of the 2007 Nobel Prize in Physiology or Medicine, October 8, 2007. Retrieved from http://www.nobelprize.org/nobel_prizes/medicine/laureates/2007/capecchi-telephone.html?print=1.
6. Interview with Toshihide Maskawa by Adam Smith, Editor-in-Chief of Nobelprize.org. after the announcement of the 2008 Nobel Prize in Physics, October 2008. Retrieved from http://www.nobelprize.org/nobel_prizes/physics/laureates/2008/maskawa-interview.html?print=1.
7. *ibid.*
8. Donnal Thomas Autobiography. (1990). Retrieved from http://www.nobelprize.org/nobel_prizes/medicine/laureates/1990/thomas-autobio.html.
9. Telephone interview with Roger Y. Tsien following the announcement of the 2008 Nobel Prize in Chemistry, October 8, 2008. Retrieved from http://www.nobelprize.org/nobel_prizes/chemistry/laureates/2008/tsien-telephone.html?print=1.
10. Telephone interview with Thomas A. Steitz immediately following the announcement of the 2009 Nobel Prize in Chemistry, October 7, 2009. Retrieved from http://www.nobelprize.org/nobel_prizes/chemistry/laureates/2009/steitz-telephone.html.
11. Lee H. Hartwell's Autobiography. Retrieved from http://www.nobelprize.org/nobel_prizes/medicine/laureates/2001/hartwell.html?print=1. Accessed on June 5, 2011.
12. Telephone interview with Harald zur Hausen immediately following the announcement of the 2008 Nobel Prize in Physiology or Medicine, October 6, 2008. Retrieved from http://www.nobelprize.org/nobel_prizes/medicine/laureates/2008/hausen-telephone.html?print=1.

13. Frost, P., & Stablein, R. E. (2004). *Renewing research practice*. Stanford, CA: Stanford University Press.
14. Barker, R. (2010). The big idea: No management is not a profession. *Harvard Business Review* (July 2010), pp. 52–60.
15. Telephone interview with Gerhard Ertl immediately following the announcement of the 2007 Nobel Prize in Chemistry, October 10, 2007. Retrieved from http://www.nobelprize.org/nobel_prizes/chemistry/laureates/2007/ertl-telephone.html?print=1.
16. Interview with Toshihide Maskawa by Adam Smith, Editor-in-Chief of Nobelprize.org. after the announcement of the 2008 Nobel Prize in Physics, October 2008. Retrieved from http://www.nobelprize.org/nobel_prizes/physics/laureates/2008/maskawa-interview.html.
17. Kaplan, R. (2011). The hollow science. *Harvard Business Review* (May, 2011), p. 1000.
18. Khurana, R., & Nohria, N. (2008). It's time to make management a true profession. *Harvard Business Review, 86*(10), 70–77.
19. Barker, R. (2010). The big idea: No management is not a profession. *Harvard Business Review* (July 2010), pp. 52–60.

CHAPTER 4

1. Dreifus, C. (2010). A conversation with Aniruddh D. Patel. *The New York Times,* 1 June, p. D2.
2. Snowball dancing to the Backstreet Boys. Retrieved from http://www.youtube.com/watch?v=cJOZp2ZftCw; Patel, A. D., Iversen, J. R., Bregman, M. R., & Schulz, I.(2009, April). Experimental evidence for synchronization to a musical beat in a nonhuman animal. *Current Biology, 19*(10), 827–830.
3. Telephone interview with Roger Y. Tsien following the announcement of the 2008 Nobel Prize in Chemistry, October 8, 2008. Retrieved from http://www.nobelprize.org/nobel_prizes/chemistry/laureates/2008/tsien-telephone.html?print=1
4. Telephone interview with Jack W. Szostak immediately following the announcement of the 2009 Nobel Prize in Physiology or Medicine, October 5, 2009. Retrieved from http://www.nobelprize.org/nobel_prizes/medicine/laureates/2009/szostak-telephone.html
5. Telephone interview with Professor Edmund S. Phelps immediately following the announcement of the 2006 Sveriges Riksbank Prize in Economic Sciences in Memory of Alfred Nobel, October 9, 2006. Retrieved from http://www.nobelprize.org/nobel_prizes/economics/laureates/2006/phelps-telephone.html.
6. *ibid.*
7. Telephone interview with Professor Andrew Z. Fire immediately following the announcement of the 2006 Nobel Prize in Physiology or Medicine, October 2,

2006. Retrieved from http://www.nobelprize.org/nobel_prizes/medicine/laureates/2006/fire-telephone.html?print=1.

8. Telephone interview with Professor Craig C. Mello immediately following the announcement of the 2006 Nobel Prize in Physiology or Medicine, October 2, 2006. Retrieved from http://www.nobelprize.org/nobel_prizes/medicine/laureates/2006/mello-telephone.html?print=1.

9. From *The New York Times*' Science section: Duncan, D. E. (2010, June, 7). Scientist at work: George M. Church, on a mission to sequence the genomes of 100,000 people.

10. *ibid.*

11. *ibid.*

12. *ibid.*

13. Telephone interview with Elinor Ostrom recorded immediately following the announcement of the 2009 Sveriges Riksbank Prize in Economic Sciences in Memory of Alfred Nobel, October 12, 2009. Retrieved from http://www.nobelprize.org/nobel_prizes/economics/laureates/2009/ostrom-telephone.html?print=1.

14. *ibid.*

15. www.edge.org

16. Snow, C. P. (2001[1959]). *The two cultures*. London: Cambridge University Press.

17. For a full list of annual questions posed by edge.org visit http://edge.org/annual-question

18. Brockman, J. (Ed.). (2005). *What we believe but cannot prove*. New York, NY: Free Press.

19. *ibid.*

20. Campbell, J. P., Daft, R. L., & Hulin, C. L. (1982). *What to study: Generating and developing research questions*. Beverly Hills, CA: Sage Publications.

21. *ibid.*, pp. 107–109.

CHAPTER 5

1. Einstein, A. (1933, June 10). On the method of theoretical physics. The Herbert Spencer lecture. London, England: Oxford.

2. Gladwell, M. (2009). *Outliers: The story of success*. Penguin.

3. *ibid.*, p. 40.

4. Retrieved from http://www.library.georgetown.edu/tutorials/research-guides/15-steps. Accessed on September 28, 2012.

5. Adapted from http://www.library.georgetown.edu/tutorials/research-guides/15-steps. Accessed on September 28, 2012.

6. Bisoux, T. (2008). The innovation generation. *BizEd*, September/October 2008, pp.18–25.

7. Kaplan, R. (2010). Accounting scholarship that advances professional knowledge and practice. *The Accounting Review, American Accounting Association, 86*(2), 367–383.

8. *ibid.*

9. Definition of "Science" according to the *Encyclopaedia Britannica*.

10. Stein, G. (2010). *Managing people and organizations: Peter Drucker's legacy.* Bingley, UK: Emerald.

11. Definition of "Art" according to the *Encyclopaedia Britannica*.

12. Einstein, A. (n.d.). "Principles of research," in *Ideas and opinions*. New York, NY: Bonanza, p. 226 as cited in Norton, J. D. (1995). Eliminative induction as a method of discovery: How Einstein discovered general relativity. In J. Leplin (Ed.), *The creation of ideas in physics*, (pp. 29–69), Kluwer.

13. Kiechel III, W. (2010). *The lords of strategy: The secret intellectual history of the new corporate world.* New York, NY: Harvard Business School Press.

14. Davenport, T. H., Prusak, L., & Wilson, H. J. (2003). *What's the big idea, creating and capitalizing on the best management thinking.* Boston, MA: Harvard Business School Press.

15. Wright, K. (2004). The master's mistakes. *Discover, 25*(9), 50–53.

16. As reported by Karen Wright in "The master's mistakes" by Karen Wright from the September 2004 Discover issue. Retrieved from http://discovermagazine.com/2004/sep/the-masters-mistakes/article_view?b_start:int=1&-C=

17. Bisoux, T. (2008). The innovation generation. *BizEd*, September/October 2008, pp. 18–25.

18. Greene, K. (2002, June 19). Publish that failure! *Science Now*. Retrieved from http://news.sciencemag.org/sciencenow/2002/06/19-02.html

19. http://www.jnrbm.com/

20. Andersen, J. H., & Mikkelsen, S. (2010). Does computer use pose a hazard for future long-term sickness absence? *Journal of Negative Results in BioMedicine, 9*, 1.

21. "We hear that …;" New Scientist. 14 December 2002.

22. Reiter, E., Roberston, R., & Osman, L. M. (2003). Lessons from a failure: generating tailored smoking cessation letters. *Artificial Intelligence, 144*(1–2), 41–58.

23. Harris, G. W. (1994). Living with Murphy's law. *Research Technology Management, 37*(1), 10; Schoemaker, P. J. H., & Gunther, R. E. (2006). The wisdom of deliberate mistakes. *Harvard Business Review, June*, 109–116; Perman, S. (2006). Some brilliant mistakes, *BusinessWeek Online, June* 30, 14.

24. Porras, J., Emery, S., & Thompson, M. (2007). *Success built to last* (p. 135). Upper Saddle River, NJ: Wharton School Publishing.

25. Einstein, A. In ideas and opinions, p. 272, as cited in Norton, J. D. (1995). Eliminative induction as a method of discovery: How Einstein discovered general relativity. In Jarret Leplin (Ed.), *The creation of ideas in physics* (pp. 29–69). Dordrecht, The Netherlands: Kluwer.

26. Reich, R. B. (2010). Entrepreneur or unemployed? *The New York Times*, June 2, p. A21.

27. Cohen, P. (2010). In midlife, boomers are happy — and suicidal, *The New York Times*, June 13, p. WK4.

28. Clancy, S. A. (2010). *The trauma myth: The truth about the sexual abuse of children — and its aftermath.* New York, NY: Basic Books.

29. Loftus, E. F., & Frenda, S. J. (2010, March 12). Bad theories can harm victims. *Science*, 327, pp. 1329–1330.

30. Loftus, E. F., & Frenda, S. J. (2010, March 12). Bad theories can harm victims. *Science*, 327, pp. 1329–1330.

31. *ibid.*

32. Grierson, B. (2003). A bad trip down memory lane. *The New York Times*, July 27.

33. *ibid.*

34. Loftus, E. F., & Frenda, S. J. (2010, March 12). Bad theories can harm victims. *Science*, 327, pp. 1329–1330.

35. Mead, M. (1928). Coming of age in Samoa: A psychological study of primitive youth for Western Civilisation. New York, NY: William Morrow.

36. Freeman, D. (1983). *Margaret Mead in Samoa: The making and unmaking of an anthropological myth.* Cambridge: Harvard University Press.

37. Shankman, P. (2009). *The trashing of Margaret Mead.* Madison, WI: University of Wisconsin Press.

CHAPTER 6

1. Telephone interview with Elizabeth H. Blackburn immediately following the announcement of the 2009 Nobel Prize in Physiology or Medicine, October 5, 2009. Retrieved from http://www.nobelprize.org/nobel_prizes/medicine/laureates/2009/blackburn-telephone.html?print=1

2. Telephone interview with Françoise Barré-Sinoussi immediately following the announcement of the 2008 Nobel Prize in Physiology or Medicine, October 6, 2008. Retrieved from http://www.nobelprize.org/nobel_prizes/medicine/laureates/2008/barre-sinoussi-telephone.html?print=1

3. Sir Alexander Fleming's speech at the Nobel Banquet in Stockholm, December 10, 1945. Retrieved from http://www.nobelprize.org/nobel_prizes/medicine/laureates/1945/fleming-speech.html?print=1

4. Noriko, H., Solomon, P., Kim, S. L., & Sonnenwald, D. H. (2003). An emerging view of scientific collaboration: Scientists' perspectives on collaboration and factors that impact collaboration. *Journal of the American Society for Information Science and Technology, 54*(10), 952–965.

5. *ibid.*

6. Porras, J., Emery, S., & Thompson, M. ((2007). *Success built to last* (p. 202). Upper Saddle River, NJ: Wharton School Publishing.

7. Tynan, B. R., & Garbett, D. L. (2007). Negotiating the university research culture: Collaborative voices of new academics. *Higher Education Research & Development, 26*(4), 411–424.

8. Napier, N. K., Hosley, S., & Nguyen, T. V. (2004). Conducting qualitative research in Vietnam: Observations about ethnography, grounded theory and case study research approaches. In R. Marschan-Piekkari, & C. Welch (Eds.), *A handbook of qualitative research methods for international business* (pp. 384–401). Cheltenham, UK: Edward Elgar.

9. Ferris, T. (1993). *The universe and eye, reflections on the new science*. London: Pavilion.

10. *ibid.*

11. Telephone interview with Professor Craig C. Mello immediately following the announcement of the 2006 Nobel Prize in Physiology or Medicine, October 2, 2006. Retrieved from http://www.nobelprize.org/nobel_prizes/medicine/laureates/2006/mello-telephone.html?print=1

12. Telephone interview with Professor Andrew Z. Fire immediately following the announcement of the 2006 Nobel Prize in Physiology or Medicine, October 2, 2006. Retrieved from http://www.nobelprize.org/nobel_prizes/medicine/laureates/2006/fire-telephone.html

13. Crafton, D. (2004). Collaborative research, doc?, *Cinema Journal, 44*(1), 138–142.

14. Crafton, D. (2004). Collaborative research, doc?, *Cinema Journal, 44*(1), 138–142.

15. Lovitts, B. E. (2008) The Transition to Independent Research: Who Makes It, Who Doesn't, and Why. *Journal of Higher Education, 79*(3), May/June 2008, pp. 296–325

16. Crafton, D. (2004). Collaborative research, doc?, *Cinema Journal, 44*(1), 139.

17. See, for example, Horsfall, J., Cleary, M., Walter, G., et al. (2007). Conducting mental health research: Key steps, practicalities, and issues for the early career researcher. *International Journal of Mental Health Nursing. 16*(Suppl 1), S1–S20; Kearney, N., Miller, M., Sermeus, W., et al. (2000). Multicentre research and the WISECARE experience. *Journal of Advanced Nursing. 32*(4), 999–1007; McCallin, A. M. (2006). Interdisciplinary researching: Exploring the opportunities and risks of working together. *Nursing and Health Sciences. 8*(2), 88–94.

18. Noriko, H., Solomon. P., Kim, S. L., & Sonnenwald, D. H. (2003). An emerging view of scientific collaboration: Scientists' perspectives on collaboration and factors that impact collaboration. *Journal of the American Society for Information Science and Technology, 54*(10), 952–965.

19. *ibid.*

20. Telephone interview with Ada E. Yonath immediately following the announcement of the 2009 Nobel Prize in Chemistry, October 7, 2009. Retrieved from http://www.nobelprize.org/nobel_prizes/chemistry/laureates/2009/yonath-telephone.html

21. Telephone interview with Venkatraman Ramakrishnan immediately following the announcement of the 2009 Nobel Prize in Chemistry, October 7, 2009. Retrieved from http://www.nobelprize.org/nobel_prizes/chemistry/laureates/2009/ramakrishnan-telephone.html?print=1

22. Telephone interview with Willard S. Boyle recorded on October 7, 2009, the day following the announcement of the 2009 Nobel Prize in Physics. Retrieved from

http://www.nobelprize.org/nobel_prizes/physics/laureates/2009/boyle-telephone. html.

23. *ibid.*

24. Manton, E. J., & English, D. E. (2007). The trend towards multiple authorship in business journals. *Journal of Education for Business, 82*, 164–168.

25. Manton, E. J., & English, D. E. (2008). An empirical study of gift authorships in business journals. *Journal of Education for Business, 83*(5), 283–287.

26. In the United Kingdom, the RAE (which has now changed name) is basically an instrument used by the U.K. government to increase returns from their investments in research. The process is based on "peer review" and results are the basis for allocating research funding.

CHAPTER 7

1. Kotter, J. (1996). *Leading change* (1st ed.). Boston, MA: Harvard Business Press.

2. Adler, N. J., & Harzing, A. W. (2009). When knowledge wins: Transcending the sense and nonsense of academic rankings. *Academy of Management Learning and Education, 8*(1), 72–95 cited in Jonsen, K., Aycan, Z., Berdrow, I., Boyacigiller, N. A., Brannen, M. Y., Davison, S. C., Dietz, J., …; Weber, T. J. (2010). Scientific mindfulness: A foundation for future themes in international business. In D. Timothy, P. Torben, T. Laszlo (Eds.) *The Past, present and future of international business & management. Advances in international management* (Vol. 23, pp. 43–69). Retrieved from http://www.emeraldinsight.com/books. htm?issn = 1074-7540&volume = 12

3. Boyer, E. L. (1990). *Scholarship reconsidered: Priorities of the professoriate.* Special report. Princeton, NJ: The Carnegie Foundation for the Advancement of Teaching; Boyer (reprint, 2004) "Chapter 2: Enlarging the perspective," *Journal of the American Physical Therapy Association, 84*(6), pp. 571–575.

4. Sharma, P. (2010). Advancing the 3R. In A. Stewart, G. T. Lumpkin, J. A. Katz (Eds.), *Entrepreneurship and family business. Advances in entrepreneurship, firm emergence and growth* (Vol. 12, pp. 383–400). Retrieved from http:// www.emeraldinsight.com/books.htm?issn = 1074-7540&volume = 12

5. Lansley, P. (2007). Making sense of research quality assessment. *Engineering, Construction and Architectural Management, 14*(1), 7–25.

6. Adler, N. J., & Harzing, A. W. (2009). When knowledge wins: Transcending the sense and nonsense of academic rankings. *Academy of Management Learning and Education, 8*(1), 72–95.

7. Peters, J. (2009, September/October). The modern day men's club. *BizEd*, pp. 68–69.

8. *ibid.*

9. Sharma, P. (2010). Advancing the 3R. In A. Stewart, G. T. Lumpkin, J. A. Katz (Eds.), *Entrepreneurship and family business. Advances in entrepreneurship, firm*

emergence and growth (Vol. 12, pp. 383–400). Retrieved from http://www.emer-aldinsight.com/books.htm?issn = 1074-7540&volume = 12

10. Peng, M. W., & Zhou, J. Q. (2006). Most cited articles and authors in global strategy research. *Journal of International Management, 12*(4), 490–508.

11. Harzing, A. W. (2010). *The publish or perish book: Your guide to effective and responsible citation analysis.* Melbourne: Tarma Software Research.

12. Peng, M. W., & Zhou, J. Q. (2006). Most cited articles and authors in global strategy research. *Journal of International Management, 12*(4), 490–508.

13. *ibid.*

14. Sharma, P. (2010). Advancing the 3R. In A. Stewart, G. T. Lumpkin, J. A. Katz (Eds.), *Entrepreneurship and family business. Advances in entrepreneurship, firm emergence and growth* (Vol. 12, pp. 383–400). Retrieved from http://www.emeraldinsight.com/books.htm?issn = 1074-7540&volume = 12

15. Frey, B. (2003). Publishing as prostitution? Choosing between one's own ideas and academic success. *Public Choice, 116*, 205–223.

16. LSE Public Policy Group. Maximizing the impacts of your research: A handbook for social scientist. Consultation draft 3. Retrieved from http://blogs.lse.ac.uk/impactofsocialsciences/the-handbook/

17. The Thomson Reuters Impact Factor, originally published in the Current Contents print editions, June 20, 1994, when Thomson Reuters was known as The Institute for Scientific Information® (ISI®), http://thomsonreuters.com/products_services/science/free/essays/impact_factor/

18. Macdonald, S., & Kam, J. (2007, June). Ring a ring o' roses: Quality journals and gamesmanship in management studies. *Journal of Management Studies, 44*(4), pp. 640–655.

19. Peters, J. (2009, September/October). The modern day men's club. *BizEd*, pp. 68–69.

20. Macdonald, S., & Kam, J. (2007, June). Ring a ring o' roses: Quality journals and gamesmanship in management studies. *Journal of Management Studies, 44*(4), pp. 640–655.

21. Starbuck, W. H. (2005). How much better are the most prestigious journals? The statistics of academic publication. *Organization Science, 16*(2), 180–200.

22. Macdonald, S., & Kam, J. (2007, June). Ring a ring o' roses: Quality journals and gamesmanship in management studies. *Journal of Management Studies, 44*(4), pp. 640–655.

23. *ibid.*

24. *ibid.*

25. Fanelli, D. (2010). Do pressures to publish increase scientists' bias? An empirical support from US states data. *PLoS ONE 5*(4), published online 21 April. doi: 10.1371/journal.pone.0010271

26. Griffith, D. A., Cavusgil, S. T., & Xu, S. (2006). An analysis of scholarship in the leading international business journals: 1996–2005. Working Paper. Michigan State University.

27. Peters, J. (2009, September/October). The modern day men's club. *BizEd*, pp. 68–69

28. Lin, T. (2012). Cracking open the scientific process. *The New York Times*, January 17.
29. Pfeffer, J. (2007). A modest proposal: How we might change the process and product of managerial research. *Academy of Management Research, 50*(6), 1334–1345.
30. Telephone interview with Elinor Ostrom recorded immediately following the announcement of the 2009 Sveriges Riksbank Prize in Economic Sciences in Memory of Alfred Nobel, October 12, 2009. Retrieved from http://www. nobelprize.org/nobel_prizes/economics/laureates/2009/ostrom-telephone.html? print=1
31. Telephone interview with Paul Krugman recorded immediately after the announcement of the 2008 Sveriges Riksbank Prize in Economic Sciences in Memory of Alfred Nobel, October 13, 2008. Retrieved from http://www. nobelprize.org/nobel_prizes/economics/laureates/2008/krugman-telephone.html? print=1
32. *ibid.*

EPILOGUE

1. Telephone interview with Venkatraman Ramakrishnan immediately following the announcement of the 2009 Nobel Prize in Chemistry, October 7, 2009. Retrieved from at: http://www.nobelprize.org/nobel_prizes/chemistry/laureates/ 2009/ramakrishnan-telephone.html
2. *ibid.*
3. Telephone interview with Professor Mario R. Capecchi immediately following the announcement of the 2007 Nobel Prize in Physiology or Medicine, October 8, 2007. Retrieved from http://www.nobelprize.org/nobel_prizes/ medicine/laureates/2007/capecchi-telephone.html?print=1
4. Retrieved from http://www.gladwell.com/outliers/index.html, accessed on October 7, 2012.
5. Porras, J., Emery, S., Thompson, M. (2007). *Success built to last* (p. 5). Upper Saddle River, NJ: Wharton School Publishing.
6. Jensen, M. C., & Meckling, W. H. (1976, October). Theory of the firm: Managerial behavior, agency costs and ownership structure. *Journal of Financial Economics, 3*(4), 305–360.
7. Martin, R. (2010). The age of customer capitalism. *Harvard Business Review*. Retrieved from http://hbr.org/2010/01/the-age-of-customer-capitalism/ar/1, accessed on October 8, 2012.
8. Social Science Research Network homepage. Retrieved from http://www. ssrn.com/, accessed on October 12, 2012.
9. Telephone interview with Professor Edmund S. Phelps immediately following the announcement of the 2006 Sveriges Riksbank Prize in Economic Sciences in

Memory of Alfred Nobel, October 9, 2006. Retrieved from http://www.nobel-prize.org/nobel_prizes/economics/laureates/2006/phelps-telephone.html

10. This section is based on the report by Gustafsson, B., Hermerén, G., & Pettersson, B. (2005). Good research practice — what is it? Report Number 1:2005. Swedish Research Council's report series.

11. Porras, J., Emery, S., & Thompson, M. (2007). *Success built to last* (p. 131). Upper Saddle River, NJ: Wharton School Publishing.

12. This section and all mentions of impressionism, the impressionist movement, and impressionists are collated from the *Encyclopaedia Britannica*. Retrieved from http://www.britannica.com/EBchecked/topic/284143/Impressionism#toc284619. Accessed on accessed on October 8, 2012.

13. Roosevelt, T. (1899, April 10). *The strenuous life*. Speech given by Theodore Roosevelt in Chicago, IL.

About the Author

Marco Busi is CEO of Carisma RCT Ltd., a U.K.-based management research and advisory company specializing in strategic and operational excellence. He regularly consults companies, government and public sector organizations, industry associations, and universities from Europe, the United States, Canada, and Asia. His research and consultancy insight have been applied to manufacturing, service, energy, nuclear, construction, and various other industries.

Marco also runs Carisma's investment arm, which aims to capitalise on high-risk and high-growth-potential business ventures. And he is editor-in-chief of *Strategic Outsourcing: an International Journal* (SOIJ), published by Emerald Group Publishing Ltd. and winner of the Emerald Excellence Award for Best New Journal Launch 2008–2011.

With a present in industry and a past in academia, Marco's main interest lies in bridging the gap between theory and practice, between knowledge and application.

Prior to transitioning to the private sector, he was founding manager of the Centre for Business Process Outsourcing, a Scottish research centre co-funded by the University of Strathclyde and Highland and Island Enterprise (regional development agency for the North of Scotland). Before moving to Scotland, he was a research scientist in the manufacturing logistics group at SINTEF Industrial Management in Trondheim, Norway, the biggest research foundation in Scandinavia.

Besides his role at Carisma RCT, he still maintains a series of academic roles at various Universities in the United Kingdom, Vietnam, and China; he serves on the editorial boards of several academic journals, and he is a member of a number of scientific committees.

His work and views on management and operations regularly appear in prominent publications including *The Times* and various international journals, books, and trade magazines.

Marco can be contacted via e-mail at m.busi@carismarct.com.